Dark Finance

Dark Finance

Illiquidity and Authoritarianism

at the Margins of Europe

Fabio Mattioli

Stanford University Press
Stanford, California

Stanford University Press
Stanford, California

Printed in the United States of America on acid-free, archival-quality paper.

Library of Congress Cataloging-in-Publication Data

Names: Mattioli, Fabio, author.
Title: Dark finance : illiquidity and authoritarianism at the margins of Europe / Fabio
    Mattioli.
Description: Stanford, California : Stanford University Press, 2020. | Includes
    bibliographical references and index.
Identifiers: LCCN 2019046789 (print) | LCCN 2019046790 (ebook) | ISBN 9781503611658 (cloth)
    | ISBN 9781503612938 (paperback) | ISBN 9781503612945 (ebook)
Subjects: LCSH: Finance—Political aspects—North Macedonia. | Financialization—North
    Macedonia. | Money supply—North Macedonia. | Construction industry—North
    Macedonia. | Authoritarianism—North Macedonia. | North Macedonia—Politics and
    government—1992– | North Macedonia—Economic conditions—21st century.
Classification: LCC HG186. N67 M37 2020 (print) | LCC HG186. N67 (ebook) |
    DDC 332.094976—dc23
LC record available at https://lccn.loc.gov/2019046789
LC ebook record available at https://lccn.loc.gov/2019046790

Cover design: Michel Vrana
Typeset by Motto Publishing Services in 10/14 Minion Pro

Contents

Acknowledgments

DESPITE WHAT COVERS SUGGEST, books, and especially ethnographies, are not individual projects. This book would not have been possible if not for the help of people at Construx and other Macedonian companies, who took me in despite my rudimentary Macedonian and my lack of useful contribution to their work. I was honored to dress in the company's blue overalls and to share, albeit from the outside, in some of their struggles.

I owe numerous intellectual debts to many people. Katherine Verdery, Michael Blim, Setha Low, Jeff Maskovsky, David Harvey, Julie Skurski, Emily Channell-Justice, David Borenstein, Naomi Adiv, Jay Blair, Juraj Anzulović, Andreina Torres, Saygun Gökarıksel, Salim Karlitekin, Rocio Gil, and others facilitated the book's inception during my years at the City University of New York (CUNY) Graduate Center. Emily Greble, Susan Woodward, Madigan Fichter, and members of the NYC Kruzhok were formidable companions of discussion with whom I shaped many of my early ideas. At the Center for European and Mediterranean Studies at New York University, the book has matured into its current shape thanks to the support of Larry Wolff, Rosario Forlenza, Christian Martin, Erica Robles-Anderson, Lilly Chumley, Sophie Gonick, Ricardo Cardoso, and Liliana Gil. But it was at the University of Melbourne that the project saw the light of day amid the lively inputs of John Cox, Debra McDougal, Harriette Richards, Max Holleran, Michelle Carmody, Carla Wilson, Kari Dahlgren, Cynthia Sear, Tammy Kohn, Cameo Dalley, Monica Minnegal, Fiona Haines, Andy Dawson, Michael Herzfeld, Amanda Gilbertson, Kalissa Alexeyeff, Erin Fitz-Henry, and many other colleagues at the School of Social and Political Sciences.

Some of the key insights of this book were developed through fleeting conversations with a nomadic community of inspiring colleagues such as Elizabeth Dunn, Larisa Kurtović, Jessica Greenberger, Sarah Muir, Neringa Klumbyte, Andrew Gilbert, Matilde Cordoba-Azcarate, Claudio Sopranzetti, Marek Mikuš, Dana Johnson, and Alan Smart. Aaron Z. Pitluck, Daniel Souleles, Paul Langley, Ana-Flavia Badue, and other participants at the Society for Economic Anthropology 2017 conference helped me develop the way I thought of financialization. Many thanks to Deborah James, Ivan Rajković, Sohini Kar, Zaira Tiziana Lofranco, Antonio Pusceddu, and Ramona Stout, who helped improve several early drafts.

I am particularly fortunate to have had the amazing engagement of a cohort of scholars of Macedonia, such as Goran Janev, Andy Graan, Keith Brown, Rozita Dimova, Dave Wilson, Vasiliki Neofotistos, Ljupco Ristevski, and other colleagues from the Institute of Ethnology and Anthropology of Skopje, who provided advice, example, and contacts over a decade of work in the country. Tijana Radeska, Petar Todorov, Gani Ramadani, and Branimir Jovanovic have been terrific in helping me access various materials and gracious enough to share them over dinner and drinks.

This book would not have happened without the enthusiastic stewardship of Michelle Lipinski and the care of the entire editorial team at Stanford University Press. At this time of turbulence in the publishing world, their commitment to intellectual exchanges and their support of early-career academics has been nothing short of exemplary. Several other institutions provided financial and logistical support to the project. Many thanks to the Council for European Studies at Columbia University, the Wenner-Gren Foundation, The CUNY Graduate Center, the Center for European and Mediterranean Studies, The Remarque Institute at New York University, and the School of Social and Political Sciences at the University of Melbourne.

The book's greatest debts, however, are owed to those mentors, friends, and comrades who helped me navigate the rough seas of intellectual, economic, and existential uncertainty. My mother, Cristina, my father, Luciano, and my brother, Federico, have supported me with their unshakable faith. The example of my grandparents—Enrico, Norfa, Beppe, and Marisa—and of Maestro Faccini taught me the value, dignity, and poetics of hard work. Bela, my companion, held strong at the rudder as we moved across three continents, taking me to unexpected places where my mind could wander and be completed by the beauty of hers. To these comrades, past, present, and future, I dedicate this book.

Dark Finance

Introduction

The Making of Illiquidity in Macedonia

WINTER 2017. Fog descends on Skopje like a deadly but merciful veil. A spectral glow illuminates the streets for the few office workers walking quickly between buildings along the city's main arteries. Behind black, air-filtering masks, blue, brown, and green eyes intermittently emerge. Cafes are open but empty—like deep sighs between regular breaths. In the smog, buildings appear and disappear slowly, their silhouettes scrambled into a thousand imaginary shapes.

When Skopje regains its senses, it is not a relief. Neo-baroque façades spread like plastic parasites on the skeletons of socialist buildings. Bronze statues of national heroes reverberate the sound of footsteps—echoing hollow promises of a grand future that are belied by the fragile shapes of decrepit schools and hospitals. A small triumphal arch points toward a patch of cramped new buildings that have mushroomed in the eastern suburbs—a win, perhaps, for the oligarchs and the government that sponsored Macedonia's urban expansion. For inhabitants, contractors, and citizens, it is a disquieting testimony to their mounting debts.

Wounded, tired, doubtful—contemporary Skopje is recovering from a ten-year-long construction hangover. Announced in 2010, the wave of urban expansion known as Skopje 2014 was supposed to keep Macedonia's economy afloat during the international recession that had followed the 2007 US mortgage crisis—an economic turmoil that, over the following decade, froze international credit markets and produced several mortgage and sovereign debt crises in Europe. In theory, the sovereign loans that subsidized the Skopje 2014 plan constituted an investment that would prevent the spread of financial

1

Figure 1. The statue of Alexander the Great emerges from Skopje's winter fog. Photo: Author

instability in Macedonia, put the country on the map, and attract global capital. In practice, few companies ever saw any cash. Money seemed to evaporate before reaching local businesses. Bills, however, did not.

As in many other global metropoles, the spirals of credit that made Skopje 2014 possible originated in the pool of liquid investments that sustain the financial architecture of contemporary capitalism. Yet the timing was odd. Global lenders had taken an interest in Macedonia precisely at a moment when investing in construction all around Europe was considered unwise. More important, their lending seemed to be targeting public agencies rather than following the same indiscriminate patterns observed prior to the global financial crisis. Paradoxically, the Macedonian government amassed debt and, in theory, cash to spend, but Macedonian businesses and citizens found it hard to get loans from private banks or even to be paid from public agencies. For them, Macedonia was not a land awash with cash. Instead, it felt like a country plagued by illiquidity and exploitative working conditions.

For those who had engineered the neo-baroque façades of Skopje 2014, however, Macedonia's construction and financial expansion had been highly lucrative. Between 2006 and 2016, Nikola Gruevski, Macedonia's prime minister; his cousin Sašo Mijalkov, head of the country's intelligence agency; and a tight circle of politicians and oligarchs leveraged the resources provided by international finance to seize assets and solidify their grip on Macedonia's state and society. The beat of sledgehammers covered networks of racketeering, forced acquisition, political violence, arrests, indiscriminate wiretapping, and intimidation. With each euro that went into Skopje's urban spaces, Gruevski's regime acquired a physical presence—appearing to be strong, real, and inevitable.

Squeezed between a lack of money and an oppressive regime, most Macedonians felt powerless. Gruevski, by contrast, seemed untouchable, able to control the country's economy and parry any protests or scandals. Even when, in 2015, the opposition released tape recordings that exposed the regime's crimes, Gruevski and his party, the Internal Macedonian Revolutionary Organization–Democratic Party for Macedonian National Unity (VMRO–DPMNE), held on—emerging as the strongest party in the 2016 elections, only a few seats short of a new majority.

And yet, when the regime seemed primed to survive yet another crisis, it suddenly fell apart. Determined to prevent a (fragile) coalition from creating a new government, the VMRO–DPMNE tried to stall, boycott, and ultimately physically occupy the Macedonian Parliament by enlisting the help of an angry mob of thugs and overzealous nationalists. In the chaotic moments of violence that followed, rumors of a coup spread like wildfire. Panicked friends and interlocutors called me in New York. They feared the army would support the regime, and they expected the president of Macedonia, Gjorge Ivanov, a close ally of Gruevski, to declare martial law. A few chaotic hours passed, yet nothing happened. In his speech, Ivanov called on everyone to remain calm. Gruevski, from Vienna, followed suit. Finally the police intervened, removing pro-VMRO–DPMNE protesters—and thus the aura of invulnerability that had surrounded the regime evaporated.

How did Gruevski's regime manage to subjugate the hearts and minds of Macedonians and yet crumble so rapidly? And if the regime was so powerful, why did it prove to be incapable of inciting overt, large-scale political violence when it mattered the most? This book suggests that the pervasive and fragile dimensions of Macedonia's authoritarianism are directly connected to the forms of financial expansion experienced at the European periphery. The ethnography of the Macedonian construction sector I put forward argues that Gruevski's regime flourished thanks to the geopolitical value that a small, peripheral country such as Macedonia acquired during the global financial crisis. Able to access financial resources during the global credit freeze, Gruevski wove complex layers of financial dependency into the urban landscape.

In the rebuilding of Skopje, financial schemes of forced credit and elusive wealth became entangled with the formal and existential processes at the core of Macedonia's political life. Rather than being a function of calculative devices or liquid capital, finance expanded through the intersections and struggles of a plurality of actors. Financial flows followed the power play of figures such as Gruevski, who was able to hijack both the expectation of profits held by global financial actors and the desire for recognition expressed by Macedonian citizens. The result, in a country subject to a legacy of financial marginality, was a specific kind of illiquidity in which credit relationships expanded but the flow of money remained centralized and restricted. For a decade, illiquidity allowed the Macedonian government to monopolize the money supply and force businesses and individuals to embrace illiberal politics. Amplifying rather than resolving the financial exploitation felt in Macedonia, illiquidity disguised the regime's structural dependencies—until the regime was no more.

Embarking on a journey with failed entrepreneurs, indebted workers, and aspiring bureaucrats, this book shows that the expansion of finance at Europe's margins transformed identities, values, and economic hopes into means of subjugation. Each chapter offers an exploration of a different site where finance and politics collided and intertwined. The narrative chronicles how Macedonia's authoritarian regime rode a wave of financial expansion to deepen its reach into Macedonian society, only to discover that, like other speculative bubbles, its domination was always on the verge of collapse.

Financialization and Politics

From food production to education, from everyday purchases to disease control and catastrophe prevention, most aspects of contemporary life are made possible by financial credit and are entangled with the expansion or contraction of financial markets. Social scientists call this expanding relevance of financial actors, markets, and modes of thinking "financialization"—a global process that has been increasingly understood as a social, rather than economic, phenomenon.[1]

While early studies of financial expansion focused on its technical and functional dimensions, the global financial crisis made it increasingly obvious that financialization intersects with formal (but also everyday) politics.[2]

As early as the 1920s, Marxist thinkers framed financial proliferation as a class project in which ruling classes used state structures to further their dominance. For Hilferding, financial expansion was caused by the emergence of large-scale monopolies that saw a convergence of the interests of the richest strata of the bourgeoisie with those of state bureaucrats.[3] Faced with endemic crises of overaccumulation, financial elites utilize political influence, legislation, and military force to open new markets and transform their productive capital into financial profits. Consequently, financialization led to dramatic political events that varied from wars to regime changes and (more or less cryptic) forms of colonialism.[4]

The proliferation and increased liquidity of financial capital, however, is also interconnected with more intimate political processes. Social scientists, influenced by Foucauldian understandings of surveillance and discipline, showed that finance affects collective and individual life by shaping how contradictory social experiences become legible, providing a new ideological framework to represent and help understand social interactions.[5] Through discursive and performative practices, mortgages, credit cards, and algorithms recast "community and family relations as cogwheels into the global speculative financial strategies."[6] These new technologies of legibility reassess "worth," reconfiguring not only standards of evaluation but also the very subjective processes through which citizens think about themselves and, ultimately, their collective aspirations.[7]

The more finance becomes a constituent of social life, the more its origins, pathways, and implications are shaped by specific historical, social, and economic contexts.[8] In this contextual view, what defines financialization and its political meanings is how it is appropriated, utilized, and moralized by specific communities of actors.[9] This is, of course, easy to see among financial professionals, elusive central bankers, and hedge fund managers,[10] who are able to mold its infrastructure according to their worldview. But there are many others whose activities are crucial in bringing finance to life: political leaders who invite or seduce global investors;[11] managers and bureaucrats who try to win, fulfill, or juggle credit-fueled contracts;[12] workers who hope to benefit from financial bonanzas or are forced to get crushing payday loans to deal with financial bankruptcies;[13] and mothers and wives who are charged with investing in or protecting their family's financial stability.[14] These actors encounter, juggle, and shape finance in a variety of contexts, riddled with moral dilemmas and contradictions, that are as much influenced by their individual backgrounds or aspirations as they are limited, or framed, by the trends set by global financiers. It is these open-ended, unequal encounters that make financialization real.[15]

This consideration leads to a conceptual dilemma: if financial expansion is operated by a variety of actors, shaped by a variety of relationships, and results in a variety of political outcomes, does it still make sense to speak of financialization as a real, singular, and coherent process? After all, most of the scenarios emblematic of financialization (that is, taking out loans, contracting debt, buying or selling stocks) do not involve individuals interacting directly with actual flows of money. In practice, encounters with finance involve interactions with bureaucrats, debt collectors, business partners, credit scoring systems, bank employees, and sometimes even software.[16]

Should we answer this conundrum by abandoning the idea of financialization as an actual existing process in favor of "financialization effects," much like when scholars in the 1970s called into question the existence of the "state" as an object of inquiry?[17] Or should we overcome the concept's ambiguous nature by specifying its limits and use financialization only to refer to the introduction of specific modes of calculation that subordinate financing processes to neoliberal markets—what some have begun to call the "financialization of finance"?[18]

Neither of these perspectives is productive for places such as Macedonia. Disposing of the concept of financialization, denying it any level of coherent existence, or restricting it to technical dimensions would impair our understanding of financial expansion in peripheral contexts, where finance appears in particularly contradictory forms compared to what is observed on London or Chicago trading floors. In these global peripheries, financial expansion can operate through different means of exchange and be directly connected to the actions of a small clique of local political leaders who "operate statecraft by deploying the methods and instruments of financial innovation."[19] Rather than constituting an abnormality, these specific political forms play out within the schizophrenic symphony of global credit and, in fact, unveil political processes that make possible some of the very abstract financial innovations that regulate life at the core of the global economic system.

The kinds of finance observed in global peripheries suggest a third option among the analytical challenges of financialization—to move away from the study of the technical dimensions of finance or the networks of its primary operators and focus instead on the political and economic landscapes that accompany financial expansion. If financialization is "generated from heterogeneity and difference, and from varied pursuits of being and becoming particular kinds of people, families, or communities,"[20] then the technical, social, and cultural processes of financial elites constitute only one of the many components that make up financialization. In this perspective, the socioeconomic process of financialization is neither a social actor, nor characteristic of a specific social group, nor a series of ephemeral effects. Rather, financialization identifies, analytically, a political and economic conjuncture that shapes, defines, supports, or structures financial expansion—the result of more or less continuous interactions, relations, and struggles—mediated by historical and material processes that intersect with statecraft efforts and reflect a society's experience of the global economic system.[21]

Organic Political Economy

Understanding financialization as a political and economic conjuncture constitutes both a theoretical and a methodological challenge. It means finding adequate ethnographic and analytical spaces to investigate how global events such as the global financial crisis interact with the political context of a peripheral society such as Macedonia. It also means giving voice to the ethnographic evidence that shows that financialization is not a one-way process emanating from New York, London, Shanghai, or Frankfurt and moving (un)evenly toward the periphery. Like the forms of colonial capitalism described by Mintz, Ortiz, and Coronil, this approach to financialization describes a dynamic of interactions[22]—a series of unequal relationships, clashes, and contradictions between the core and the periphery, between liberal leaders and would-be dictators, and between global financial institutions and local workers.

To analyze and reconstruct this interactive dynamic, I have disassembled the process of financial expansion in Macedonia into five analytical components, which describe its historical and geographical trajectory, its proliferation through multiple credit logics, and its entanglement with individual and collective identities. These five analytical spaces not only provide different ethnographic viewpoints but also identify various kinds of entanglement—diverse relationships that weave financial forms into social life and generate unequal but "meaningful connections between people."[23]

To illuminate the relational nature of financialization requires a combined effort, an approach where the expectations of profits of financiers is juxtaposed with the experience of other social actors, such as distressed workers and calculating political leaders. In the Macedonian context, this means understanding why international financial institutions such as Deutsche Bank, Citibank, and the International Monetary Fund (IMF) decided to invest hundreds of millions of euros in Macedonia,[24] in light of Gruevski's branding and legibility strategies; the growing ability of oligarchs to bank on illiquidity in relation to the dreams of citizens stuck for decades in endless cycles of economic stagnation; and the smooth integration of pernicious financial schemes on the blueprint of benign, socialist informal credit. Without these parts of the story, it would be impossible to comprehend why financial expansion sped up dramatically during the global financial crisis, giving birth to elusive financial riches and a fragile but pervasive authoritarian regime.

Despite the analytical clarity that this approach presents, collecting the data necessary to identify and research these five spaces of entanglement was made particularly messy by the progressive expansion of authoritarian politics in Macedonia. In 2013–2014, when I conducted twelve months of ethnographic research in Skopje's construction sector, the political contours of Gruevski's rule were very fuzzy. Interlocutors whispered of politically motivated beatings; of public contracts manipulated by the government; of the possibility that businessmen and foreigners were actively surveilled by intelligence operatives; and of homophobic attacks against the lesbian, gay, bisexual, transgender, and queer communities. These rumors fueled a widespread climate of fear and suspicion. Many complained—offering "philosophical" diagnoses of a political backdrop that they felt was increasingly oppressive—but were reluctant to reveal names, sums, or, sometimes, concrete examples, which might reveal their own involvement in illegal deals.

These suspicions made my fieldwork an extremely frustrating and anxious experience. Was I being surveilled? Were my participants honest in their accounts? Why did many keep on using fictional examples? Was it my shortcoming as an ethnographer? It was not until several visits later, after the release of tape recordings emboldened critics and the opposition, that I realized that keeping conversations abstract and general had often been an act of care, an attempt by my interlocutors to protect us both from exposing dangerous details. More important, the spectral landscape they evoked became a crucial analytical tool for understanding the intensely political and contradictory nature of financialization and its connection to Gruevski's rule. Vague and yet perniciously suspended "across the line of the real and the fake,"[25] these rumors accompanied every failed deal, conjuring Gruevski as a powerful shadow—not as that of a solid, autocratic state but as a regime built on elusive contradictions.

As I collected data, the expansion of Gruevski's authoritarian government permeated the study beyond my analytical concerns. Several companies who had expressed interest in participating during my preliminary research retracted their involvement, frightened of the political implications of describing their financial ties. Faced with a hostile landscape, I shortened stints of participant observation in some organizations and decided to concentrate on Construx, a middle-sized construction firm in financial trouble that remained on the periphery of the VMRO–DPMNE political network. Spending time on its construction sites, waiting with idle workers for deliveries of evanescent materials, and accompanying some of its (would-be) subcontractors, I listened to the laments of men who were trying to navigate a series of poor financial choices. To identify the sources of their anxieties, I interviewed stakeholders who played a role in building Gruevski's financial schemes, following the chains of financial flows that connected male workers to male administrators, managers, and professionals at several public agencies and ministries, local and international construction companies, and domestic and global financial institutions. Ultimately, these links brought me back to Construx and its administrative offices, where I kept company with (or distracted) architects, planners, and assistants, whose female perspectives represented a rather different side of financialization.

The resulting narrative begins with gendered accounts of workplace-related dilemmas that help to explain the contradictory relationships embodied by financial expansion.[26] Gender aspirations, conundrums, and fears appeared to animate often unrelated encounters that brought finance to life. To delineate this intrinsic dimension of financial expansion, I utilized the disturbing experiences of women as a lens through which to tell the story of a masculine world where financial contradictions tied together Macedonian workers, bureaucrats, and even Italian investors in mutual oppression. While this choice meant giving a less direct voice to women, it enabled me to highlight a common experience in postindustrial contexts in which the privileges that defined men's identity evaporated, leaving them struggling to find new sources of social worth. In Gruevski's Macedonia, the ability to access finance became both a proof and a tool to overcome the feeling that workplaces and, more broadly, society were becoming feminized—as if intercepting global finance could provide new avenues for predatorial, male domination.[27] Unsurprisingly, it was not hardened, working-class men who led the protest against Gruevski but young women who, as figure 2 shows, faced off against the riot police and defied, physically as well as symbolically, Gruevski's financial magic.

Figure 2. One of the symbols of the Colorful Revolution: a Macedonian woman defies the regime, using a policeman's shield as a mirror. Photo: Ognien Teofilovski

This book contextualizes the gendered specter of illiquidity in a broader historical and geographical context, engaging directly with the evolution of Macedonia's political economy. I spent significant time analyzing formal indicators used by economists to describe the general state of the Macedonian economy (and that of neighboring countries) and mining data from the Macedonian National Archives, the Central Intelligence Agency (CIA) archives, and other similar sources to explore the past circumstances that framed Gruevski's regime and his financial networks. The book is deeply shaped by comparative questions that were elaborated during dialogue with political economists and financial professionals about my archival and quantitative findings. The result is a syncopated narrative that intersects numerical and comparative issues with the existential struggle of Macedonian workers and managers—an organic approach to political economy, inspired by the critical philosophy of praxis present in much of heterodox Marxist literature[28] that describes the micro genealogies connecting everyday actions to macro changes.[29] In this relational perspective, ruptures such as the oil shocks of the 1970s, the postsocialist transition, or the global financial crisis of the past decade are never just economic changes. Instead, they emerge from the ordinary occurrences of social lives, opening and closing spaces for political action and imagination.[30]

Crucial to this story was the global financial crisis. To prevent it from spreading, financial institutions extended precautionary credit loans to small, peripheral countries like Macedonia. Gruevski leveraged those loans, increasingly hard to get for independent companies, to capture the Macedonian economy. Bad financial solutions and delayed payments consolidated the relationship between authoritarian leaders and oligarchs and transformed how workers and managers related to each other. Broke, isolated, and challenged in their gender and professional identities, workers and managers tried to reconstruct their personhood on the bases of the illiberal moral values that the VMRO–DPMNE utilized to rule Macedonia. One bad deal at a time, individuals found themselves tied ever more tightly to the regime, a financial leash that seemed to be everywhere but often failed to materialize.

Postsocialism and Financial Crises

To understand why finance became so important for Gruevski's regime, it is necessary to trace its roots in the Yugoslav political economy and its connection to the networks of power that mediated socialist Macedonia's reliance on global imports and aid. Between 1945 and 1991, Macedonia constituted one of the least developed regions of the Socialist Federal Republic of Yugoslavia (SFRJ), a country that also comprised Slovenia, Croatia, Serbia, Bosnia and Herzegovina, Montenegro, and the two autonomous regions of Kosovo and Vojvodina. Thanks to the Yugoslav state's non-aligned status, which allowed the SFRJ to deal with both the West and the Soviet bloc, Macedonia's lack of development was offset by accessing highly affordable business and personal loans.

Yugoslav finance demarcated a space where political leaders, businessmen, and intelligence operatives manipulated international credits in hard currency to keep domestic production alive and ensure that workers could experience a rise in their living standards. This financial bonanza slowed down in the 1970s, in a climate of stagnation and inflation that was aggravated by a sudden rise in oil prices and global interest rates—known as the Volcker and oil shocks. As international credit dried up, European partners veered away from Yugoslav products and, in the early 1980s, implemented a more restrictive lending policy. Unable to find new international loans, Yugoslavia found itself crushed by external debt and hyperinflation, paving the way for bailouts orchestrated by the IMF and international creditors, in exchange for sweeping austerity and structural reforms.

In the 1990s, with the collapse of the socialist system, Yugoslavia, and Macedonia in particular, lost their geopolitical status and fell into a spiral of financial contraction. Wild privatization schemes, prescribed by international organizations and enacted by former communist leaders, fragmented the domains of political power and the country's economic infrastructure.[31] As Verdery and Humphrey noted, rather than bringing about liberal social structures and virtuous cycles of economic competition, the transition from socialism gave rise to a semi-feudal era, characterized by political segmentation and social decay.[32] This transitional environment was, by all accounts, saturated by chaotic and dramatic conflicts. Oligarchs, mafia, and gangs competed to assert power over the spoils of socialist states.[33] In the interstices of these struggles, apparatchiks, international organizations, and common citizens relied on old and new interpersonal relations to overcome economic and bureaucratic roadblocks through illegal but moral compromises.[34] Pushed to the brink of economic collapse by geopolitical instabilities and criminal privatizations, these informal financial processes became particularly evident in peripheral places such as Macedonia, where not only marginalized communities but even state agencies came to depend on gray forms of finance and kinship networks.[35]

If Macedonia did not descend into the same kind of open war as did many of its neighbors, it was thanks to the shrewd leadership of its first president, Kiro Gligorov, and his consolidated networks of former socialist associates. As a minister of finance, Gligorov had shaped some of socialist Yugoslavia's constitutional reforms and had negotiated debt restructurings during the late 1970s and early 1980s. These international connections helped Gligorov obtain the peaceful withdrawal of the powerful Yugoslav National Army (JNA) from Macedonia. But they also allowed Gligorov to deal with networks of former secret agents and import/export directors and supply Macedonia with the resources needed to establish a reserve for its national banks and ensure the supply of other crucial services, including drugs, fuel, and food previously provided by other Yugoslav republics.

Gligorov's influence, however, did not last long. After he was incapacitated by a car bomb in 1994, Macedonia's early years of transition saw the rise to power of the Social Democratic Union of Macedonia (SDSM). Under the leadership of Branko Crvenkovski, the SDSM sped up the process of industrial privatization. Incompetent or dishonest managers, backed by the SDSM, bankrupted hundreds of companies and pocketed the revenues, leading to the loss of thousands of jobs. Simultaneously, Macedonians found themselves cut off from their regional and European markets by the Yugoslav wars and by two embargoes imposed by Greece. On the brink of economic collapse, Macedonia faced Greece's refusal to recognize its name,[36] Bulgaria's denial of the existence of a Macedonian nation, and Serbia's opposition to acknowledging the existence of an independent Macedonian Orthodox church. Isolated economically and politically, Macedonian citizens who used to travel the world freely thanks to their red Yugoslav passports discovered that their postsocialist freedom was symbolically encapsulated in the smuggling of resources in and out of the small country in which they were trapped.[37]

While Macedonians tried to organize themselves in the informal economy, the political elites started following the advice of international organizations that argued for joining the European Union (EU) as the best economic and political option to end the country's financial stagnation. To become a candidate for the EU, right- and left-wing governments reduced the country's debt, implemented structural reforms, reduced public investment, and harmonized the country with European legal and economic norms. By 2006, when Gruevski was elected, the country was heralded as a poster child of neoliberal reforms in Eastern Europe and as the next North Atlantic Treaty Organization (NATO) candidate. But in 2008, everything changed. At the NATO summit in Bucharest, at the onset of the financial crisis, Greece vetoed Macedonia's entrance into the alliance and signaled its readiness to do the same in talks regarding accession to the EU. Humiliated, Gruevski changed his priorities.[38] The time of postsocialist austerity was over.

(Il)liquidity and the Regime

It is hard to evaluate whether the 2008 NATO summit fractured Gruevski's relationship with the West or simply sped up an authoritarian process already in the making. What is clear, however, is that living under Gruevski's expansive rule differed radically from what citizens had experienced during the trajectory of political decline and financial disarticulation typical of the early transition. Paradoxically, Gruevski's regime resembled a process of partial rebirth, where a particular brand of (oppressive) politics utilized financial means to expand and centralize the Macedonian state and infiltrate interstitial and informal relations that had become spaces of solidarity and meaning in the previous decades.

This novel configuration of power was, partly, a result of Gruevski's unstable hold on the state. During the 1990s, Gruevski's political clique had occupied a relatively marginal position. His family's connections to the networks of oligarchs and secret service operatives that had emerged from the transition had been undermined by the death of his uncle, Jordan Mijalkov. Between 1997 and 2002, as a minister of finance, Gruevski managed to accumulate personal contacts and resources to begin his own climb to power. Yet, it was only with the global financial crisis that Gruevski and his clique had an opportunity to overcome and mask their lack of centrality within Macedonia's postsocialist power brokers.

Unlike countries where a rapid financial expansion had made it easy to contract unsustainable debt, the banking system of postsocialist Macedonia had been very conservative. Before the global financial crisis, global investors, funds, and even organizations such as the World Bank and the IMF had shown little interest in the country, preferring instead more lucrative markets elsewhere—an isolation that led many to conclude that Macedonia weathered the storm "with minimum impact on the domestic economy."[39] During the global financial crisis, however, Gruevski's neoliberal profile and his government's branding campaigns caught the attention of international investors. While the architecture of global liquidity crumbled, the Macedonian government found itself able to access investments from actors interested in diversifying their portfolios or committed to preventing a Balkan-wide contagion of the debt crisis that had begun to wreak havoc in Greece.

A significant portion of that new public debt was funneled toward large-scale construction projects. Conceived as ways to stimulate a sector in crisis and raise the international visibility of Macedonia, "kitsch" and "unproductive" urban projects such as Skopje 2014 raised concerns about Macedonia's ability to repay its debts. To maintain an appearance of fiscal discipline, Gruevski and his regime devised clever strategies of delayed payments, forced credit, and creative public (sub)contracting. For oligarchs, these conditions worked well insofar as they offered opportunities for creative dispossession. For managers and workers in smaller companies, however, Gruevski's promises of enrichment often meant exploitative working conditions, which forced them to lose both time and money.

The failed deals and elusive riches that punctuated this increasingly unequal context induced many businessmen to attribute all sorts of financial hiccups, quasi-bankruptcies, and sudden fortunes to the VMRO–DPMNE influence. As a dark operator of Macedonia's finance, Gruevski's regime appeared to be a sprawling political entity, a spectral presence that had taken control and expanded the reach of the Macedonian state to the point where it could affect every business deal. Fueled by both facts and rumors, illiquidity came to be embedded in an aura of fear and hope that citizens attributed to Gruevski's regime, an economic expression of a palimpsest of collective expectations, credit trends, and political scheming.

At a basic level, the ghastly form of illiquidity experienced in Macedonia reflected changes in the flows of international credit, from the private to the public sector, that followed the global financial crisis. But Macedonian illiquidity also embodied a second, political process. Delayed payments and dysfunctional deals were understood as tangible proof of Gruevski's authoritarian presence in an array of everyday encounters—almost as a diagnostic tool for his expansive power over Macedonian society. From the perspective of workers, businessmen, and citizens living in Macedonia's stagnant postsocialist economy, illiquidity came to reinforce and amplify anxieties, contradictions, and other forms of social precarity—a third, existential social dimension—by which illiquidity helped to saturate intimate relations with a sense of oppression and desperate expectation.

These three aspects of illiquidity, reflecting a global rearticulation of credit, a chain of political dependencies, and a series of existential doubts, defined a post-postsocialist form of political magic—a political and economic conjuncture—that made Gruevski's regime real not despite but *because* of its contradictions. The simultaneous presence and absence of money allowed Gruevski's authoritarian rule to become material, concrete, and unified; the promise of financial reckoning with global powers, and its constant delay, made Gruevski a necessary presence, or a scapegoat, an almost demonic entity whose financial ties kept Macedonians in a suffocating embrace. Prefiguring a gendered vindication that could never be fully realized, illiquidity legitimized Gruevski's rule on an emotional level, an existential apogee that folded financial and political misgivings within layers of extractive oppression. A desperate situation, illiquidity turned Gruevski's regime into the citizen's last hope. By submitting to him and the VMRO–DPMNE regime, Macedonians would be pulled from the ditches of history.

What follows, then, is an account of the contradictory relations that allowed Gruevski to piggyback on a particular form of financialization, in which entangled, unwanted, and centralized flows of credit constituted "the norms and operation of power."[40] If liquidity defines a knowledge process performed by material techniques, discourses, or devices that normalize risk and "a false sense of security and optimism,"[41] illiquidity—understood not as a property

of assets or a form of knowledge that allows assets to be sold on the market but
as a set of forced credit relations—framed a desperate, semi-lucid assessment
of Macedonia's geopolitical context as a collision between the postsocialist pe-
ripherality and the global financial crisis.[42] In a landscape populated by contradictions, illiquidity became an arrhythmic dance of ad hoc and exploitative financial ties that did not fool anyone but were dramatically embraced
because there seemed to be no alternative. The existential hopes, fears, and
forms of dispossession pooling around illiquidity kept authoritarianism alive.
As a conjuncture of conjunctures, illiquidity became the condition of possibility as well as one of the outcomes of Gruevski's centralized rule, a financial
space between promises and reality, between the safety of paternalism and the
reality of violence, that allowed VMRO–DPMNE to seem to be forever—until it was no more.

Chapter Outlines

Until 2015, Macedonia's authoritarian regime received international coverage
largely in relation to the Skopje 2014 project. Consisting of hundreds of new
buildings and statues that celebrated a fictional Hellenic and neo-baroque
past, the project's origin and rationale were a mystery. Since then, investigations have tried to uncover how much it cost, which companies had won
contracts, and who were the architects who envisioned the plan's kitsch aesthetics. Chapter 1 tells another, hidden story, one that sees shady businessmen collude with former secret agents, plot to ruin former socialist companies, and invest in a wealth of real estate developments in Skopje. The chapter
describes the financial networks that are at the core of Skopje's construction
expansion, their connection to the socialist era's need for foreign currency,
and their crucial role in supporting Gruevski's political ambitions. Following
their trajectory through the transition, the chapter shows how the built environment has become a magical device through which dirty money is made
clean and ambiguous power relations are recast as national identity.

Post-transition Macedonia is a country with few natural resources, high
unemployment, and few value-adding industries. Where did the money for
Skopje 2014 and other construction-related public investments come from?
Chapter 2 details the international conditions that favored and structured the
inflow of capital in Macedonia, focusing on two pillars of financial expansion at the periphery (that is, the role of foreign direct investment [FDI] and
aid funds). It describes why international investors and agencies decided to

provide funds to the Macedonian government, despite the lack of credit that characterized the global economy. The chapter also follows the peregrinations of a group of Italian businessmen who tried to escape global illiquidity by intercepting international investments in Macedonia. Their stories portray the domestic, rent-seeking structures put in place by Gruevski's rule and illustrate how an increasingly unequal and subdivided EU generates financial peripheries and supports authoritarian regimes.

How did international loans translate into domestic power for Gruevski's government? In Chapter 3, I explore the characteristics of Macedonia's domestic financialization, focusing on the non-payment crisis that followed the global financial crisis, which prompted a reemergence of in-kind exchanges, locally known as *kompenzacija*. Outlining the trajectory of kompenzacija after socialism and its relation to the Macedonian banking system, the chapter describes how politically disconnected companies receive payments in goods they do not want. These objects, such as apartments or eggs, lose value, thus obliging businesses either to absorb losses or offload these properties onto subcontractors and workers. By describing the political coercion and financial dispossession that ensues, the chapter shows that kompenzacija constitutes a form of forced credit fully integrated within global financial flows. At the periphery of European and global financial systems, the need to convert value across means of payments allows authoritarian regimes to increase their power by reaching deep into people's social networks.

Time has long been recognized as one of the crucial forces that transformed Fordist workplaces into tools of governance and shaped the existential experiences of work. In a financial context permeated by illiquidity, production is not constant but rather is subordinated to the rhythms of debt repayment. Chapter 4 focuses on the disruption of daily routines that takes place once illiquidity makes manual work close to irrelevant. Based on a fine-grained description of the actions, rituals, discussions, and pauses that characterize work under illiquidity, this chapter details the strategies used by workers to regain agency and meaning. The chapter narrates the poetic resilience of workers and their capacity to generate spaces for empathy in the interstices of financial uncertainty. Filled with potential for social transformation, the tempo of workers' acts, jokes, and conversations does not remain merely performative. Framed by financial precariousness, their tricky conversations slide toward opportunism and reduce their moral capacity to oppose the Gruevski regime.

Illiquidity affects not only workers' self-conception but also their collective identity. Chapter 5 shows how contemporary illiquidity renders heteronormative and patriarchal masculinity impossible, despite the regime's insistence on aggressive masculinity as a fundamental component of Macedonian identity. The chapter follows a group of male Macedonian construction workers as they try to restore patriarchal authority within their company, despite being unable to provide for their families and faced with economically ascendant ethnic Albanian males. Their failure, and the director's refusal to assume responsibility vis-à-vis their labor, leaves them exhausted. Scorn and mockery emerge as hierarchical ways to keep male solidarity alive, forcing workers to consume their energy in containing their increasing microaggression. The chapter details the workers' existential uncertainty as a new model of speculative masculinity that parallels the docility and aggression typical of Gruevski's fragile authoritarianism.

In Chapter 6, the conclusion returns to the last breaths of Gruevski's regime to suggest a different way of reading the book. At first glance, the book follows the (historical) trajectory of finance from global centers into Macedonia's institutions and everyday life. The conclusion, however, presents a different approach to financialization—one in which financial expansion is the outcome of dialectical relationships—made and remade by different actors operating simultaneously, but with different capacities to act, within the Macedonian political economy. Hijacked by an authoritarian project and materialized in in-kind exchanges, monumental buildings, and existential doubts, financialization amplified contradictions nested within postsocialist Macedonia. This perspective suggests the usefulness of an expansive concept of financialization, able to incorporate the different forms and shapes that finance takes at the periphery and core of the global economic system, rather than limiting it to the "financialization of finance"—that is, to the increasingly market-driven functioning of the financial market, now driven by reliance upon equities rather than stock.[43]

1 The Magic of Building

THE STATUE OCCUPIES the middle of the square and stands thirty-five meters high. Atop a white marble fountain, defended by a cohort of bronze hoplites, sprayed by water mists, and colored by disco lights that shift between red, blue, and yellow tones, Alexander the Great casts his shadow over Skopje—a shadow that blends with that of the Gruevski regime. In a city rebuilt following the Skopje 2014 plan, Gruevski's major urban investment, one can find all sorts of historical figures of Macedonia's contested historiography. With its eighty marble and bronze statues and monuments, the plan does not distinguish between genocidal maniacs and national heroes—from Tsar Dušan to Goce Delcev, they are all welcome in the "capital of Kitsch."[1]

The new aesthetic of the city center is designed to repudiate socialist and brutalist architectures and the crumbling dreams of progress they represent. Most buildings that overlook the main square or nearby streets have already been covered by neo-baroque balconies and columns of plaster, including the seat of the executive government, a prize-winning piece of architecture that Gruevski had physically and symbolically separated from the rest of the city by an ornate iron fence. Other masterpieces of brutalist architecture met the same fate. According to the most recent estimates, Skopje 2014 consisted of 137 objects, including twenty-eight buildings, five squares, eight multilevel or subterranean parking lots, four bridges, two fountains, close to eighty statues and monuments, a triumphal arch, and a replica of the London Eye, at a minimum total value of 683 million euro. Practically, Skopje 2014 looked like a replica of Las Vegas, only in one of the poorest and least touristic cities in Europe.

Figure 3. Some of Skopje 2014's neo-baroque and neoclassical buildings. Photo: Author

As soon as the plan was disclosed in January 2010, architects, activists, and common citizens took to the streets to oppose various phases of the project. The protests began with a group of around 20 activists who were then able to gather a further 100 urbanites and intellectuals. From that first "architectural uprising,"[2] more people came to object to the VMRO–DPMNE's urban policies, and in 2015 and 2016 the project became a catalyst for daily protests by tens of thousands. Middle-class citizens, some of whom initially thought of Skopje 2014 as a project that added value and dignity to their decaying city, came to see it as a loss—a loss of public money, public spaces, and finally, of their own political agency. By 2013, 67.3 percent of the population opposed the project.[3] In 2014, local organizations in the neighborhoods of Debar Maalo and Karpoš 4 started to organize to stop the renewed building spree that came with it and threatened to transform parks and other parcels of land into residential buildings.[4] But the VMRO–DPMNE did not relent. More statues representing dubious heroes from Macedonia's past were erected; new façades were built, and more trees and public spaces were eliminated and replaced by building sites—sometimes at night and under heavy police escort.

Why was the regime so invested in rebuilding the center of Skopje? What was the meaning of its neo-baroque aesthetic, described by many as kitsch?

This chapter argues that Skopje 2014 embodied a specific form of financial fiction that simultaneously hid and showcased the contradictions of the political and economic conjuncture that empowered Gruevski's regime. Neo-baroque urban forms masked and even improved Gruevski's historically tenuous relations with socialist-era financial networks that had enabled the first wave of Macedonian oligarchs. At the same time, the spectacular forms of urban renewal highlighted the growing inequality and murky politics of financial expansion at a time of global crisis. Caught between awe, fear, and absurdity, citizens felt disempowered and paralyzed—not because they embraced the new aesthetic but because of the contradictions it embodied.

Despite its antisocialist aesthetics, Skopje 2014 maintained an element of continuity with the financial fictions of socialist Yugoslavia. Since the 1960s, urban investments and currency tricks helped camouflage the structural deficiencies of the Yugoslav and especially Macedonian economy in the eyes of international partners. Starting with the rebuilding of socialist Skopje and the growth of Macedonia's construction sector, this chapter chronicles how various financial practices permitted and masked the growth of a substrate of gray, quasi-legal relations between the Yugoslav intelligence and business communities—which, until the 1980s, kept the local economy afloat and, after the transition, influenced the trajectory of postsocialist oligarchs and of Gruevski and his allies.

Unlike Vladimir Putin, a former high-ranking officer of the KGB, one of the most well-known Soviet intelligence agencies, who could mobilize armed support and discipline unruly oligarchs,[5] Gruevski gained power unsteadily. His family had accumulated political influence during the 1970s and 1980s, largely through Gruevski's uncle, Jordan Mijalkov, who worked as a director for a large Macedonian import/export company and had extensive contacts with the Yugoslav security apparatus. Their political trajectory derailed quickly in the early 1990s, when an internal fight between former Yugoslav security forces empowered rival businessmen and the social-democratic party. In a structurally fragile position, cut out from the negotiations between former socialist managers of import/export companies and socialist intelligence agents, and reliant on a rural electorate, Gruevski found in Skopje 2014 a perfect project to buy the support he needed. At once, the renewal project offered lucrative contracts for postsocialist oligarchs and had the potential to enshrine Gruevski's rule by making Macedonia a world-class city in the eyes of both international investors and domestic citizens.

The explicit political dimension of urban financial speculations aligns

Skopje with other postsocialist cities such as Batumi, Astana, Baku, Sofia, Perm, and Moscow, where monumental buildings with a Disney-like aesthetic supplanted the previous socialist urban fabric. In most of these cities, urban transformations included extensive construction of façades. In Batumi, Georgia, and Astana, Kazakhstan, futuristic or neoclassical façades were affixed to older socialist ruins, contributing to a schizophrenic atmosphere of hope wedded with cynicism.[6] A similar tone dominated conversations among Azeri citizens, for whom the "technologically sublime" façades of the new Baku, Azerbaijan, combined hopes for the end of postsocialism with suspicions about the provenance of the wealth of the new oligarchy.[7]

As a spectacle or as a distraction, postsocialist façades reconfigure the relationship between state and citizens, the latter finding themselves at once attracted and repulsed by the grandeur and illicit nature of their new urban settings. Against this common background, the stakes of (re)building different urban aesthetics are dictated by the local political contexts. In Azerbaijan, a country dominated by a single party/family since the fall of communism, building a new capital diverted attention from the country's dependency on oil. In Bulgaria, an incoherent series of Vegas-like developments, known as "Mafia Baroque," signaled the rise of a new entrepreneurial class connected to local bosses who supplanted architects as the main urban decision makers.[8] In Uzbekistan, spectacular architecture filled the theatrical void of Karimov, a ruler who embraced Soviet-era surveillance and bureaucratic practices.[9] In Putin's Russia, the shiny architecture of the new Moscow bolstered a cult of personality that captured collective frustration and muted the explicit forms of violence and social control enacted by the country's new tsar.

In the case of Skopje, the entire city was designed to constitute a new façade—not only for the local citizens but for oligarchs, the regime, and international investors. Skopje 2014, with its neo-baroque, white plaster buildings, allowed Gruevski to hide flows of money in and out of shell companies owned by old and new allies. By engaging them in the rebuilding of a city, Skopje 2014 gave Gruevski the opportunity to offer established oligarchs profit in tandem with symbolic legitimacy, whereby illicit deals of the past could be converted and hidden through real estate investments. As an aesthetic form, Skopje 2014 provided a way to reaffirm the symbolic belonging of Skopje on the world stage while also suggesting a new narrative for the whole Macedonian people—ethnically purged of Ottoman, Muslim, or Albanian influences and rooted in a new historical continuity with Alexander the Great. Façades transformed Skopje into Gruevski's own backyard—one that at the same time amplified his power and concealed his regime's shortcomings.

But if this new financial fiction was effective in generating consent, it was not only because of its spectacular, abstract, or affective characters.[10] Certainly, citizens felt that Skopje 2014 stripped them of their own city in a deep, existential sense that for many translated to a constant fear of the regime's ruthless machinations. That existential angst, however, stemmed directly from Skopje 2014's materiality. Façades were a physical manifestation of the political and economic contradictions of the regime and of highly personal forms of domination and corruption rather than of abstract, numeric financial flows. This subjective process, however, did not become operational by introducing a third layer of affective agency between citizens and the regime. On the contrary, Gruevski's neo-baroque façades and other urban projects dislodged citizens from their urban rhythms and forced them to inhabit new material spaces that kept on evoking the regime's crass corruption and their inability to change it. In its plaster physicality, Skopje 2014 oversaturated urban life with a new national narrative and *eliminated* the existential distance between the nation and the regime—not because it was successful at convincing the population that they were all descendants of Alexander the Great, but because it forced them to be trapped in an increasingly illiquid financial and urban landscape, completely separated from the glittering world of global finance.[11]

Unlike other peripheral cities, where citizens were captured by the seductive replication of innovative aesthetics,[12] Skopje 2014 never managed to transcend its own contradictions. Designed to literally encase Macedonians in a new urban and national narrative, "reinventing the city character and tradition through [a] globalist megaproject,"[13] Skopje 2014 appeared every year more absurd in its scale, cost, and execution. Neo-baroque plaster façades failed as a "broker between being and becoming,"[14] constantly reminding Macedonians that Gruevski was giving them an urban facelift instead of functional hospitals; that they, themselves, were often complicit with the crooked planning schemes of the regime—a far cry from the idealized image of true, rational European subjects. Rather than producing a credible global identity for Macedonia, "facelifting Skopje" revealed the constructed and contradictory dimensions of Gruevski statecraft—material proof of an authoritarian state that citizens felt powerless to stop.

Over time, the atmosphere of incapacity, inconsequence, and unaccountability fostered by the project gave way to a diffuse sense of anger. Citizens' struggles to inhabit ill-designed urban spaces and national narratives stopped fueling fear of a ruthless regime. Instead of a quasi-magical tool for statecraft that disguised and supplanted the frailty of Gruevski's grip on power, urban façades became a rallying force, a target for protests against the regime's brutality, and a scapegoat for Macedonians' collective shortcomings in opposing the regime.

Construction and Power

If Skopje 2014 was so effective in monumentalizing Gruevski and his regime, it was largely because of the secrecy and rumors that surrounded its finances. Despite having drawn an unrivaled amount of criticism and scrutiny, the price paid by the government and other public institutions for the Skopje 2014 project remains shrouded in secrecy. Initially, Skopje 2014 was described as an innocuous Keynesian stimulus to the economy worth approximately 200 million euro. In 2015, when daily protests had thrown the legitimacy of the regime into an international crisis, journalists revealed that the project had begun in January 2007, soon after Gruevski had gained power, and that by 2017 it had cost taxpayers over 683 million euro.

In interviews, economists close to the regime suggested that Gruevski's insistence in funding such a gigantic real estate scheme was an attempt to rescue a sector in danger of collapse. But the reasons Gruevski chose to invest in construction are far more complex. Even more than other firms that worked outside Macedonia, construction companies were a centerpiece of the socialist state. Giants such as Beton or Granit employed thousands of citizens, embodying Yugoslavia's aspiration to building a better future in a landscape of international solidarity. Already in the 1960s rebuilding Skopje had been a crucial part of the socialist state's strategy to mask its own economic problems, attract more investments, and promote global and local consent. Aware of their history, Gruevski utilized Skopje 2014 as a unique political bait: to gain the support of oligarchs who had privatized the sector thanks to their connection with the SDSM[15] while appealing to citizens' sense of nostalgia for a lost global relevance.

On the other side of a T-shaped table, looking obliquely at a map of Macedonia, sat a man in a carefully crafted blue suit. Unlike many other managers, Dragi was at ease in his leather chair and smiled calmly as he welcomed us into his office, at the core of Beton, a construction company I was interested in for its rumored connection to the government. Dragi was a hard man to meet. I had seen many managers who worked at Beton, but they had all been afraid of participating in my study without his permission, which they were too scared to ask for. After weeks of unanswered calls, Caci, a good friend, mobilized a contact who occupied an important position in the city administration. "They will have to respond to that; after all, they are the ones who give them work," she told me.

And there we were. The meeting itself was extremely cordial. I briefly outlined my interest in the company, the kind of observations concerning workers' everyday experiences I hoped to conduct, and my intention to look through the company's archives to document socialist financial practices. Dragi was particularly eager to explain the exemplary systems they had in place to guarantee workers' safety. He repeated at least three times that they abide by each International Organization for Standardization (ISO) 9001 or 45001 standard norm. "Of course, you realize, we cannot just let you go into the archives by yourself. We need somebody, say, a lawyer, to help you out," he suggested toward the end of the conversation. I assured him: I would only operate with their agreement. Finally, we stood up. He gave me his card and shook my hand. "I hope we became new friends today, and that we can remain friends, whatever happens."

In fact, nothing happened. For days, weeks, then months after our meeting, Skopje 2014 continued to grow, and I continued to receive no answer. Dragi was supposed to discuss the matter with the board of directors and then get back to me, but he never did. After a couple of months, when I had already started my work at Construx, one its chief engineers casually overheard a frustrated conversation I had with Caci and offered to call Dragi, an old friend of his. The day after, the engineer looked at me with pity. "Did you really have to mention financial practices?"

Like other financial aspects of Skopje 2014, Beton archives are shrouded in secret—an active illusion that affirms rather than denies the agency of people such as Dragi as gray eminences that could affect Macedonia's everyday life if they so wished. I started wondering: Was there anything in those archives that connected Gruevski to Beton as far back as the 1970s? Did socialist financial practices facilitate underground collaborations between oligarchs and businessmen that eventually empowered the VMRO–DPMNE? Masking the archives, like the masking of Skopje's financial sources, made the regime not only real but also expansive in both time and space.

Indeed, Beton had been a politically significant company since socialism, when the Macedonian construction sector had enjoyed years of expansion, encouraged by the twelvefold growth of Skopje during the twentieth century.[16] This rapid expansion had accelerated after 1963, when a devastating
earthquake severely damaged 75 percent of the city center. Capitalizing on its
unique position between the East and West, the Yugoslav leadership seized
this dramatic tragedy to direct flows of international aid, grants, and domestic investment toward the rebuilding of the city. Thus Skopje "resurged," mor-
phing its urban fabric from a "backward" regional center into a "city of solidarity," where companies such as Beton, Granit, Pelagonija, and Mavrovo
realized the plans of Kenzo Tange and other star architects and demonstrated
the (re)generative power of Yugoslav socialism.

By 1981, the Macedonian construction sector had expanded to 61,896 workers, while Yugoslav construction as a whole occupied 689,297 individuals—the
third largest sector of employment after industry and agriculture.[17] Together
with Pelagonija, Mavrovo, Ilinden, and Granit, Beton had become one of the
main companies active in rebuilding Skopje. When the reconstruction of
Skopje slowed down in the 1970s, Beton and other Macedonian construction
companies started to participate in projects abroad, generally as subcontractors of larger, Yugoslav import/export companies.[18] Beton built over twenty-
five industrial plants, bridges, clinics, administrative buildings, and hotels
in the Czech Republic. The company was also active in Libya in 1978, where
it built two university complexes and various other residential buildings. In
1980, Beton built military installations and the Iraqi Ministry of Oil.[19] Officially, these construction operations were part of a broader strategy that positioned the SFRJ at the center of the non-aligned bloc. Construction companies such as Beton participated in strengthening the defense, educational, or
housing capabilities of non-aligned countries in collaboration with the powerful Yugoslav Army. A series of political collaborations and low-profit financial flows that approximated what Johanna Bockman calls "socialist finance,"
or the attempt to construct a different financial system, centered on ideas of
solidarity rather than profit.[20]

But just like the reconstruction of Skopje, building ventures abroad did
more than "democratize international economic relations."[21] Instead, developing infrastructure in non-aligned countries sustained a global admiration
for the Yugoslav model, widely acclaimed as an economic success. The physical manifestations of socialist finance helped Yugoslavia shield its domestic production problems from the sight of international actors and access the

hard-currency payments and credit from international partners it desperately
needed.

In the 1990s, after the collapse of the SFRJ, Macedonian construction companies had to radically scale back the size of their operations. Without the lo-
gistic support of the Yugoslav Army and the financial backing of Yugoslav
banks, companies such as Beton and Granit were unable to recuperate their
machinery and their investments abroad, which remained largely unpaid. As
Yugoslavia descended into chaos and war, Macedonian companies stopped
being a symbol of the country's progress and became a testimony to its downfall. Without capital, international customers, or a sizable domestic market,
construction companies were preyed upon by unscrupulous investors who
took advantage of lax oversight of privatization schemes to buy workers out
for pennies on the dollar. Pelagonija went bankrupt shortly after its privatization; Mavrovo collapsed in size and relevance and was recently bought
by the Croatian company with which it had historically collaborated. Ilinden
survived privatization but came to face enormous financial challenges and
shrank to a negligible size. Only Beton and Granit maintained a semblance of
their political and economic relevance in postsocialist Macedonia.

After socialism, Macedonian construction companies depended financially on their ability to profit from the transition of other Eastern European
countries. Beton, for instance, fired more than half of its 6,000 employees and
took on construction jobs in Bulgaria and Russia, Mavrovo in Ukraine and
Russia. Granit built heavily in Russia, Bulgaria, and Kosovo. Even Construx,
originally an offspring of Mavrovo, worked in Kosovo and Bulgaria and later
recruited workers who had gone abroad as independent contractors. Around
the time of the global financial crisis, however, work abroad declined abruptly,
plummeting from a value of 74.3 million euro in 2007 to 14.5 million euro in
2012.[22] Without investments in productive processes and machinery, Macedonian construction companies found themselves unable to compete in a
global market wary of construction bubbles.

The critical situation of construction companies, which lost an estimated
5,000 jobs at the onset of the global financial crisis, created an opportunity
for the regime. It was only thanks to the Skopje 2014 project that the downward trend was contained; the industry managed to retain approximately
40,000 jobs throughout the crisis and even to expand to 50,000 employees
after 2013.[23] Companies such as Beton and Granit were literally saved by the
Skopje 2014 project. For Beton, owned by the magnate Minco Jordanov, the
project came to constitute almost the entirety of the company's profits in 2011.

Skopje 2014 also represented 30 percent of Granit's profits, although the company's overall income was complemented by other public investments that took place concomitantly, such as the building or rehabilitation of Macedonian highways.

A Baroque Network

Beton, like most other construction companies, had been privatized in the early 1990s through murky practices that had taken place during the SDSM government of Branko Crvenkovski. The cadres of Beton and Granit had cold relationships with Gruevski's VMRO–DPMNE before 2006. Having built his fortune on the import and export of steel-related products, Jordanov had earned notoriety as a deputy prime minister in a former SDSM government. After buying Beton in 2007, however, Jordanov took a more conciliatory approach toward the VMRO–DPMNE—a move that allowed Beton to profit enormously from the construction expansion promoted by Skopje 2014.

Like other construction moguls, Jordanov found himself increasingly entangled in a small network of oligarchs who commanded both deference and fear, in large part because of their connection to Gruevski's family. Among these businessmen, a key figure was without doubt Orce Kamcev. Son of a powerful socialist-era manager, Kamcev owned a business empire, which included the textile company Orka Holding, the bank Stopanska Banka AD-Bitola, the private hospital Sistina, and the Ibis Hotel in the center of Skopje. These business interests allowed Kamcev to gain significant international influence and enlist the help of powerful international politicians, including the United Kingdom's (UK) former prime minister David Cameron.[24]

The most influential oligarch, however, was not Kamcev but one of his business associates—Sašo Mijalkov, the head of the Agency for Security and Counterintelligence (UBK).[25] Described in urban folklore as a violent man, Mijalkov joined the military intelligence in 1998 and immediately worked toward solidifying strong personal connections between intelligence operatives. When he became director of the UBK in 2006, Mijalkov deployed these connections and turned the UBK into the surveillance arm of the regime. Under his watch, the agency mounted a large-scale, illegal operation that wiretapped 20,000 Macedonian citizens, businessmen, journalists, foreign diplomats, and even high-ranking members of the VMRO–DPMNE.[26]

Mijalkov's influence extended far beyond his official capacity as head of Macedonia's domestic intelligence. As the de facto owner of Security Group

Services (SGS), a private security firm, Mijalkov retained an almost uncontested monopoly over public contracts in the security sector.[27] According to my interlocutors, SGS extended their "protection" to private companies. Some of those who declined SGS's protection awoke to fires, broken windows, and other mysterious accidents—a modus operandi shared with the famous Bulgarian Multigrup during the 1990s.[28] Even popular cafes known to be meeting points for Skopje's intellectuals, some of whom engaged in active protests against Skopje 2014, were protected by SGS.

For many oligarchs, being in business with Mijalkov could turn into a double-edged sword. The income (and fear) generated by the SGS racket allowed Mijalkov (and Kamcev) to purchase profitable and strategic companies, such as the agricultural company Pelagonija and the dairy factory Zdravje Radovo, whose owners were secretly forced to sell their stakes to shell firms.[29] Through companies such as Finzy and Eksiko, registered in the US or Belize; owned by proxies in Cyprus, Switzerland, or the Czech Republic; and managed by low-profile, unknown Macedonian directors, Mijalkov and Kamcev amassed a small fortune. Between 2012 and 2015, Finzy and other companies were involved in dozens of international triangulations, which allowed oligarchs close to the regime to supply overpriced goods to Macedonian institutions and redirect their profits into their offshore accounts without leaving a trace.[30]

But shell companies had a larger role that interested oligarchs more than making money disappear. Finzy and Eksiko were crucial to bringing illegal money back to Macedonia in the form of investments in real estate businesses. Over time, Finzy and Eksiko acquired stakes in companies owned by Kamcev, including Beton Štip, one of the main players in Skopje 2014; the Ibis Hotel; and the residential complex Panorama Residence, alongside other fast-growing construction companies such as Iskra and Adora Grup.[31] In addition, Eksiko was linked to various construction and real estate moguls in Prague, where Sašo Mijalkov had resided for a significant amount of time. Kosta Krpac, the only witness able to provide evidence of Mijalkov's involvement in this network of offshore and real estate investments, was found dead in his home in April 2016, days before his scheduled appearance in court.

Foreign Currencies and Socialist Finance

For a decade Skopje 2014 diverted public scrutiny away from the networks of business interests that supported Gruevski's rule and toward issues of urban nationalism and contemporary corruption. The conspicuous absence of financial transparency reinforced a sense that neo-baroque buildings and plaster façades were indeed part of a massive money-laundering scheme, which involved building companies such as Beton, smaller subsidiaries, and ultimately the regime. This sense of inescapable interconnection, however, largely exaggerated the regime's strength and mystified contradictory relations with the networks of businessmen and intelligence operatives—whose financial deceits had kept the Yugoslav miracle and Macedonia's precarious finances flowing during socialism and the 1990s.

Cicko (uncle) Tito, as he called himself, had the gentle and clever manner of a man used to facing difficult problems. He welcomed me into his home, a modest two-story residence located in an ordinary part of Crnice, an expensive neighborhood overlooking Skopje, with a glass of excellent *rakija*, a strong kind of brandy. "I make it myself, you see, when I go to the mountains, where I have a plot of land. It's good for nothing, but at least I can distill good rakija there."

Given his connections to an import/export company based in Titograd (today's Podgorica in Montenegro) and Italy, I was curious to get Cicko Tito's perspective on the origins of Gruevski's power. How did Gruevski and his regime find the resources to set up these economic (and political) schemes? According to some sources, the network of shell companies utilized by the regime was inscribed in Gruevski's family's longstanding association with the world of intelligence and import/export companies. Yet others suggested that Gruevski's family had been relatively small fish, sidelined by oligarchs during the early transition. How did Gruevski manage to gain support from oligarchs and postsocialist intelligence operatives? Cicko Tito suggested that to understand how Skopje 2014 intersected the world of clandestine finance, it was necessary to retrace the steps of Gruevski's uncle Jordan Mijalkov, the father of the UBK director Sašo Mijalkov and a representative of one of Macedonia's biggest textile companies, Makoteks, in the Czech Republic. According to Cicko Tito, it was not by chance that "managers like Jordan Mijalkov became powerful. They had bank accounts in foreign countries, and when the country collapsed, who knows what they did with that money."

Directors and managers of import/export companies occupied a crucial position in the economic structure of socialist Yugoslavia as the brokers who kept the appearance of Yugoslav's economic miracle alive. Between 1950 and

1979, after abandoning Soviet-style policies, the Yugoslav economy achieved an average annual rate of growth of 6.3 percent,[32] elevating the living standards of citizens throughout the republics.[33] Consumption per capita, disposable household income, and real wages more than doubled over the thirty-year period,[34] leading many, even in the West, to admire and study the Yugoslav model of self-management.

This economic miracle relied heavily on foreign capital. Since the 1950s the SFRJ had run a deficit in its balance of payments that was covered by foreign, and especially American, grants and humanitarian aid.[35] The expectation of the Yugoslav leadership was that, over time, the country would become "economically responsible" and gradually replace international capital with home-grown funds.[36] But the Yugoslav economy never reached the pace necessary to overcome its dependency on foreign finance. As early as 1961, Yugoslavia needed to refinance its (hard currency–denominated) debt.[37] By 1964, the country experienced another debt crisis when the bulk of domestic companies' net income ended up servicing foreign debt. Paradoxically, the situation seemed to ease amid the general economic turmoil of the 1970s thanks to remittances from the Yugoslav diaspora in Western Europe. After the 1973 oil shock, the SFRJ took advantage of the low-interest loans made available by Western countries to subsidize stagnating growth and fuel domestic consumption.[38]

The expectation that Yugoslav society would improve by introducing a *sloboden pazar* (free market), regulated by "economic coercion"[39] and independent from foreign capital, would prove particularly unrealistic in the Socialist Republic of Macedonia, one of the least developed republics of the SFRJ. Data I collected show that the Macedonian economy was plagued by illiquidity and losses from the 1950s onward, especially in the crucial agricultural sector. A 1956 report from the Secretariat for Commerce lamented that transporting products from Macedonia to the Yugoslav border cost 30 USD per ton, while "from the Yugoslav border or port to the furthermost unloading port abroad, be it New York, Italy, Ceylon, Beirut, does not cost more than 20–25 USD per ton." Consequently, "while they are in season, one kilogram of tomatoes sells on average for 40 dinars in Munich, while [if exported from Macedonia] . . . the lowest price is 55 dinars, which means a loss of 15 dinars per kilogram."[40] The old socialist infrastructure, which included non-refrigerated and poorly ventilated railroad cars, left much of the produce to spoil, thus forcing tomatoes, peppers, and similar produce to become much more expensive.

Things were not much better on the manufacturing front. In the SFRJ, most advanced industries and processing centers were located close to the border with Western Europe. Bosnia, Kosovo, the south of Serbia, and Macedonia saw a concentration of mining, heavy industry, and energy production. Large enterprises, such as the nickel plant Feni and the steel plant Železara, built thanks to international loans contracted by the SFRJ to promote development in Macedonia, never recovered the sums that were initially invested—in part because of planning mistakes, in part because they were completed at a time when the global economic system favored small, light industry.[41] Out of sync with the global economy, Macedonian manufacturing exports lagged in quantity and quality and were not supported by a strong commercial network. In 1983, after thirty years of investment, Macedonia had the third highest percentage of foreign debt in relation to social product and the third lowest percentage of export in relation to foreign debt in Yugoslavia, better only than Kosovo and Montenegro.[42]

In a context of growing international debt, the SFRJ depended heavily on import/export companies to buy the foreign technologies needed by domestic manufacturers[43] and to sell abroad products that were (sometimes) inconsistent in quality and (often) overpriced.[44] While the rebuilding of Skopje had offered diplomatic cover for negotiating assistance without ruining the country's international reputation,[45] the problem became increasingly pressing for Macedonian companies. In 1975, the Federal Currency Inspectorate (*Savezni Devizni Inspektorat* or SDI) of Skopje reported significant problems with companies getting payments for exported goods. Because Macedonian companies had "little creditworthiness and low financial capacity,"[46] their products were often defective, and foreign partners did not want to pay without significant discounts. Consequently, Macedonian businesses were forced to increase their presence abroad, sending directors or managers "to secure payments and solve other issues."[47]

Payments in foreign currency rendered import/export companies structurally crucial for the functioning of the Yugoslav economy. Dependent on foreign imports, Yugoslavia relied on its reserves of deutschmarks, US dollars, and other foreign currencies to stabilize the country's currency and maintain a (fictive) exchange rate that could reassure international lenders even if its balance of payments was not always positive.[48] When exports decreased, it was the creative practices of import/export managers who manipulated currency flows that inflated the apparent health of the Yugoslav economy. Between 1970 and 1973, companies such as Jordan Mijalkov's Makoteks sold Macedonian textile products, including faux leather jackets and other leather goods, to their own branches in Germany, Austria, and Italy—where large sums of foreign currency disappeared. Other import/export companies such as Agromakedonija reported large unpaid contracts—or at least, sums of "foreign currency that were not brought into our country."[49] Investigators suspected that these accounting practices signaled forms of corruption that allowed import/export directors and managers to hide foreign currency. Agromakedonija, for instance, had over twenty international debtors, including its own branch office in Belgium, which pocketed half of the commission earned representing the German company Frisch, approximately 500,000 deutschmarks. Agromakedonija Sofija utilized annexes to increase the price of goods and appropriated the difference.[50]

All sources suggest that import/export companies systematically bypassed Yugoslav currency regulations. Some companies would import products from the Eastern Bloc, re-export them to their companies in Western countries in a fictitious sale, and then sell them within Yugoslavia, thus obtaining hard currency instead of *klirinški dolari*, a fictive currency used for intrasocialist exchanges.[51] Others did the opposite. They declared their imports as originating from Western countries to access import subsidies, while they were buying lower-quality products from the Eastern Bloc, often via a clearing agreement.[52] False invoices, underreporting imports or exports, whereby products were paid for but not imported or exported but unpaid for, were so extensive that some claim that Yugoslav aggregate statistics became totally unreliable.[53]

From the perspective of inspectors in Skopje, these manipulations of foreign currency damaged the Yugoslav economy and meant that Yugoslav companies were, de facto, "providing credit and financing foreign companies."[54] Cicko Tito had a different interpretation. To him, fictive sales were crucial to support the Yugoslav economy and keep the confidence of international partners alive. Fake invoices allowed a certain amount of currency to disappear from official circulation. That foreign currency would then be sold at a much higher exchange rate than allowed by the Yugoslav banks, either domestically or abroad. The profit realized would balance the export company's account or would be used to support other struggling companies. In fact, as various restrictions limited the amount of imports to a percentage of exports (typically around 80 percent in the 1970s), companies were incentivized to export at a loss if that allowed them to import parts crucial to the production processes of their Yugoslav partners.

Supplanting Yugoslav institutions as "the intermediary between the foreign contractor and the domestic producer,"[55] import/export companies, their financial directors, and foreign representatives engaged in financial practices that kept alive the illusion of the Yugoslav miracle and enabled the survival of domestic companies, especially in Macedonia. This is where foreign representatives acquired esoteric powers. Instead of condemning unviable Macedonian businesses to bankruptcy, foreign representatives transformed the losses of overpriced exports into gains by regularly converting, disappearing, and transforming foreign currencies on the global market—enabling Yugoslavia to preserve its inflated exchange rate and maintain access to international loans.

These financial illusions started to crumble during the 1980s. The second oil shock (1979–1985) put Yugoslavia under tremendous pressure from international creditors. Foreign lenders forced the SFRJ to adjust its currency exchange rate to a real value,[56] making imports costlier. Desperate to "raise hard cash by hook or by crook" to avoid the collapse of the dinar, the Yugoslav currency, and the blockage of foreign loans, federal organs of control started to shift their oversight strategies. Import/export companies were encouraged to export massively, even if that meant circumventing official regulations or generating losses.[57] At the same time, the inspectorate escalated its controls aimed at individuals. In 1981, the SDI found 9,173 code violations (up 20 percent from the previous year) and implemented a "stricter fining policy."[58] At this point, concert halls, tourist agencies, sports clubs, and even circuses and fairgrounds were subject to investigation.[59]

In a memo dated August 23, 1982, and classified as top secret, officers in Skopje were instructed to control banks that issued foreign currency accounts. The memo states that banks were supposed to deposit 15.9 or 20.9 percent of foreign currency inflows into a special foreign currency account of the National Bank of Yugoslavia—to "secure payments for gasoline and cooking oil, settle down the obligations of the federation, and to secure the necessary resources to settle fixed and guaranteed liabilities with foreign countries."[60] The tone was urgent. Without foreign currency, the survival of the entire Yugoslav federation was at stake.

Men of (Many) Services

While the import/export directors' sleights of hand delayed Yugoslavia's economic disaster, they were ultimately not able to avoid it. By the mid-1980s the

Yugoslav economy was paralyzed by a skyrocketing 19 billion USD in foreign debt, falling imports, and alarming rates of inflation of over 3,000 percent in 1990.[61] In 1991, Slovenia and Croatia declared independence, plunging the region into a bloody civil war. Yet for import/export companies this fragmented landscape represented an opportunity. With access to personal connections in multiple countries, flush with liquid cash in hard currencies, and accustomed to financial tricks to navigate blurry networks of financial relations, import/export directors such as Jordan Mijalkov were in a prime position to become crucial economic and political players. But there were other actors who were working to provide former Yugoslav republics with access to foreign currencies, foreign accounts, and business networks—many of them tied to the powerful Yugoslav security apparatus, especially the Agency for State Security (*Sluzba za Drzavna Bezbednost* or SDB) and the Yugoslav Army Counterintelligence Service (*Kontraobaveštajna Služba* or KOS).

Many rumors circulate regarding Jordan Mijalkov's political career. What is known for certain is that after his stint as director of Makoteks's Prague bureau, he was appointed as minister of the interior in the first government of independent Macedonia in 1991, where he rejoined family friends such as Minister of Justice Gjorgi Naumov and Prime Minister Nikola Kljusev. While this *Štipska vrska* (the connection through their hometown of Štip) is certainly important, it is rather bizarre that a crucial role in the new government, which included responsibility for managing powerful security structures such as the Yugoslav secret services, was entrusted to a civilian with no prior experience in police activity. Reports published in newspapers throughout the 1990s suggest that there was more to Mijalkov than met the eye—including connections to the powerful KOS.

The first thing I noticed about Eva were her eyes—benign and lively as if they belonged to a young adolescent rather than a former KOS agent. Yet when I introduced my research into our conversation, her smile faded almost imperceptibly, and I found myself looking at the enigmatic face of a marble statue. Now her eyes, as clear as a pristine mountain lake, were locked on my every expression, scorching my skin as they judged my intentions. Somehow, I forced myself to continue. I had been told by a former employee of Makoteks that Jordan Mijalkov was known to receive SDB operatives in his office even before his post in Prague. Others placed him within the circles of those right-wing sympathizers who formed the core of the VMRO–DPMNE—a group that operated largely underground during the socialist period. Eva lowered her voice and suggested that "if this is true, and if he was working with the services as well as the nationalists, then he must have been a double agent, a *dvojnik*."

I exchanged glances with Nikola, a Macedonian scholar who had been helping me in this delicate phase of my research. Eva was the first to mention that Jordan Mijalkov could have been working as a double agent—either for nationalist groups, or, as others suggest, for other countries. But who were these other entities? Eva was not sure: deals that involved the army involved KOS personnel, but she was not well positioned to help us further in civilian issues. Makoteks was surely within the SDB domain.

It was not until we met with Cicko Vanco, a former SDB operative, that we gained other insights into Mijalkov's career. A well-dressed man, Cicko Vanco appeared comfortable telling us *pikanterii* (spicy anecdotes) and details of operations that involved long-deceased people—he was the opposite of Eva, who carefully cultivated a nondescript, evasive demeanor. After a couple of hours of conversation, I asked him if Jordan Mijalkov was indeed a collaborator with the Yugoslav secret services. "*Pa da*," he erupted. "Of course, he was our collaborator! He has a dossier taller than himself!" His candor took us by surprise. Nikola jumped at the opportunity and pushed it further. Was he a *dvojnik*? Cicko Vanco hesitated a little. "Well, he worked for KOS, so we kind of let the army deal with him." According to Cicko Vanco, the SDB kept tallies on most directors of companies that worked outside of the country.[62] The agency did not control the companies' operations per se, but "we knew what they did. Mijalkov was a small fish; he sold currency on the black market. But we tolerated that because it did not hurt the country."

There might have been other reasons why the Yugoslav secret services tolerated (or possibly protected and encouraged) such schemes with foreign currencies, at least after the services were reformed in the late 1960s. For instance, they could have leveraged import/export companies as covers for illegal operations either to steal foreign technology or to smuggle weapons, alcohol, and drugs (especially amphetamines) in exchange for much-needed US dollars or deutschmarks—a documented occurrence in the Bulgarian socialist-era security services.[63]

Similar schemes popped up throughout the region during the wars of the 1990s and the early phases of privatization.[64] Socialist Yugoslavia, however, did not need to utilize underground channels to trade with Western countries or with the non-aligned bloc. The SFRJ routinely struck weapons and construction deals with non-aligned countries in exchange for dollars or natural resources.[65] Since the 1970s, however, reports from the SDI repeatedly referred to *crni fondovi*—unnamed black funds possessed by foreign representatives of Yugoslav companies. Former directors suggested that such funds were made up of small amounts of gold and foreign currencies available for the discretionary expenses of top managers. The SDI seemed inclined to believe that black funds were the result of embezzlement or fraud on the part of rogue directors. Cicko Vanco believed that most black funds were utilized by the Yugoslav secret services. In his narrative, unaccounted for and untraceable stashes of cash, as well as accounts in German, Swiss, or other Western or Eastern banks in the name of Yugoslav firms, were necessary to run covert operations between the East and West.

The different functions of black funds did not need to be exclusive. Even more than in Bulgaria or Romania, where the security services were known for their repressive tactics, collaboration with the Yugoslav secret police implied a two-way relationship. KOS, SDB, and their various incarnations provided their collaborators with useful services, ranging from "expediting access to the tangled bureaucracy to overlook . . . smuggling operations,"[66] in exchange for viable information. Indeed, import/export directors recount tense but convivial relations with intelligence operatives. After all, they operated in similar ways: import/export directors were accustomed to moving and manipulating currency through relationships, while for Yugoslav security operatives, relationships were quite literally currency.[67] This convergent way of seeing and operating in the world made import/export companies natural vehicles for covert operations—a nexus that made security agencies crucial to the myriad companies entangled in the fiction of Yugoslav currency manipulation.

With the rise of regional and ethnic tensions in the 1980s, intelligence operatives started to position themselves for a potential economic and political meltdown, which reconfigured the relationships between security services and import/export companies. As Yugoslavia fell apart and pivoted toward a gray-market economy in the early 1990s, these entangled collaborations evolved toward productive business enterprises, often in a ragtag fashion and without explicit planning. Cicko Vanco himself understood that his way of doing police work was outdated for the current political scenario. Like many of his colleagues, he left the agency and started various businesses in which he utilized his network of former contacts and colleagues to build (more or less) successful business ventures.

Macedonian operatives from KOS, however, were not so lucky. Between 1992 and 1996, news outlets such as Plus and Fokus exposed alleged KOS plans to generate incidents that could justify a Serbian invasion of Macedonia. In these allegations, the well-known supranational character of KOS and former Yugoslav Army officers was turned into proof of ethnic ambiguity. After the breakup of the SFRJ, former Yugoslav officers were recast as foreign agents plotting against the Macedonian people. Soon enough, these campaigns prompted political action, whereby the new government cleansed police, intelligence, and army ranks of these occult influences, firing, demoting, or "eliminating" various Macedonian officers who had served in the Yugoslav Army and security services.[68]

Plus and Fokus never published names or plans linked to the other main Yugoslav spy agency, the SDB. According to most of my sources from the intelligence community, this was not an accident. Instead, the selective publication of names in the Macedonian press indicated a collaboration between Kiro Gligorov, the powerful communist leader and first president of independent Macedonia, and the SDB to decapitate the leadership of the newly formed Macedonian Army, including its intelligence department.[69] This was the natural outcome of decades of close interaction between the SDB and local political leaders, who after the 1960s were able to "control the selection of republic SDB directors and fully control the activities of lower level SDB offices within their purview."[70] More important, liquidating the former cadre of the KOS allowed Gligorov and the SDB, now called the UBK, to become the only players who could influence international networks of trade and smuggling and the primary interlocutors for any aspiring Macedonian oligarch.

In the early 1990s, international networks of gray trade were crucial to the economic and political life of Macedonia. Unable to trade with its most important partner, Serbia, because of the various embargoes that followed the Yugoslav wars, and then paralyzed by a Greek economic blockade, independent Macedonia desperately needed access to foreign markets. On the institutional level, the Macedonian National Bank needed hard-currency reserves to stabilize its currency, while the state needed hard currency to import crucial goods, including drugs and military equipment. Thanks to the alliance between the UBK and Gligorov, Macedonia's former network of security officers and import/export companies turned into an infrastructure for smuggling oil, cigarettes, and weapons throughout the Balkans—allowing whoever managed it unprecedented influence in the country.

Gruevski and his family did not have a prominent place in Gligorov's plan. In December 1991, after only nine months as minister, Jordan Mijalkov died in a car accident. Newspapers began drawing associations between the VMRO–DPMNE, Mijalkov, and the KOS, suggesting that Mijalkov had been involved with anti-patriotic and pro-Serbian plots.[71] In 1994, Mijalkov's party, the VMRO–DPMNE, lost the parliamentary election, leaving free rein to Gligorov and his successor, Branko Crvenkovski, the leader of the postcommunist SDSM, who rose to power after a car bomb injured Gligorov in 1995.

With the support of the UBK, Crvenkovski completed the first wave of privatization, paving the way for a first generation of "legitimate" oligarchs. Under the permissive SDSM government, managers were able to privatize companies indiscriminately. By 1995, half of the socially owned companies had been sold to private investors, who paid, on average, 6.5 percent of their estimated value.[72] Among the businessmen who emerged, Trifun Kostovski and Minco Jordanov came directly from the import/export world, where they worked in Poland and Russia for the company Technometal Vardar—a company described by Yugoslav-era security operatives as one of their primary hubs for undercover operations. International networks were also at the root of the fortunes of other tycoons, including Šterjo Nakov, owner of the television channel Alfa, the winery Skovin, and the transport company Feršped; Hari Kostov, director of the Komercijalna Banka; and Velija Ramkovski, owner of various media including the television channel A1.

The first Macedonian oligarchy did not come into being without heated contestation. Between 1994 and 1998, newspapers reported daily scandals, bankruptcies, and layoffs that resulted in staggering unemployment, economic stagnation, and daily strikes. Increasingly frustrated with this level of corruption, Macedonian citizens punished Crvenkovski and the SDSM in the 1998 election, which consigned a majority to the VMRO–DPMNE. Things, however, did not take a turn for the better. Indiscriminate privatization continued to be allowed, and Macedonia became the main entry point for smuggling oil, weapons, drugs, and other resources in and out of Serbia during the NATO bombings in Kosovo in 1998–99.[73]

At this critical juncture, Gruevski and a group of trusted associates exploited his position as minister of finance to regain a foothold in the gray landscape of oligarchs and intelligence operatives.[74] Opposed by the early oligarchs connected to the SDSM camp, Gruevski and his clique began reactivating Jordan Mijalkov's connections inside the Macedonian intelligence community, accessing crucial information about the deals between import/export companies, secret services, and other oligarchs.[75] Some suggested that Gruevski did more than amass compromising information and utilized murky schemes to appropriate capital from three medium-sized banks, Eksport–Import Banka, Almako Banka, and Rado Banka; the latter ultimately went bankrupt and lost over 50 million euro of capital.[76]

While it is hard to evaluate these rumors, it is not unthinkable that Gruevski and his new allies from the Macedonian security services utilized Makedonska Banka or the other failing banks to orchestrate movements of capital and create or consolidate old and new business networks in the Balkans. Dimitrov, for instance, suggests that it was common for former secret services in Bulgaria to utilize failing banks to move capital abroad.[77] At least one of the failed Macedonian banks, Makedonska Banka, systematically channeled its funds toward Euroaksis Banka, a Russian entity opened with Serbian capital and owned by a controversial Serbian businessman.[78] While no conclusive evidence has been provided in relation to this case, there are signs that these bankruptcies might have allowed the VMRO–DPMNE to build partnerships with a host of foreign security services, including the Serbian Security Agency. Perhaps for that reason, agents of the Serbian Security Agency were among the mob that stormed the Parliament in 2017.[79]

Kitsch, Finance, and Urban Speculation

Security operatives inhabit a landscape in constant twilight, where truth, facts, and relationships are not starkly defined but dance and shift like shadows. In this world of penumbra, socialist networks of import/export managers overlapped with the Yugoslav security apparatus and shaped the trajectory of postsocialist oligarchs. As a minor player from a peripheral country, Jordan Mijalkov opened the door for his son, Sašo Mijalkov, and for Sašo's cousin, Nikola Gruevski. Now it was up to them to cast their own shadows on the gray landscape that had been created by already established oligarchs. To do that, they needed a strong, blinding light—something like impressive neo-baroque buildings and gigantic bronze statues.

Skopje 2014 built on the socialist legacy of financial schemes to create new alliances between Macedonia's first oligarchy and Gruevski's tight circle of associates. Most of the powerful oligarchs of the early 2000s had been linked to the SDSM and felt little enthusiasm for Gruevski. On the other hand, these oligarchs were enticed by the potential profits to be made from urban speculation. They knew that unresolved denationalization practices or bankruptcies had collapsed the value of land plots in Macedonia. Those parcels that did have private titles were often in the hands of individuals who did not have the capital needed to exploit them.

While this context presented prime opportunities, those oligarchs who had invested in real estate started to fear that a collapse of the market might reveal the origins of their fortune. Others were cautious about investing, afraid of inviting additional scrutiny by national and international authorities. The best scenario for appeasing the oligarchs' anxiety was a flurry of investments in the construction sector. Skopje 2014, with its spectacular, kitsch dimension, went beyond even the rosiest prediction. Acting as a branding device, the plan's excessive aesthetics allowed oligarchs to exploit gaps between current land prices and future profits, based on the growing cost of housing and land rents. With a little bit of luck, the renewed exuberance surrounding Skopje's urban fabric could hide or even erase the origins of their fortunes.[80]

Besides hiding the frailty of the regime and providing an avenue for urban speculation, Skopje 2014 was designed to reconfigure how working- and middle-class citizens experienced their urban surroundings. With the pretext of making the city more beautiful, the gargantuan urban redevelopment plan limited what people could do within the space around them and anchored Macedonia to the masculine figure of Alexander the Great and to the melancholic aura of pre-war Central Europe. Skopje 2014 unsettled urban sentiments about the city and the nation's identity, revamping an aesthetic irredentism that appealed to working-class citizens but not to urban elites. When workers fell out of love with the excess of Skopje's 2014 design, *Skopjani* found themselves engulfed in spaces they did not recognize, part of a national narrative they could not appropriate and in a surreal landscape that made them feel trapped and worthless. This new context prompted fear, doubt, and suspicion—not about the origins of the money involved in urban investments and the networks of oligarchs but about citizens' own urban belonging. As an existential and physical process, urban speculation started to corrode citizens' sense of autonomy and convinced them that Gruevski's government was not a small, fragmented oligarchy, but rather an invincible and omnipotent regime.

The National Archives was built to project a European aura and stake

Figure 4. The basement (and depository) of the Macedonian National Archives after a water leak. Note the binders of documents on the floor, close to water marks. Photo: Anonymous

claims on Macedonia's ancestral heritage. Yet just like most of Skopje 2014, the building was designed poorly and constructed cheaply. Despite its hefty price tag of 42 million euro, the façade featured a very thin layer of marble and a lot of polyester. Bathrooms for an entire floor had no running water and were built with second-rate stained marble or ceramics. The building's complex ornaments provided a comfortable abode for hordes of pigeons who left evidence of their habitation on the building's white exterior. The basement, which was supposed to host the Archives' actual depot, flooded regularly—forcing workers to utilize the older depot and manually transfer documents (see fig. 4). Considering workers' complaints of insufficient sunlight and air circulation, along with a flimsy door and windows and a poorly designed interior space, the Archives building did not sound like a great investment.

Most Skopjani seemed more affected by the symbolic and material weight of the Archives and the other buildings of Skopje 2014 than by the poor quality of construction. According to middle-class residents, the project forced them to assume uncomfortable positions and severely restricted how they circulated through, inhabited, and imagined the city. Through the new urban semantics of neo-baroque monuments and nationalist heroes, citizens were told that their city was now bigger, better, and more European. Yet they could no longer stroll along the riverbanks, now occupied by monumental buildings such as the National Archives, nor in proximity to the Government Building, which was now enclosed by fences. If they wanted to rest on public benches close to the old train station, they could no longer sit in socialist-era small parks but had to circumnavigate shiny new white façades and sit on the benches around the new VMRO–DPMNE headquarters.

Most of the people who inhabited the center, especially middle-class citizens, resented Skopje 2014. "This is not my city," young professionals and older retirees told me repeatedly. Interlocutors who had spent their youth sitting in grassless parks or sliding down decrepit concrete banisters knew the ins and outs of the modernist city where they circulated, greeting people at every step. In the words of scholar and architect Srdjan Jovanovic-Weiss, these Skopjani had identified beauty in their environment, even in the midst of abandonment, because "some of its most futuristic public spaces are in such wonderful neglect that they remain what they are no matter what happens to them."[81] In Dorina Pojani's study, longtime city dwellers adored the "dark beauty" of Skopje. In its 2014 incarnation, however, the city made them feel "'choked,' 'stuck,' 'usurped,' or 'suffocated.'"[82] Instead of propelling citizens toward an (unreachable) future, neo-baroque buildings chained Skopjani to a set of antique symbols that spanned from 1930s Serbian-built neoclassicism back to Alexandrian Greece. The result of these urban interventions was to glue a new layer of plaster identities on older socialist symbols, fracturing the relationship between people and space—in ways that evoked the forms of violence through which gentrification expelled residents from urban centers.[83]

For working-class citizens, however, Skopje 2014 had a different appeal. The speculative building spree that had accompanied the project allowed cash-strapped citizens to access housing through various credit schemes, thus

Figure 5. One of the most famous spaces of "wonderful neglect," inhabited and repurposed by young adults in Skopje. Photo: Author

redressing some of the difficulty that workers had encountered in accessing adequate housing since the socialist era.[84] As Dimova's work shows, the bombastic and unique character of kitsch aesthetics mimicked but also distorted the world of European luxury—a form of symbolic revanche that appealed to workers who had been disenfranchised by the postsocialist transition.[85] "Before, you had nothing to see in Skopje, nothing to take pictures of," a worker summarized—as if posting an Instagram of her daughter on a neo-baroque lion constituted a small but important moral victory.

Construction workers found that Skopje 2014 brought back blemished memories of their importance during the socialist period. Workers from Beton and Granit whom I interviewed were all critical of the regime and especially of the overall cost of the project, yet they found its aesthetics interesting. Buzo, a specialized construction worker, commented that "making some of the electrical wiring inside the bridge was hard. We were working suspended in very uncomfortable positions. But it was also interesting. It is not often that you get to create such a different project, so I enjoyed it." One of the architects, whom I will call Konstadin, was candid: "It was a hard project. It had different surfaces, different materials, and we needed to use particular techniques.

I enjoyed the challenges of the project; it was stimulating." As a follow-up, he continued to tell me about some makeshift solutions he had to come up with, and then he suddenly shifted to other ingenious fixes he had utilized in the past during the Yugoslav era.

These voices capture how Skopje 2014 foregrounded an "intensive political desire for world recognition"—a recognition that workers had lost in the aftermath of the postsocialist transition.[86] Yet as time progressed, these desires proved to be somewhat fleeting. Lights and singing fountains were great for taking pictures and for pretending to live in a beautiful city. My interlocutors found them less pleasant when they were attacked by swarms of mosquitos or flies that proliferated in the wet, luminous environment created by Skopje 2014. Pictures also did not look good in the copious "fog" that, since 2013, had become a constant of winter life in the Macedonian capital. Caused by high levels of particulate matter (PM_{10} and $PM_{2.5}$) in the air, this fog had led to weeks of flight cancellations and even a sizable number of premature deaths. According to the Macedonian Institute for Public Health (2015), "Approximately 1,350 deaths per year in the country are due to particulate air pollution. . . . The pollution particles cost the Macedonian economy about 253 million euro or 3.2 percent of GDP in 2011."[87]

Uncomfortable Communities

An electric energy permeated the streets of Skopje in the summer of 2016, when thousands of people marched daily, demanding the resignation of Gruevski. "Today is the day, we are going to occupy the Parliament," commented a woman. "Enough! Support to the Special Tribunal," chanted another. Following a different path each time, the protest always terminated at one of Skopje 2014's landmarks. When assembled, protesters utilized homemade elastic slings to throw paint bombs against the Parliament or other government buildings or water pumps to spray the new, neo-baroque façades of monuments and ministries with colorful dyes.

The idea of coloring the fountain below the statue of Alexander the Great with red paint, symbolizing the blood shed by the VMRO–DPMNE regime, had surfaced at least a year earlier in a meeting attended by no more than a dozen activists. The mood was somber and the room filled with doubt, suspicion, and fear. "We should blow up the whole damn project," said one of the women seated, exaggerating her own exasperation. Others listened to her outburst, uncomfortable, as she continued to lament the lack of reactions among the citizenry. Despite years of protests against the regime and its urban politics, activists had very little success in thwarting Skopje 2014. Over the years, the government was not prevented from cutting trees, erecting new statues, and procuring doubtful subcontractors. "But what can we do? The [Macedonian] people are just an aimless herd. We lack a critical mass, that is the problem," finished the activist, before turning away and lighting up a cigarette. In that meeting and many others that preceded it, activists turned from considering possible actions to voicing endless critiques that targeted not the regime but themselves and their fellow Skopjani—in particular, their inability to act collectively.[88]

From the activists' perspective, their inability to act was a direct consequence of the sheer materiality of Skopje 2014. Not unlike the urban theatrics implemented by other authoritarian or fascist regimes,[89] neo-baroque urbanism enforced a strict division of the city's urban space that reoriented the Macedonian nation along ethnic lines.[90] Despite significant protests,[91] statues of hoplites, Christian icons, and controversial anti-Albanian leaders filled the city center—a bubble of Macedonianness within the older socialist city that erased non-Christian Macedonians from the nation's memory.

But Skopje 2014's pernicious effects also extended to those subjects who were included within the new definition of Macedonianness. At the core of its nationalist bubble the project placed the historical VMRO movement, an anti-Turkish group of rebels active during the nineteenth-century Balkan wars whose heritage was claimed by the VMRO–DPMNE. In propaganda materials such as the publicly aired documentary series *Skopje Prodolzuva* ("Skopje Continues"), the building of a new Skopje was presented as a necessary outcome of the Macedonian struggle for independence, finally achieved thanks to the VMRO–DPMNE. The Macedonian nation was led, or rather menacingly escorted, to its new home by Gruevski, Mijalkov, and the VMRO–DPMNE inner circle—a scene that was depicted in the fresco commissioned by Gruevski to adorn the VMRO–DPMNE headquarters.

Despite its socialist-realist style, the painting was strikingly accurate. Just as in other authoritarian states in Eastern Europe,[92] Mijalkov and Gruevski were, in effect, at the center of a kinship system that generated Skopje 2014 and its network of shell companies. Nikola Kljusev, the first prime minister of independent Macedonia, was *kum* (best man) to Jordan Mijalkov. Sašo Mijalkov, Jordan's son and Gruevski's cousin, was *kum* to Žarko Lukovski, who owned Eksiko, one of the shell companies that directed investments throughout Macedonia. Sašo Mijalkov was also *kum* to Orce Kamcev, owner of Orka Holding and co-investor with Eksiko in multiple shell companies and the richest person in Macedonia.[93]

Creators, profiteers, and ideologues of the new Skopje, Gruevski and Mijalkov used Skopje 2014 to promote a new urban and national identity that was saturated with their own family. Initially, this definition of Macedonian identity appealed to newcomers and working-class citizens. But what kind of honest Macedonian could feel truly at home in a city, and by extension a nation, that seemed to belong to a single family? Instead of fostering a new, unified national identity, the sheer scope of Skopje 2014 and its failure to mask corrupt deals made more evident the constructed nature of Macedonian nationalism—together with the class, gender, and urban cleavages that fragmented the ethnic Macedonian community.

Activists and second- or third-generation Skopjani found themselves questioning their ability to connect with fellow Slavic-speaking, ethnic Macedonians who appeared to embrace kitsch aesthetics. In activists' discussions, Skopje 2014 seemed to have unleashed a right-wing, working-class apocalypse, the worst in Macedonia's troubled postsocialist history. Could activists expect anyone, and especially disenfranchised working-class citizens, to oppose Skopje 2014's new national identity, whose promises were literally being carved in stone-like plaster? "Maybe, Skopje 2014 is what we deserve," suggested some activists—as if a kitsch, made-up identity might be well suited to what they had naturalized as their inability to act.

The symbolic incorporation of the Macedonian nation within Gruevski's lineage effected by neo-baroque monuments and façades dissolved in 2015, when damning recordings exposed the regime's oppressive tactics and its widespread violence. Suddenly, façades were not perceived as proof of the regime's omnipresence but of its crass brutality—a material manifestation of Gruevski's contradictions that empowered waves of protests. When activists threw barrels of red dye into the main fountain and started painting its plaster monuments with impunity, the VMRO–DPMNE became an object of ridicule—a fragile political structure unable to stop the desecration of the urban spaces that it had invested with so much meaning. That act of defiance energized other protesters, who quickly took up painting and defacing Skopje 2014 monuments as a distinctive symbol of the new, colorful revolution. It was as if coloring and soiling the white neo-baroque surfaces broke the regime's aura of invulnerability. In the words of a close participant, "It was like a weight had

Figure 6. Skopjani take to the streets during the Colorful Revolution. Photo: Vanco Dzambaski

been taken off our back. We took to the streets, threw paint and dyes against those monuments, and suddenly it was like an explosion of energy, and joy."

To Disneyland and Back

There is little doubt that finance follows the global laws of profit. Once it intersects with the lives of human beings, however, finance becomes part of a complex web of social relations.[94] Financial products such as mobile money, microcredit allowances, and mortgages are entangled with and shaped by the lives of customers and citizens who use them to produce or contest boundaries, even in face-to-face interactions.[95] With the Skopje 2014 plan, the interweaving of finance with social life assumed a monumental shape. Incarnated in neo-baroque façades, gigantic statues, and a host of dense, subpar residential buildings, financial speculations unsettled the urban rhythms of Skopje by enveloping citizens in a new, decidedly uncomfortable national narrative—one that helped reify Gruevski's regime.

At first, many Macedonians, especially working-class citizens, appreciated the kitsch nature of Skopje 2014. As an aesthetic of excess, kitsch seemed to embody their demand for recognition—one that working-class citizens felt extended to the entire nation.[96] But that feeling changed with the proliferation of statues and the worsening of atmospheric pollution. By 2014, most interlocutors felt constrained by the boundaries of the new, financialized Skopje, its dysfunctional architecture, and its poorly planned spaces. Instead of affirming Macedonian identity and celebrating Gruevski's family, Skopje 2014 came to be perceived as a veneer for corruption—a testament to Macedonians' inability to trust one another and to act collectively.

Behind the neo-baroque façades lay a series of rather unpatriotic relationships. Skopje 2014 was the recipient of an impressive flow of public investments, explained to international investors and donors as an innocuous Keynesian stimulus to offset the global financial crisis and support domestic companies cut off from global markets. Instead, the Gruevski regime utilized Skopje 2014 to funnel public investments to companies offshore and strengthen its network of allies.

When Gruevski took power in 2006, the VMRO–DPMNE government did not control enough economic resources to compete with other Macedonian oligarchs. Mijalkov's family, the most prominent in the regime, had operated in the import/export world during socialism—a sector that had achieved considerable influence thanks to Yugoslavia's structural dependency on foreign technology and currency. Under the watchful eye of Yugoslav security agencies, managers such as Jordan Mijalkov stretched the limited amount of foreign currency gained by Yugoslav exports to cover the increasing needs of Yugoslav businesses and institutions. When Yugoslavia fell apart in the early 1990s, Mijalkov and other oligarchs-to-be were caught in the fight between former Yugoslav intelligence agencies—the beginning of a decline that lasted until the election of Gruevski as prime minister. By the time the VMRO–DPMNE regained its foothold in the Macedonian security services, a strong oligarchy had coalesced around the SDSM. By that point, Skopje 2014 investment schemes proved to be a useful political instrument. The speculative urban bubble allowed the VMRO–DPMNE regime to enlist the support of other Macedonian oligarchs, who could now cleanse their gray capital through investments in real estate.

This historical context highlights the political causes of urban speculation in Macedonia. Inside the Skopje 2014 bubble, however, Yugoslav currency manipulation, postsocialist thefts of property, and current-era extractive financial schemes were partially hidden from the public eye. Shady socialist financial networks and fictions were replaced by a hyper-real construction

Figure 7. A man looks, perplexed, as workers assemble Alexander the Great's horse. Photo: Author

landscape that forced Skopjani to inhabit uncomfortable physical and existential positions. While Gruevski imagined neo-baroque aesthetics as a glorious narration of his family's role within a revanchist, grand Macedonia, older middle-class residents of Skopje felt threatened by the very fabric of their own urban communities—whose unity Skopjani could recognize in the Skopje 2014 landscape but could not identify with.[97]

Somewhat akin to socialist financial schemes, where currency speculations and urban redevelopment had helped disguise the country's economic weakness and broker international aid, Skopje 2014's deception was directed toward Macedonian citizens. Through the project, Skopjani experienced "the visible normality of apparently unrestrained power—of grandiose plans, loose commitments, illegal actions."[98] Faced with their own powerlessness, citizens did not question the legacy of the project but wondered who among their fellow Macedonians was profiting from it and why they had failed to support each other against Gruevski's aggressive urbanism. Paradoxically, the failure of neo-baroque façades to produce a coherent, credible "all-encompassing nation-building mechanism"[99] over time did not empower critics of the project. Instead, knowing that a veneer for shady deals among postsocialist oligarchs such as Skopje 2014 continued to exist impelled activists and citizens to turn an increasingly critical and disquieting gaze on themselves. It was as if Skopje 2014 prompted both economic and existential speculation—an epistemic conundrum in which critical questions about citizens' complicity or incapacity to resist the regime hid the fragility of Gruevski's power.

To build such a speculative real estate bubble required significant and constant investment. Luckily for Gruevski, the global financial crisis had prepared a fertile international audience interested in new, low-risk opportunities for investment—including speculations in Skopje's urban landscape. Making Macedonia readable to international finance, the Skopje 2014 real estate bubble allowed for the convergence of two separate sources of financial flows—one rooted in Yugoslav-era illiquidity, currency manipulation, and secret deals, the other mediated by global illiquidity. More complex than a "subordinate" relation, this encounter became a crucial part of the VMRO–DPMNE regime and its extractive landscape.

2 Peripheral Financialization

Seventeen companies announced they will build factories in Macedonia; we are in close contact with all of them. They are working actively to prepare the projects and everything else they need to build the factories. The investments that are already in place, such as Dräxlmaier, Johnson Matthey, and Johnson Controls, have produced 11,000 jobs and many more indirect ones. Those we just announced will create 13,000 new jobs combined. There is significant interest for more investments. Every week I, or someone from the foreign investments team, meet with at least one or two companies that want to come [to Macedonia].

Nikola Gruevski, November 22, 2014

WHEN FINANCE MOVES from the center to the periphery, it rarely follows abstract calculations of profits. Instead, it embodies dreams, expectations, or nightmares. In thriving Eastern European cities, mortgages or consumer loans express middle-class appetites for consumption and cosmopolitanism. In more depressed parts of the periphery, finance becomes enmeshed with subterranean histories of stagnation in which hopes of profit and realities of loss are often two sides of the same deal.

In this chapter, I highlight the social paradoxes that led Macedonia to become a destination of international financial speculation. From the perspective of global investors, until the global financial crisis there were very few reasons to consider investing in Macedonia, a country that had been transformed into a financial wasteland through decades of political and economic instability. To reverse this trend and put Macedonia "on the map," Gruevski's government launched a branding campaign that seemed to reflect the developmental priorities outlined by international organizations: transform the country into a labor reservoir for companies interested in relocating production. Conjuring an onrush of greenfield investments in manufacturing, Gruevski's pompous speeches and inflated statistics portrayed Macedonia as a country awash with international investment opportunities—implying the existence of a productive renaissance that promised to become a financial bonanza for savvy global investors and Macedonian citizens alike.

To an extent, Gruevski's branding campaign was successful. Between 2006 and 2015, several global companies started to invest in Macedonia, propelling the country into the top ten best economic reformers. Financial organizations followed suit, offering loans to strengthen the country's infrastructure and betting on its continuing openness to foreign finance. Between 2007 and 2015, Macedonia's public debt had tripled in absolute terms from around 1.3 billion euro (20 percent of gross domestic product [GDP]) to 4.10 billion euro (46 percent of GDP)[1]—a much faster increase compared to other countries in the region.[2]

Yet global investors were much more cautious when it came to the private sector. Most found Macedonian business practices illegible, and started rationing credit lines to companies in anticipation of financial instability. Excluding a few multinational groups, most foreign businessmen I met in Macedonia were not the international billionaires or global managers evoked by Gruevski's speeches. Cash-strapped, hurt in their personal and professional lives by the European crisis, male entrepreneurs came predominantly from countries that had slid toward the European periphery and saw Macedonia as their last resort. Instead of bringing jobs and money, these foreign micro-"investors" brought anxious hopes—dreams of wealth fed by the inflow of European aid, loans, and investments that had fostered Gruevski's government's building spree.

Once in Macedonia, however, foreign businessmen quickly realized that intercepting international finance was a painful and sometimes dangerous process. Micro-investors found themselves in a chaotic landscape, cut off from larger European corporations or institutions and surrounded by business partners who tried to scam them out of money they did not have.

If micro-investors found themselves as targets rather than beneficiaries of financial extraction, it was often thanks to Gruevski's manipulation of Macedonia's subterranean history of economic decline. Once part of socialist Yugoslavia, a country at the political and financial heart of Europe, Macedonian businessmen and administrators had seen their social lives unravel since the collapse of socialism. Greek embargoes, criminal privatizations (see Chapter 1), and ethnic conflicts had excluded Macedonians from accessing the sudden and potent inflow of cheap money that had benefited the middle classes in countries such as Portugal, Ireland, Italy, Greece, and Spain (derogatorily referred to as PIIGS).

By 2010, this social context seemed about to change. The global financial crisis exposed the vulnerability of rising Southern and Eastern European countries. Micro-investors moved further eastward, searching for cheaper labor, sensual pleasures, and public contracts, and triggering new hopes in the stagnant Macedonian economy—as if their arrival constituted a sign of wealth to come. Banking on the decade-old thirst for social recognition, Gruevski and his regime fueled these expectations and painted European investors as cash cows to be squeezed for rent—but only under the patronage of the VMRO–DPMNE regime.

What ensued were tortuous encounters mired in different expectations of profit, a rentier landscape where businessmen and administrators from Macedonia and the EU tried to utilize their geopolitical positions to extract monetary and existential benefits. Unlike classic examples of rent, which refers to unearned income generated by ownership, the friction that different predatory hopes generated within the circulation of finance became politically productive for the regime—precisely because of their contradiction.[3] Instead of fueling processes of abstraction, where financial flows disembedded economic relations from their social contexts, encounters between European investors and functionaries or local businessmen and administrators generated a chaotic environment filled with physical violence and exploitation. Exposed to unpredictable and constant threats, larger investors and European institutions entered into tense, conflicting, but ultimately symbiotic relationships with the VMRO–DPMNE regime—a cultural and political convergence that amplified the rentier approach already fundamental to European aid. Distant from sudden riches or the proverbial wall of money, financialization at the European periphery unraveled a collection of failed deals and more or less fictional rents that framed the emergence of a powerful and yet fragile authoritarian regime.

Leaving the Sinking Boat: Italian Hopes for an Eastern El Dorado

It was a strange request. The director of Construx, the construction company where I did most of my research in 2013 and 2014, wanted me to come to his office. His assistant wouldn't say more on the phone, but it had something to do with Italians.

In the director's office I found Marco and Giovanni, two middle-aged businessmen from the Italian northeast, accompanied by Nikola, a Macedonian associate who acted as their translator. Sitting close to the director, I listened to Nikola discuss the thermal and acoustic insulating mortar material that the Italians had developed. The director, nicknamed Moustache by his workers, seemed unimpressed by Nikola's chatter. Yet every time that he asked Marco and Giovanni directly, in slow but accurate Italian, to see certificates that proved the characteristics of the materials, Nikola would jump in and dodge the question with some vague answer. "Then we'll talk again after we see them. Meanwhile, you'll be in touch with Fabio—he's my right-hand man in these matters," concluded the director. "Find out what you can about them," he whispered in my ear as we walked out. "I trust you."

After the conversation, the director forgot about the Italians. Marco and Giovanni, however, took him at his word. The following week I received a call from Marco. They were nearby, finishing the external flooring of a new eight-story residential building together with a crew of young Albanian men from the nearby city of Tetovo, and they wanted to meet to explore possibilities of collaboration. I could do little for them, but we decided to sit down for a drink of *salep*, a typical winter drink of Turkish origin, while talking about their business.

Marco had moved to Macedonia after the Italian company he worked for at home went bankrupt in 2010. First working as a consultant, Marco had realized that Macedonia had abundant supplies of high-quality sodium carbonate, which he could develop into a proprietary material with excellent thermic and acoustic isolation capabilities—something that construction companies in Macedonia would be very interested in purchasing. In 2012, he moved to a city in the western part of the country. There he found an intermediary who could work for him, mixing products he bought through resellers from different mines in the region—a complex arrangement necessary to preserve the secret of his formula and circumvent the monopoly held on sodium carbonate by international companies who owned the Macedonian mines.

Marco was telling me how he had enlisted Giovanni to help him out with the logistics when Giovanni interrupted us, pulling Marco's arm and pointing outside. "I saw him . . . there, behind . . . I think it is him." Marco looked worried for a second, then he waved his hand, "No, it is not. Come on." Still worried, Giovanni shrugged his shoulders and took over the narrative. "I was selling electrical stuff, you know, everything from lighting systems to décor and chandeliers. But with the crisis I had to close down, so here I am." In the winter of 2013, they had not yet started full-scale production of their material and worked mostly with small quantities. With the help of Nikola, their local partner, the pair took on some small jobs, mostly related to giving the final touches to external paving and flooring, which would help them develop their contacts. That side of the business was curated by Lollo, who had previously worked in Italy and who acted as their "insurance" thanks to his close contacts with the local police.

At first, Marco and Giovanni seemed to embody the quintessential expression of the logic of capital. Coming from a country at the core of the global economy, the duo had moved east to look for new opportunities as profits within the Italian market fell. In Macedonia, they had developed a new product with materials they did not own, hoping to turn a profit by exploiting the country's inexpensive workforce.

And yet the duo were fundamentally different from most of the investors who typically do capital's dirty work. They had no money. Like thousands of other Italians, both Marco and Giovanni had recently lost their jobs and had faced periods of precarious underemployment as the country experienced a growth in unemployment (12.5 percent in 2013, with peaks over 40 percent for those under twenty-five years old).[4] The crisis had been particularly impactful in the Italian northeast, where Marco and Giovanni lived—where the region's network of small and medium-sized enterprises, once one of the economic engines of the "third Italy," turned into a landscape of economic devastation.[5] In the period from 2007 to 2016, Italian industrial production decreased 22 percent and the country's public debt increased from around 100 percent of GDP in 2007 to 130 percent of GDP in 2014.[6] From 2008 to 2013, over 59,000 companies closed, with an average of two bankruptcies every hour.[7]

In the depressed economic climate of postcrisis Italy, entrepreneurs such as Marco and Giovanni had no place. They were too old to be considered for entry-level jobs, too young to retire, and too unqualified for some of the high-tech ventures where new positions were available. Faced with the need to support his family, Marco had taken technical positions with companies operating abroad—leaving behind his partner and two children. Giovanni, on the other hand, had jumped from odd job to odd job, building up frustration that, over time, estranged him from his wife and daughter.

Rather than money, then, micro-investors such as Marco and Giovanni brought to Macedonia a set of hopes and aspirations. For them, Macedonia represented a second chance—a frontier where they hoped to turn around not only their economic fortunes but also their social ones. For micro-investors like the Italian duo, the low standard of living in Macedonia meant that, even without much capital, they could afford to mingle with other entrepreneurs, attend parties, and have a respected role in society—as entrepreneurs rather than unemployed citizens.

To properly succeed as businessmen and gain the respect they felt they deserved, Marco and Giovanni were interested in more than money. Like many other expats working in Eastern Europe,[8] Marco and Giovanni were particularly troubled by their inability to affirm their manhood in Italy. In Macedonia, instead, they could boss around (underpaid) workers or casually hang out with other male, foreign investors. There, their Europeanness, status, and small investments allowed them to engage in flirtatious encounters with Macedonian women, who embodied their ideal of white, European, or Mediterranean beauty—all with relatively little competition.

One night, I accompanied Marco and Giovanni to the opening of an exclusive lounge bar that aspired to attract some of the nouveau riche close to Gruevski's government. As I squeezed past the mass of tightly packed bodies, Giovanni pulled unceremoniously at my shirt. "Look at him," pointing at Marco and his housekeeper hitting it off. "Now I have to get lucky too," he insisted. I followed his glance as it scanned the room and landed on the generously filled dress of a striking middle-aged woman. Shortly, Marco, his housekeeper, and a friend left to get a drink at another place. Giovanni, however, insisted I stay on as his wingman, as he scribbled his number on a piece of paper ripped from a cigarette package and prepared to make his move. Still, he hesitated. That small, fragile piece of paper carried the weight of a world in disarray.

Unable to force his feet to move, Giovanni started to confide in me—as if speaking about his family could dissolve the images that had just filled his mind. Giovanni told me about his tense relationship with his daughter and about the difficult life that Marco had back in Italy with his family. For a moment, he even took his eyes away from his Macedonian crush, lost in a labyrinth of thoughts. Finally, his arousal triumphed. He walked up to her, struck up a conversation, delivered the piece of paper with nonchalance, and walked away. In our taxi, he was exhausted. Had it been a good idea? Would she call? Had he been too direct? We continued to examine all the possibilities until we reached a Cuban bar, where Marco was dancing avidly with his housekeeper and their other Italian friend was working his charms on three very young girls. Hugging Giovanni and me in a friendly gesture, he introduced us all and then ordered one more bottle of white wine. "Pretty good, ah!" he screamed to us, his face red. "Oohohoooo!" answered Giovanni, his glass in hand. I raised my glass, a shadow of shame lurking in my half-smile.

Illusions and Infrastructure of Finance

Marco's and Giovanni's gendered trajectory offers a complicated view of what happens when finance expands at the periphery. Their profiles are very dissimilar from those of financial investors—if not in their predatory aspirations, at least in their ability to harness global finance. So what makes microinvestors agents of financialization, if they have no significant sums to invest in Macedonia? This constitutes one of the first paradoxes of financial expansion at the periphery: financial expansion can, in fact, feed off the presence of cash-strapped investors, because financialization is not premised on the actual transfer of capital but on its illusion.

In productive processes, adding value and generating profit takes place through the transformation of capital and labor into services or products. In the case of finance, however, it is not necessary to produce anything to generate value. In fact, quite the opposite is true. Less capital can increase the monetary value of stocks or other financial products. As Karen Ho famously demonstrated, stakeholders' evaluations can push stock value up during downsizing when the productive parts of a company are dismantled.[9]

As investors suggested during my interviews in both Macedonia and the US, similar sets of expectations frame how financiers decide whether to invest in a country. It is not so much the quantity of capital or its productive context that makes a country attractive for investment. Rather, it is the expectation that other investors will also be investing in it, driving up the value of early financial moves. What is needed to generate financial expansion, then, is an infrastructure of dreams, expectations, and hopes that are articulated around a specific understanding of what counts as value—a sort of cultural infrastructure of both words and appearances[10] that, given the right material circumstances, can turn a peripheral economy into a legitimate destination for investment.

In countries such as the US or elsewhere in Eastern Europe, risky economic practices can become productive opportunities to extract rent through the deployment of specific technologies of evaluation. In the work of Martha Poon and many other sociologists of finance, credit scores, rating standards, and other similar calculative tools allow international investors to make equivalences between debt products and to calculate profit margins on domains of life that are, by themselves, completely disparate.[11] With adequate models of forecasting, investors can feel confident about betting on the chances of rainfall in Paraguay, the profitability of housing bonds in Sacramento, or the likelihood of Ebola prevention in Sierra Leone.[12]

The kind of data needed to construct reliable evaluation tools was mostly unavailable in postsocialist Macedonia. Afraid of high unemployment and political and economic tensions, financial institutions had been historically cautious with liquidity requirements for lenders and interest rates for new loans, resulting in a rather depressed formal financial landscape. In the early 2000s, despite a need for new housing, only 2 percent of Macedonian households possessed mortgages,[13] relying instead on a variety of formal or informal financial arrangements such as pooling family credits or rescheduling socialist loans. By the mid-2000s, the economic situation was so fuzzy that it was impossible to utilize credit-rating tools or even more conventional metrics based on property to showcase the country's readiness as a destination for international finance.

To counter the opacity of Macedonia's economy, Gruevski had run on a platform of transparency and economic reform that had been widely praised by the international community, especially for its intention to open Macedonia to foreign investment. At the beginning of his mandate, Gruevski created *Invest in Macedonia*, an agency dedicated to marketing Macedonia as a safe haven for global finance. Staffed with a team of at least twenty-five economic promoters under the direct supervision of the prime minister, Invest in Macedonia regularly scouted international fairs abroad, dedicated personalized attention to foreign companies interested in relocating, and prepared the terrain for the government's roadshows, where Gruevski directly brokered business deals—with the goal of bringing to Macedonia at least 138 factories and 62,700 new jobs, for a total of more than 3.8 billion euro of investment.[14]

To capture the attention of global investors, the agency had spent heavily on a rebranding campaign aimed at improving Macedonia's international reputation.[15] *Invest in Macedonia* regularly bought airtime on major international channels such as the British Broadcasting Corporation (BBC), put up billboards at international airports (including Istanbul Atatürk), and created and circulated dozens of video clips showcasing Macedonia's natural beauty. These clips, directed by the world-acclaimed artist Milcho Manchevski, presented Macedonia's history as a continuum between the empire of Alexander the Great and Gruevski's Macedonia. Leveraging the new historical and kitsch architecture of neo-baroque Skopje, Macedonia was presented as an exotic and yet sensually futuristic tourist destination, reachable through inexpensive flights. Unbeknownst to the public, Gruevski subsidized Wizz Air, a low-cost Hungarian airline specializing in Eastern Europe, and struck a questionable deal to renovate the Skopje Alexander the Great Airport. Airlines such as Turkish Airlines, and more recently, Alitalia, Qatar Airlines, and Emirates, began to offer worldwide flights to Macedonia via Istanbul, Paris, Milan, Venice, Doha, Dubai, and other cities.

But the focus of *Invest in Macedonia*'s promotional material was the country's high-quality, skilled, yet inexpensive workforce. In pamphlets, graphs, and charts, the agency went out of its way to signal that Macedonian workers were not only cheap but also skilled and educated—ready to be exploited for any entrepreneur savvy enough to take advantage of the four special economic zones built in Skopje, Štip, and Tetovo, or the nine more planned throughout the country. Companies that decided to invest in these zones could take advantage of a ten-year tax break, discounts on utilities, up to 500,000 euro in construction incentives, and land with ready-to-use infrastructure. Companies paid no VAT (value-added tax) or customs duties if producing for export and no personal or corporate tax for the first ten years, after which they would be subject to a 10 percent flat tax rate.[16]

To an extent, portraying Macedonia as an accessible and commodified labor reservoir was a strategic decision that utilized a well-known global indicator, FDI, as a predictive measurement of the financial opportunities and future profits.[17] Branding Macedonia as a destination for FDI in the manufacturing and software sectors reinforced global fantasies about Eastern Europe—a space at the same time "primitive" enough to constitute one of Europe's frontiers but closer and easier to navigate compared to other developing countries.

Despite this global resonance, Gruevski's highly publicized investments in urban renewal and his branding campaign worked only partially. Gruevski managed to attract a few larger international conglomerates: Johnson Controls produced car seat covers; the Belgian Van Hool produced buses; and the multinational chemical firm Johnson Matthey produced emission control catalysts in Macedonia and has become the most important exporter of goods from the country. By and large, however, Gruevski's strategy attracted entrepreneurs such as Marco and Giovanni who came from other European peripheries with very little financial capital to invest.

Over his ten years of government, this inflow of small-scale investors led to only 579 million euro of FDI in Macedonia, one-sixth of what Gruevski had expected.[18] Instead of constituting a crucial source of financing as it had in other Eastern European countries,[19] this kind of FDI-driven financialization cost the Macedonian state over 159 million euro in subventions and promotional activities. Companies invested 92.1 million euro in salaries and pocketed 235 million euro of profit. Practically speaking, "Macedonian taxpayers' money [was] used to generate profits for the foreign companies."[20]

Peripheral Financialization Between East and West

In the decades that preceded the global financial crisis, many European entrepreneurs had reacted to financial challenges by relocating their activities abroad, investing first in the southern edges of Europe and then further east in former socialist countries. Macedonia had been a latecomer to the game of attracting foreign investors. Other European countries such as Ireland, Greece, and Spain had seen mirages of riches materialize and achieved dreams of self-realization almost a decade before Gruevski's branding campaign. So why had entrepreneurs such as Marco and Giovanni moved to such a peripheral space—one where the construction boom paled in comparison to the Spanish or Irish real estate bubble? What kind of cultural tools prompted micro-investors to imagine Macedonia as a ready-to-be-exploited, feminized frontier replete with potential wealth and sensual pleasures?

The strange appeal of Gruevski's Macedonia had its roots in yet another financial paradox, namely the increased inequality that had come to plague the domestic and international life of countries within the EU. Contrary to the popular perception, most of the problems that European economies faced in the second decade of the twenty-first century were not only a result of the global financial crisis. Instead, the experience of peripheral countries such as Macedonia shows that the global financial crisis amplified forms of inequality that had spread since the 1990s—when a bifurcated path separated a core and a peripheral Europe based on countries' ability to access, manipulate, and profit from financial deregulation.

Officially, the European reforms that began with the Maastricht Treaty (1992) were designed to support the bloc's political and economic integration and an (ongoing) process of eastward enlargement. Together with the introduction of the euro as the union's common currency and the subsequent Stability and Growth Pact signed in 2011, these reforms promised to bring political stability and economic prosperity to the whole continent. Yet the newly integrated mechanisms did little to address the different economic capacities and performances of its member states. In fact, imposing specific limits on

public spending and relying more on market dynamics, the EU actively followed a path that empowered the economies of certain member states at the
expense of others. What looked like economic stability for Germany meant
austerity and economic stagnation for countries at the Southern and Eastern
periphery—economic policies that led them to be vulnerable to the crisis and
facilitated the subsequent rise of populist leaders.[21]

Centered on maintaining a strong euro and fostering competition, EU regulations introduced in the 1990s benefited export-driven economies such as
Germany and financial tax havens such as Luxembourg, the Netherlands, and
the UK.[22] Reliant on large companies that could invest in advanced technologies, Germany consolidated its export primacy and allowed its companies to
accumulate record profits that eclipsed EU competitors thanks to a politics of
stalled wages. In Southern European states (PIIGS), however, small and medium enterprises started to lose ground to their Northern European competitors—whose size allowed them to amplify their profits on financial markets.[23]

But if Northern European conglomerates were able to gain record profits,
it was precisely thanks to the economic decline of Europe's Southern bloc. Enabled by permissive EU regulations, Northern European banks loaned their
newfound money to their Southern neighbors,[24] whose increasingly uncom-
petitive private sector, especially households, began to rely on growing levels of debt.[25] Amid cuts to public investment demanded in the name of financial stability, the common currency area facilitated unrealistically low interest
rates on debt and fueled a perverse form of financial unification based on debt
bubbles in the South and profits and capital in the North.[26]

When their speculative bubbles imploded, Southern European countries
were thrown into an ongoing political and economic crisis—the very crisis
that Marco and Giovanni had experienced in Italy. Instead of addressing the
structural inequalities and lending practices that facilitated the expansion of
debt bubbles, postcrisis EU economic policies addressed only in a "limited,
piecemeal and incremental fashion"[27] the dominance of Northern European
financial interests.[28] Under threat of financial capital flight[29] and in a regula-
tory environment characterized by revolving doors and intense lobbying by
financial institutions,[30] the European Central Bank (ECB) started to purchase
public debt through a mechanism called quantitative easing—providing some
relief to highly indebted countries by paying creditors rather than reducing
debtors' burden. Meanwhile, in agreement with other international institutions, the EU forced disciplinary austerity packages upon Ireland, Spain,

Portugal, Greece, and to a certain extent Italy—supporting the rise to power of conservative leaders and unleashing a wave of stagnation and bankruptcies among small- and medium-sized enterprises.[31]

In this context, Marco and Giovanni had few incentives to relocate from Italy to other Southern European countries. Instead, they looked east, intrigued by the opportunities opened up by the eastward enlargement of the 1990s. The incorporation of Eastern Europe in the EU had sped up a massive decline in production, wealth, and prosperity in former socialist economies. Shock doctrines and criminal privatizations, imposed on postsocialist states by international organizations and supported by the EU, led to the dismantling of much of the socialist economic and political infrastructure. Faced with rising unemployment and mounting debt, Eastern European countries turned to foreign, and especially European, investors—an opportunity for entrepreneurs looking for cheaper labor that widened rather than diminished the economic gap between the East and the West.

The economic and material decay of postsocialist Europe unearthed the region's longer history of subordinate entanglement with Western Europe[32]— a peripheral status that marked Eastern Europeans as semiprimitive, criminal, hypersexual, prey, or predators.[33] These perceptions were aggravated over time by a series of policies that transformed cultural biases into legal discrimination. For instance, even after joining the EU in 2007, citizens of Romania and Bulgaria were subjected to work restrictions; when these limitations were officially lifted in 2014, individual EU countries (including the UK, France, the Netherlands, and Belgium) maintained special requirements for Romanian and Bulgarian citizens, including special applications for work permits.[34] Unsurprisingly, Eastern European citizens found themselves the target of widespread racism on the part of their "civilized" cousins—a relationship that some increasingly describe as neocolonial.[35]

On the economic level, Eastern Europe found itself dragged onto the bifurcated path of its Western cousins. Postsocialist countries that had geographical ties to Central European economies such as Poland, Hungary, Slovakia, and the Czech Republic received significant industrial investment, especially from German car and telecommunication manufacturers.[36] Baltic economies (including Estonia, Lithuania, and Latvia) that had undergone sweeping hyper-neoliberal reforms instead attracted interest-bearing capital from Germany, the Netherlands, and other Northern European countries, feeding a significant expansion of consumer credit and, in particular, mortgages.[37]

By the early 2000s, European finance had re-created in Central and Eastern Europe many of the same financial vulnerabilities that had emerged in Southern European countries. Only Yugoslav republics, especially places such as Serbia, Bosnia, Kosovo, and Macedonia, distressed by ethnic wars and fragmented into small, dysfunctional markets, had remained marginally integrated in European financial flows—a peripheral position that turned into an asset in the wake of the global financial crisis when countries that had experienced forms of mass financialization started to show signs of financial instability.

When household debt and non-performing loans skyrocketed in Croatia and Slovenian banks appeared to be on the verge of collapse, international institutions started to become more interested in households in less leveraged countries such as Macedonia and Serbia. From 2003 to 2010, Macedonian and Serbian households increased their credit portfolio from 2 percent and 4 percent of GDP to 18 percent and 20 percent of GDP, respectively (see fig. 8).[38] As shown in figure 9, Macedonian bank assets grew from 38 percent of GDP in 2000 to 60 percent of GDP in 2008 and 75 percent in 2014,[39] demonstrating a later but continuous accumulation of financial capital in the country when compared to others in the region—one that was perhaps too timid to catch the eye of global developers and hedge funds but that investors from other peripheralizing areas of Europe hoped to capitalize on.[40]

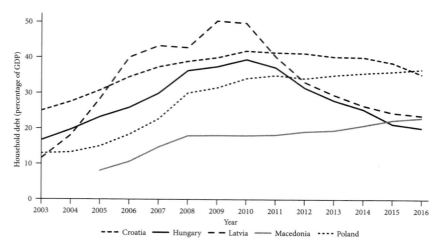

Figure 8. Household debt as a percentage of GDP for selected Eastern European countries. Source: IMF

	2000	2014
Poland	61	89
Hungary	67	100
Russia	32	109
Croatia	63	123
Serbia	53	85
Macedonia	60	76

Figure 9. Bank assets as a percentage of GDP for selected Eastern European countries. Source: Raiffeisen RESEARCH, NBRM

Paradise Lost: The Dangers of Authoritarianism

Motivated by the timid expansion of consumer finance, the promises of state investments, and the branding of the country, European businessmen like Marco and Giovanni tried their luck in Macedonia, often armed with semi-workable ideas and little savings. Once they began to invest in Macedonia, however, businessmen realized rather quickly that to generate profits from the country's financialization, they had to face dramatic contradictions sponsored by an increasingly oppressive regime.

During our last evening at the bar, Marco and Giovanni offered me a ride home to Italy for the Christmas holidays. As December progressed, however, the two Italians kept postponing their departure and finally stopped answering my calls and texts altogether. Not until March of the following year was I contacted by Marco, who claimed to have lost his phone and invited me to visit his new company in Struga, a city in the western part of the country. When we met, he was with Besart, an enthusiastic and charismatic Albanian investor who ceremoniously drove and introduced Marco around as the brain and soul of their new joint venture. In private, Marco told me that it was all a necessary charade:

> Do you remember when Giovanni was nervous, in the café? Well, he thought he had seen our Macedonian partner, Nikola. Some months before meeting you, we closed a deal for almost 50,000 euro, but neither Giovanni nor I had a registered company in Macedonia. So, we talked to Nikola: we would use his company's name to take on contracts, and he would be in charge of finding us clients—you know, everybody gets a cut, everybody is happy. After a couple of months our workers told us that they had never been paid! We went to the developer and he showed us the receipts of his deposits into Nikola's account! The bastard did not pay us, not even the workers! As it turned out, Nikola had

massive debts and his bank had blocked his account. We gave him an ultima-
tum, and he finally scraped together some money in cash, some in euro, even
Swiss francs and US dollars. . . . He probably went door to door to his friends
and relatives to get it!

That was just the beginning of their misadventures. Since then, Nikola tried to
steal some of the tools they worked with, organized the meeting at Construx
behind their backs, and harassed them when Marco and Giovanni decided to
cut him out of the small job they were working on when I met them. Although
it was a small amount of money (around 5,000 euro), they desperately needed
the cash to pay for materials consumed on bigger projects. Plus, it was Christmas, and they had no money to pay for gas and go back home.

Finally, on December 24, Marco and Giovanni were paid. With the 5,000
euro in hand, they drove back to their house to pack a few things and try to
make it to Italy before the Christmas celebrations. In the middle of the highway between Skopje and Tetovo, a black car cut them off. It was Nikola with
two thugs. "They got out of the car, beat us, and took the money, plus our
phones and watches. You know I was in the military, right? I did not react
because I was scared that they had a gun—so I let them beat the hell out of
me." Marco and Giovanni immediately went to their partner and friend Lollo,
their insurance. "And by the end of the day, they found them! You know, with
our money, in cash, our phones, everything they had stolen from us! And
you know what they said? Lollo and his friend in the police can't do anything
about it. And then I understood. They fucked us."

Without money, without work, without even the gas to reach Italy, Marco
and Giovanni were broken—physically and mentally. They talked to Besart,
who gave them some money to go home and forget all about their business.
Giovanni quickly took his advice. He had no interest in fighting with Lollo or
other Macedonian partners. Unable to mobilize support from the Italian embassy, Macedonian courts and institutions, or other international organizations, Giovanni felt that they had hit the limits of what the Macedonian market and society could offer them; remaining there would have put them in
danger without any certainty of profit.

Marco, however, had invested too much in Macedonia. Emotionally, he
had rediscovered pleasures and sides of himself he thought he had lost. Plus,
his material was almost ready and could make a big splash in the construction
market—or so he convinced Besart, who welcomed him to Struga and into
the Albanian social world. "You know, here among Albanians I feel protected.

They have my back, for real. And I know Besart sent word to Nikola and others not to mess with me again."

Besart did everything he could to present Marco as his revered guest and partner, partly to make him and everyone else forget about his past misfortune (and gullibility) but also to cement their partnership. Besart not only financed the production of Marco's material and inserted him into his own business network, but he also started to build a factory for chemicals and other related products. Besart's eyes lit up when he brought me to see the factory's construction site and he sparkled with pride and joy, noting that twenty years earlier he had nothing to eat, and now he would own a factory that produced things. Adding a fancy Italian technician to his deck of cards added prestige, if not immediate returns, to his expanding business vision.

Conflicting Expectations

Conflicts such as those experienced by Marco and Giovanni were not unheard of for other Italian investors who operated in Macedonia—although they rarely escalated to explicit forms of violence. After a period of idyllic hedonism, many investors reported being subjected to scams or having to navigate expectations of additional payments—a hostile climate that had forced some to abandon the country.

At the center of most of these disagreements were divergent evaluations regarding how to properly share the often meager profits captured by the inflow of European finance. Macedonian partners expected international investors to contribute additional sums of money that went beyond what was established in official agreement—payments that they considered legitimate given the country's decades of postsocialist peripheralization. For international and Italian businessmen, however, these rents constituted proof of corruption inherent to Macedonian society.

"Why is it that a cubic meter of cement costs the same in Macedonia and in Italy? We know that here in Skopje you pay workers 300 euro per month, while in Italy it is four times that. But the price of the cement is the same." I did not have an answer to Gennaro's question. After all, he was the expert: he had been managing the Macedonian office of an Italian company that specialized in the supervision of public works for a year now, after periods in Cambodia and Uzbekistan. I had just spent twelve hours under the summer sun following him on the construction site of a major infrastructural project, and we were both tired enough to share some pearls of wisdom in a run-down

parking lot. "Because certain costs," said Gennaro, rubbing his thumb and index finger in a very Italian gesture alluding to money, "cannot be squeezed. In
other words, here you pay less for labor, but you have added costs for . . . you
know . . . !?"

Barely able to listen, I looked at him with empty eyes. Bothered by my lack
of reaction, Gennaro shrugged and decided to speak plainly.

> I mean that you have to bribe them. That money you cannot recover. And it is
> not just the bribes for getting the contract. It is all that comes with that! We
> recently participated in a call for offers regarding an important project. We
> offered a low price, by our standards. The company that won offered one-third
> of our sum. For them it makes sense: once you are the supervisor, you decide
> if a finished work is approved. You can withdraw approval, say, if the contrac-
> tor uses a certain product. Usually you need to provide technical reasons—
> like, one product has a given mechanical set of properties that the other does
> not offer, or it can guarantee better performance over time. But sometimes
> the products are equivalent, and you can still force the contractor to choose
> one if the company that sells that product pays you something under the ta-
> ble. So even if you lose money on the contract, as a supervisor you have other
> ways to make money.

Expecting payment to authorize one product instead of another equivalent
one; extracting money for having obliquely facilitated deals; requesting bribes
to access construction materials; for Gennaro, Marco, and Giovanni, these
expectations of profit constituted illegitimate practices because they did not
create new value. Instead, they appropriated, skimmed, and diminished the
worth of existing contracts. Italian investors understood rent as unproductive, unearned, and pernicious "return independent from labor"[41]—generated
by their partners' abilities to monopolize not land or means of production but
access to the social and political infrastructure needed to monetize one's participation in Macedonia's tight financial landscape.[42]

Macedonian businessmen with whom I spoke admitted that a strange atmosphere of hostility had come to surround international investors and that
some of the means utilized, such as rigging the system of international grants,
were indeed illegal. And yet many justified these actions. What were a few
thousand euro for international businesses who were about to earn millions
thanks to public grants given to Macedonia? Even if they wanted to act, there
was little that Macedonian subcontractors could do: calls for projects were

rigged from within the Macedonian Ministry of Finance, a ministry that was tightly controlled by Stavrevski, one of Gruevski's closer allies.

Officials who worked within public institutions agreed. VMRO–DPMNE officials had fostered a hostile approach to international partners, businessmen, and more broadly, financial opportunities. An administrator in charge of EU projects, for instance, recalled that colleagues "who bought the regime's view of doing things" were encouraged to take advantage of their position and liberally use EU resources for questionable expenses. My interlocutor was forced to approve vacations as European-funded study trips or team-building exercises. Officials from a different ministry recalled being lined up, screamed at, and then fined for up to 30 percent of their salary for sharing information with international funding partners. Instead, as former VMRO–DPMNE ministers told them, they should have squeezed their EU partners so hard that "they wouldn't even know how to get out of the meeting room."

In a work environment that had lost its veneration for European governance, several administrators found playing hardball with international institutions enjoyable—as if extracting rent from international partners could make up for decades of unfulfilled promises and paternalistic lecturing about "proper" economic practices. Extracting rent allowed Macedonian businessmen and administrators to take advantage of their unequal partnership with Europe and turn their subordination into profit—a game that Gruevski and his clique encouraged Macedonians to see as zero-sum, in which their own existential or material desires for (normal) wealth and political recognition could only be expressed through desperate forms of scams or extractive actions that necessarily collided with foreigners' own aspirations.

Landscapes of Extraction

The extractive landscape encountered by international investors in Macedonia constituted a new paradox of Gruevski's strategy. The international inflow of foreign investors was crucial for the regime as it inflated statistics about jobs and employment in Macedonia, contributing to a general sense of opening of the Macedonian economy to neoliberal reforms that made the country more appealing for international donors and agencies. So why was Gruevski so keen on making international investors' lives complicated, exciting Macedonian administrators' and businessmen's hopes of wealth and pitting them against their international partners? What was gained by transforming financialization into a game of positions, a trench warfare of rentier anticipations?

As it turned out, the misadventures of micro-investors such as Marco and Giovanni were politically very productive—not for Macedonian partners but for the regime and, to a lesser extent, for large and institutional investors. Stories of micro-investors' vulnerability circulated broadly among the international community, leading even international managers to feel exposed to unpredictable and constant extractive expectations. To avoid these looming misadventures, international investors and managers of larger companies agreed to enter into complex relationships with the VMRO–DPMNE regime. As Gennaro told me,

> You saw how it was the other day on the worksite. You know they are going to screw you. You just have to decide what to pick on and what to allow. What you will accept and what you will not because you'll be too ashamed to tell your children about it. For instance, you saw the plant they wanted to use to provide us with concrete. It was barely functional. They had no capacity to deliver a consistent standard. And I would need to use *that* material for a capital infrastructure? Now the contractor called the ministry, for whom I supervise the site, and now *they* are telling me that it is okay. Of course, nobody would ever write it down in an official letter. . . . It is all this formal, but really informal, way of saying things, so that you will be the one who makes the decision.

"There's a constant pressure," he continued—a pressure that Gennaro felt was becoming personally unbearable. Bribing and pressuring others was not what he wanted to do for a living. As he went deeper into his history, Gennaro then took a deep breath and settled back in his black leather desk chair. "I requested a transfer from my company. I was about to go, but then the whole Ukraine thing happened, and I couldn't move there anymore. But you see, my predecessor couldn't take it either. You either move, or you end up like him, with three lovers, spending every other weekend in Thessaloniki to fuck them."

Tullio, a manager of another Italian company that had worked on a politically sensitive urban redevelopment project, was also very troubled by the increasingly extractive dimension of Macedonia's economy—a concern that verged on paranoia. In the middle of one of our meetings, he lowered his voice, leaned heavily on our table, inviting me to come closer. In a conspiratorial tone, Tullio said,

> You have to be careful. See, the other day I was in Gevgelija, on my way to Greece, to take a break from this mess here in Skopje. I enter a grocery shop and it turns out that the owner's daughter speaks Italian. She tells me that she

is working for the Ministry of the Interior, translating conversations of Italian businessmen in Macedonia! Our phones are under control, you see! And yet, I receive calls from the Ministry of Transport or the Ministry of Education, in which the ministers themselves tell me to come, meet the person they want me to hire if I get the project, or how much money I should give them both! It is so in your face, so transparent!

While at the time I dismissed these concerns, Tullio was right. Phones of international businessmen were indeed under surveillance, as recordings leaked to the press confirmed several years later (see Chapter 1). Unlike micro-investors such as Tullio or Giovanni, businessmen who collaborated with the regime faced more direct threats, which allowed them to devise strategies to deal with dodgy collaborators. As Tullio admitted, the forms of extraction that larger investors faced in Macedonia's economy were "transparent." He knew which calls for projects were likely to be rigged, and thus he could decide whether to avoid them or, conversely, decide to participate—not to win, but to drive down the price of public contracts and screw over their Macedonian "partners."

Knowing with relative clarity when administrators requested bribes or favors, Tullio or Gennaro had options and, paradoxically, benefits. Those who paid gained extensive access to the VMRO–DPMNE regime. Some large-scale investors had the prime minister's mobile phone on speed dial. But even investors such as Gennaro or Tullio who did not have these perks were able to use their "transparent" extractive relationships with the regime to cut out the likes of Marco and Giovanni, who were stuck in violent tugs of wars with other desperate businessmen. Instead of having to compete for financial opportunities, large-scale investors could find common ground with members of the regime in parallel rentier endeavors—endeavors that fit comfortably under the umbrella of the EU and its assistance to candidate countries such as Macedonia.

Rentier Aspirations in the European Project

Between 1992 and 2017, Macedonia received a total of 3.2 billion euros in assistance projects, mostly through low-interest loans, trade credits, development grants, and structural European funds—assistance capital that the government paraded as proof of its growing success in and commitment to attracting foreign investors. To this, the government added significant loans from organizations such as the IMF (234 million euro), the World Bank (277 million euro), the International Bank for Reconstruction and Development (229 million euro), and other private national and international banks—organizations that had a wealth of eyes on the ground and were all very well informed about the regime's way of doing business. So, if the international and especially European institutions knew about the regime's penchant for extractive and authoritarian methods, why did they continue to support Gruevski, funneling aid and funds that helped the regime last for over a decade?

In a moment of candor, Tullio gestured toward a convergence of approaches and interests between EU aid, Gruevski's authoritarian regime, and large Italian investors—an extractive closeness that was as uncomfortable as it was evident. "Look," he told me, "I am an Italian, right? It's not like these kinds of things don't happen in Italy." *Not everywhere*, I remember thinking. But before I uttered my dismay, I realized that his remark was not expressing a stereotype about Italians but constituted an actual commentary about the kind of work that investors like himself did in Macedonia—a kind of extractive work that was not all that incommensurable compared to the expectations of rent fueled by VMRO–DPMNE officials.

Despite having a larger portfolio than Marco and Giovanni, Tullio (and Gennaro) were not in Macedonia to invest and create greenfield ventures out of their own money. Their investments were conditional on intercepting European grants, international aid, or Macedonian public contracts. But to do so, managers such as Tullio and Gennaro relied on the surprising and sometimes conflicting collaborations between businessmen such as themselves, Eurocrats, and Gruevski's regime—relationships that were predicated on fueling and excluding micro-investors, while, at the same time, supporting the rise of an increasingly authoritarian regime.

Managers such as Marco and Giovanni felt betrayed by this apparent convergence, which they suggested explained why Italian institutions seemed so unsympathetic toward their problems. But for businessmen such as Tullio and Gennaro who managed mid-sized portfolios of investments, this collaboration was crucial. Preliminary calculations of Instrument for Pre-Accession Assistance (IPA) funds disbursed between 2009 and 2011 suggest that only 54 out of 460 million euro were contracted directly to Macedonian beneficiaries, institutions, and companies. By and large, contractors from Germany (52 million), Austria (19 million), Spain (16 million), France (15 million), the UK (10 million), and Italy (8 million) benefited the most from EU funds in Macedonia, excluding a 200-million-euro highway contract won by a Greek contractor, and around 20 million euro of cross-border and local investments obtained by Bulgarian contractors.[43]

Maintaining these tense yet symbiotic relationships was at the center of the Eurocrat's mandate. Accustomed to inhabiting a space of competition between peripheralizing political and economic systems, Eurocrats understood their financial aid as a tool to generate visibility and produce profit for the EU while also benefiting the specific country who had won the project—a game that different European countries played in symbiosis with Gruevski to generate economic returns, more than stability.[44] This could only be done if Macedonian officials were satisfied—a circumstance that led to very close interaction and collaboration, often fraught with tension, around the management of myriad projects aimed at strengthening and harmonizing Macedonian institutions. Both the tension and close collaboration between Eurocrats and officers of the Gruevski regime resulted in one of the final paradoxes of financialization in Macedonia—a syncopated resonance between the extractive strategies of Macedonia's regime and those of European countries, as exemplified in the "Sustainable Fishing Project," an IPA-funded initiative between the "Maritime Ministries" of Rome and Skopje.[45]

The Sustainable Fishing Project was conceived as an opportunity to extract economic and existential value from European aid for the periphery. For the project's manager, Antonio, that opportunity concerned primarily his future career opportunities. With about seven years of experience in the Italian Maritime Ministry, he was a young, energetic, and hardworking official who had already served in other European postings. To convince his Macedonian counterparts to select the Italian proposal, Antonio had lined up renowned Italian experts on fishing—packaging their expertise along with a streamlined project and an opulent post-pitch dinner. After all, Antonio was "the biggest *paraculo* around," as he liked to remind me—a manager able to adapt to unexpected challenges and manipulate others and still land on his feet. It was that *paraculo* attitude that the Italian Maritime Ministry counted on to generate extractive synergies with Macedonian bureaucrats and find mutually beneficial ways to access further European funds.

Once in Macedonia, Antonio hired Martina, a manager/assistant, and Sofija, a female translator; as he told me, he had hired women because they were "easier to work with, more precise," and more accepting of hierarchical roles. But that gendered statement was not the only way in which Antonio affirmed his authority. In the first of many scuffles, he defied the Macedonian minister who had promised the jobs to protégés. While they were willing to compromise, the Italians were still in charge.

Most of the team's activity consisted of flying experts from Italy to Skopje to help Macedonians design legal instruments that regulated and promoted fishing. This meant scheduling seminars, organizing field visits, and entertaining Italian experts in Macedonia. For Antonio, however, the value of the project exceeded its technical or even financial aspect. He had in mind a much more ambitious plan for the team, which corresponded to Rome's idea of utilizing the project to showcase the new direction of Italian international cooperation in the Balkans. While the team worked hard to promote changes in the legislation on sustainable fishing, Antonio, Martina, and their other collaborators tried to make the project a reference point for broader investments between Italy and Macedonia—a crucial effort to allow Italian institutions to be part of talks about financial flows that moved between the Balkans and Europe. Antonio quickly grew close to the new Italian ambassador, who suggested contacts and consortia to involve at cocktail parties, opening ceremonies, and international cultural events. Most important, he socialized with both Italian experts and local administrators, bringing them to clubs or dinners and making sure that their wishes were fulfilled.

While other Eurocrats were offended when collaborations hinged on favors or "benefits," Antonio banked on these expectations and their emotional dimension. After working on other European projects, he had realized that encouraging and satisfying some of the material desires of local administrators was the most effective way to move his own agenda forward. Without deep cultural connections to the local society,[46] Antonio relied on Martina's cultural (and often organizational) sensibilities. Charming and energetic, Martina spent much of her time smoothing over the misunderstandings that arose from opposite extractive expectations of Italian and Macedonian colleagues—a managerial and emotional labor that was compensated by a somewhat generous salary (by Macedonian standards) but especially by the opportunity to be independent from the rapacious control of VMRO–DPMNE officials. Taking active part in cultural events and diplomatic soirées, Martina felt part of an exclusive circle of global elites—a taste of a diplomatic lifestyle that perhaps could give her a chance to showcase her true worth. Putting up with odd hours, overtime work, and the occasional flirtatious passes of Antonio was a small price to pay to reset years of economic disadvantage.

In general, Macedonian beneficiaries appreciated and exploited Antonio's strategy. The team's effectiveness, along with Antonio's and Martina's anticipation of local administrators' wishes, allowed them to develop synergies for legitimate as well as extractive purposes. But Antonio had to be careful not to be *too* generous. Administrators with an irredentist view of European finance could easily push the extractive envelope too far—asking him to pay for completely random expenses or to create a scene over other colleagues' benefits. These conflicts were particularly acute for those events that embodied the power hierarchy between European countries—such as study visits. Going to Italy on a visit reversed the roles of hospitality between Macedonians and Italians. For once, it would be the Macedonian experts and not the Europeans who would be pampered as guests of honor—an opportunity that VMRO–DPMNE administrators would not give up, even if that led to conflicts so bitter that the entire visit had to be cancelled.

Besides appeasing Macedonians, Antonio and his team had to reckon with other sets of expectations. For Rome and Brussels, the fishing project offered opportunities to extract strategic, political profits. Rome sent "important" experts to Skopje, a reward that came with generous travel allowances and VIP treatments paid by the project's funds. The Maritime Ministry wanted the project to succeed so that they would have better chances of winning future projects, securing money from Brussels, and maintaining political influence in European circles. EU officials, on the other hand, placed significant emphasis on the project's visibility strategy. The project had a budget for things such as mugs, agendas, calendars, and other promotional material with EU flags and titles of the project, but it could not invest in productivity tools such as smartphones or research. In a way, the EU conceived of the project as a means to legitimize its own presence, claiming a civilizing value that hid the other extractive processes promoted by the inflow of assistance capital.

Backed by this institutional support, the project provided managers who led it with a degree of success. Macedonian beneficiaries within the Maritime Ministry and beyond loved both the project and Antonio to the point that they requested him for two follow-up projects lasting two years after the original contract expired. Most of the team remained to work with Antonio, while Martina utilized the experience to begin a career in international development abroad. Antonio impressed his superiors in Rome and created a network of contacts that allowed him, when he returned, to move up the ministry's hierarchy—although not without a significant dose of delay, frustration, and struggle.

Financial Extraction and Recursive Peripheralization
Developing an idea to avoid bankruptcy and remake one's manhood; intercepting European grants; transforming European aid into prestige and political visibility—these different, sometime conflicting goals pushed Italian

businessmen, investors, and Eurocrats toward Macedonia's construction boom in the hope of intercepting the financial capital that had flowed toward one of Europe's last economic peripheries.

Ranging from existential dilemmas to rational calculations, these extractive aspirations capture the social context that accompanies financial expansion at the periphery—a tortuous path by which Italian investors tried to flee the European crisis eastward. The movement of European investors and businessmen was favored by Gruevski's branding of the country as a safe haven for international capital—a well-timed effort that ultimately failed to attract large sums of productive investments in the form of FDI. Instead of wealthy financiers, cash-strapped adventurer "investors" moved to Macedonia—not to bring a wall of money but to try and intercept European assistance capital contracted by the Macedonian state to build Skopje 2014 or other projects.

Within Macedonia, however, the hopes of international entrepreneurs collided with the extractive dreams of local businessmen and administrators—founded on experiences of loss stoked by the VMRO–DPMNE irredentist posture and made possible by what appeared as a radical transformation of the EU. After decades of economic and social stagnation in the postsocialist world, the global financial crisis had finally demonstrated that it was not only Eastern Europe that had been ravaged by unscrupulous privatizations and deals. Speculative endeavors had fractured the very core of the European project, magnifying inequalities between different productive systems and punishing the economic fabric of Southern economies in a purgatory of austerity. Finally, during the global financial crisis, being at the periphery had turned into an asset—one that Macedonians could use to extract material and moral benefits from their international partners.

The tensions produced by such different expectations of profit and rent constituted the existential ground of financialization that the VMRO–DPMNE relied on to recast its own regime as inexorable and oppressive. For foreign entrepreneurs as well as local administrators, financialization corresponded to a landscape of reciprocal exploitation saturated with pressures and scams, hard to avoid because they originated from many, often unpredictable, directions. In this loosely identifiable but existentially oppressive atmosphere, the regime seemed to be everywhere, anchoring Macedonians and foreigners alike to mutually corrosive relationships.

If these rentier expectations proved politically useful, it was precisely because they were often impossible for individuals to realize. Managers such as

Marco and Giovanni who fled the economic ruin in Italy and followed the trail of money that led to Macedonia managed only to see it dissipate behind what they understood as the regime's machinery. Their bad deals and partial successes bolstered the illusion that there was copious financial opportunity—one needed only to join the VMRO–DPMNE to reap its benefits. But even those who did manage to gain access to international finance thanks to their new positions in the VMRO–DPMNE administration were undermined, conflicted, and often unable to gain real privileges. After all, being a member of the regime did not solve the piecemeal, insufficient, and highly controlled character of financial deepening in Macedonia.[47]

Eurocrats and managers of larger European companies found creative ways to benefit from the oppressive dimension of financial expansion in Macedonia. Officials from the Italian state realized that they had a lot in common with VMRO–DPMNE administrators, particularly when it came to skimming EU funds for their personal or political interests. Closing an eye to or even banking on the VMRO–DPMNE's extractive approach, Eurocrats and larger European investors were able to limit the international competition for European grants—a convergence common at the European periphery, where financialization brings together different extractive aspirations in an uncanny, uncomfortable symbiosis. Riddled with conflict and deceit, such interdependency showed the parallel, somewhat recursive dynamic of financialization—a process that, as will be explained, was rooted as much in monetary gains as it was in existential paradoxes.

These uncomfortable ties and aspirations also constituted a limit to Gruevski's power. Similar to the geopolitical structure of Putin's Russia, centered on incorporating and sabotaging the political viability of rival states, including Ukraine, Georgia, and more recently, the US,[48] Gruevski's central technology of domination appropriated the dysfunctional characteristics of financial expansion at the periphery. The VMRO–DPMNE regime turned EU-promoted financial deepening into a landscape permeated by extractive hopes but deprived of the consequent liquidity—a scenario of aspirations that could only be fulfilled by Gruevski himself. Until Macedonians believed in Gruevski's quasi-magical power and pervasive threats, and international actors found it convenient for their own strategy, the regime continued to manipulate the inflow of foreign finance and turn it into domestic forced credit. Once the equilibrium fell out of sync, however, Gruevski found himself with little solid ground to support his authoritarian machinery.

3 Forced Credit and *Kompenzacija*

DURING THE GLOBAL FINANCIAL CRISIS, most countries that had experienced a construction bubble were in total disarray. In Spain, Greece, and Ireland, construction sites stood motionless while investors and mortgagers scrambled to avoid bankruptcy. Yet Skopje's real estate and financial sectors began to thrive precisely at such a critical moment, when most global finance steered away from crediting construction enterprises.

There was an additional oddity to Skopje's financialization. Unlike other real estate bubbles, Skopje's thriving construction industry did not translate into widespread wealth, increased salaries, or even massive availability of credit. Contrary to what happened in other financialized economies such as Spain or the US,[1] where cheap loans and mortgages temporarily increased wages, living standards, and the amount of money circulating in the economy, in Macedonia salaries stagnated and inflation went negative. Most of the businessmen I interviewed lamented that Macedonia's economy was widely illiquid (*nelikvidna*), and that such illiquidity caused the business sector to rely upon in-kind payments called *kompenzacija*.

On the surface, kompenzacija could be understood as a form of barter, whereby companies supported each other by exchanging goods during a critical time of crisis. This was the common starting point for narratives offered by the managers of many companies, including Construx's director. After a long explanation of his profit margins, he suggested that the smartest way to conduct business was to exchange apartments for services. With kompenzacija, contractors and subcontractors could help each other and bypass the transaction costs imposed by Macedonia's famously hawkish banking sector.

As I continued collecting accounts of kompenzacija, however, this benevolent image became sinister. Construx's financial director confided that kompenzacija was utilized as a reverse path to gain money, rather than exchange services, even by his own company. First you identified who had money, then you tried to find an exchange sequence that allowed you to convert labor, and goods, into money.

"Kompenzacija?" asked Ilco, a businessman I had just interviewed. "Oh, we need to sit down for a whole day to talk about this." He continued:

> You can't imagine how often I did kompenzacija with other people. But most of the time, when someone mentions kompenzacija, you immediately know that something is wrong. I did it myself, you know, I also screwed people with kompenzacija. But let me tell you this: If people who owe me money want to give me, say, toilet paper, well that's okay. I can sell toilet paper in a second. I make a couple of calls, and bam, it is gone. No problem at all. But nobody wants to give you toilet paper. They could sell it themselves. You get stuck with other things. . . . What do you do then? Listen now—once I did the worst kompenzacija ever. I had sold some stuff to this guy, but for about six months he hadn't paid me; he always had something coming up—some problem with the bank, some issue with the family, something. One day I go to his house, and I tell him that I can't wait any longer. I also have my own problems, and I'm about 100,000 euro in debt to other people. So, I tell him that I really need to get paid *now*. He has no money, he tells me. But then he says, "I can give you some stuff, we can do kompenzacija." I ask him, "What kind of things?" "Eggs," he says.

At this point Ilco stopped, turned to me, and passed his hand over the sweaty surface of his bald head.

> Can you imagine that? *Fresh* eggs! I get the eggs in the van, there might have been thousands of them, and I start driving back home. But you know how our villages are—it was far from Skopje, in the middle of the mountains, and the road was so poor that . . . You can't imagine the condition my van was in when I got back here. Half of the eggs were broken, and I spent more to clean the van than the whole load was worth. [He paused briefly, then he stared at me.] *THAT* is kompenzacija.

Ultimately, most businessmen agreed with Ilco. While kompenzacija as a term was often used to describe an elastic continuum of relationships, including beneficial, horizontal exchanges, by 2013 it generally designated forced transactions that often devalued the labor of those who received goods. If you were paid in kompenzacija, my interlocutors insisted, you were likely to end up with things you did not want, which would make you lose money.

If kompenzacija was such a pernicious kind of exchange, what made it so ubiquitous? This question is even more puzzling given that economic aggregates seem to suggest that the country was not facing a major liquidity crisis. Official data shows that Macedonian banks were well capitalized. The national banks, and some companies, had substantial reserves of cash both in Macedonian denars (MKD) and in other foreign currencies. Companies I worked with, however, were unable to get paid, faced constant cash-flow problems, and were often part of kompenzacija deals—especially if they were not connected to the VMRO–DPMNE regime.

In this chapter, I analyze kompenzacija deals to understand how financialization can operate without widespread money. Monetary scarcity in Gruevski's Macedonia had a longer history that stemmed from socialist-era underdevelopment and Macedonia's peripheral role in the global economy. While Macedonian businesses experienced the worst of the global credit squeeze, the Macedonian government had expanded access to global debt. Gruevski and his allies utilized this money, meant to stabilize Macedonian finance, to force companies into poisonous deals that were not paid on time or were paid with goods—resulting in monetary credit to the regime and associated oligarchs in exchange for in-kind, depreciating, and unwanted goods. Extending the extractive landscape in the business sector (see Chapter 2), kompenzacija allowed the VMRO–DPMNE to monopolize the money supply and to cement the idea that in Macedonia there was no money—an illusion of illiquidity, to paraphrase Nesvetailova, whereby the VMRO–DPMNE regime appeared unavoidable and omnipresent.[2]

In part, kompenzacija became so toxic because it had been a normal feature of the Macedonian economy since the socialist era. As a peripheral country with a scarcely competitive economic system, Macedonia had suffered through multiple incidents of economic collapse. While kompenzacija had emerged at different critical junctures, its meanings and implications differed widely. During socialism, kompenzacija facilitated production. In the early years of postsocialism, kompenzacija distributed capital accumulation and helped networks of informal transactions survive the dramatic fragmentation of political and economic life. Under Gruevski, kompenzacija allowed the VMRO–

DPMNE regime to transform international credit, a consequence of postcrisis mitigation measures, and turn international loans into domestic forced credit.

Many Shades of Barter

Most of the anthropological analyses of in-kind exchanges focus on two specific economic processes—"primitive" money and barter.[3] The first body of literature suggests that, rather than constituting a rudimentary and backward means of exchange, primitive money such as brass rods, cloths, and cowries takes part in very complex payment systems. Often some of these kinds of money are utilized only for specific types of exchanges (pertaining to subsistence or prestige) and coexist with other means of exchange employed in other spheres.[4]

In the context of capitalist societies, however, anthropologists have generally understood the reemergence of in-kind exchanges and barter as an alternative, rather than a complement, to general-purpose, fiat money. In Eastern Europe, Latin America, and more recently Southern Europe, the resurgence of networks of in-kind and favor exchanges has been explained as a consequence of political and economic crises. In economies where cash is suddenly unavailable, barter becomes a means to ensure everyday survival.[5]

As a class of in-kind exchange practiced by equal and free partners with incommensurable interests, barter allows people to match their wants through competitive, rational, and self-interested calculations.[6] While it fulfills market needs, the cultural evaluation of the intrinsic quality of objects is what matters in barter transactions. By contrast, when exchanges are conducted through impersonal currency, the specific qualities of the objects exchanged are erased by the abstract value of a currency that can be used to purchase any object.[7]

In this perspective, barter is construed as the opposite of financial debt. "One of the possible schema used for the distribution of what economists would term goods and services,"[8] financial debt identifies a hierarchical process of social death, which eliminates the communal relationships of human economies.[9] Abstracting communities from their ancestral land or subjecting a country to the economic rationality of a balanced budget inevitably leads to devastation, as cultural forms of reciprocity are eradicated in favor of monetary interests.[10]

Yet an increasing number of ethnographic studies show that the difference between in-kind and financial debt might be exaggerated, insofar as neither financial debt nor in-kind transactions require abstraction to generate oppression. In their studies of convertibility across different means of payment and commodities, both Ferry and Rogers note that monetary and non-monetary forms of debt can coexist to reproduce international hierarchies and reinforce the precariousness of vulnerable populations.[11] In other words, converting material or even immaterial forms of value across different systems of payment provides opportunities for profit and political power to those who can monopolize the process—a point that is increasingly evident in the emerging literature on payment platforms.[12]

The same is true for financial debt. As Stout argues, mortgages can be inscribed in moral relationships that, simultaneously, reiterate systemic inequality.[13] In fact, financial debt is often central to social relationships, which makes it circulate and stick to different communities. For instance, as Palomera demonstrates, the progressive indebtedness of low-income migrant households in Spain was made possible by the informal knowledge shared by migrants of similar ethnic backgrounds.[14] Similarly, studies of microcredit show that poor women "have absorbed the work of seeking out and repaying credit into existing regimes of domestic labor," often working themselves into unsustainable levels of debt to fulfill gendered expectations.[15]

As a type of in-kind transaction that is directly connected to monetary credit, kompenzacija inhabits the space between abstract financial debt and socialized barter. Being forced to accept unwanted eggs or apartments is tangible, personal, and often ambiguous—a pernicious bond that can make embedded debt even more insidious.[16] As a form of payment, kompenzacija interrogates the nexus between worth, value, and labor and highlights how financialization provides political and economic elites with a multiplicity of tools to arbitrarily decide on the "deserved recompense for labor."[17] Its capacity for connecting and translating social and financial logics is framed by broader political and social processes, which, in the Macedonian case, made it progressively exploitative as the country pivoted from the Yugoslav model toward an increasingly neoliberal and authoritarian political economy.

Socialist Kompenzacija

Since 1945, in-kind exchanges constituted an important part of the international trade of socialist countries and were generally classified in three different ways. The first was classic barter, in which goods were directly exchanged, "as in the case of 5,000 British passenger cars for Hungarian manufactured articles."[18] The second was sometimes referred to as "switch trading" and was aimed at rebalancing accounts between countries that had clearing agreements. In cases such as Yugoslavia and Albania or Austria and the USSR, the two countries had agreed to directly exchange goods whose cumulative value would cancel itself out over a given period. When that was not possible, one of the countries would sell a "clearing unit" to a third country that was willing to buy goods from the deficit country. The last type of in-kind exchanges was kompenzacija.

> A third category of barter, known as "compensation" trading, generally calls for the Western supplier to be paid partly in cash with the balance in counter deliveries of goods. This type of barter arrangement has been used with increasing frequency in contrast with the declining use of the two previously mentioned forms. According to recent reports, it is not uncommon for a Western partner to accept 10 percent or 15 percent of the value of its sales in counter purchases. . . . A variation on the compensation-type transaction . . . involves a combination of credit and barter. Thus, the Western supplier extends a medium- or long-term credit to the Eastern partner and is to be repaid partly or wholly in goods, often goods produced from the plant and equipment provided on credit.[19]

Sometimes referred to as "buy-back" agreements by analysts,[20] kompenzacija complemented monetary and financial payments between socialist and capitalist countries. In fact, kompenzacija constituted an in-kind exchange and accounting practice that completed circles of outstanding credit. Certainly, countertrade increased during the period of financial crises, especially during the 1980s, when it helped Eastern European countries save a crucial amount of hard currency and reduce their debt.[21] Yet kompenzacija was never a residual practice. Rather, it appeared to be a method to reduce market uncertainty and overcome export fluctuations—so popular that "in Europe, merchant banks [had] compensation departments"[22] even during the period of credit expansion in the 1970s.

While CIA documents stressed its relevance in mediating international exchanges,[23] kompenzacija also had an important role to play in the Yugoslav domestic economy. A solution to companies' problems with receiving payments, kompenzacija helped the socialist system survive its sluggish productivity and awkward integration within the global economy without cutting back on salaries and benefits provided to workers.

Like most socialist economies, Yugoslavia suffered from significant oscillations in its production. Unlike Romania or the USSR, however, these fluctuations were not the result of a rigid economy that forced directors to hoard materials to avoid being punished if they failed to meet the (unrealistic) objectives stipulated by a plan.[24] To a greater degree than other Eastern European countries, Yugoslav fluctuations depended on the country's integration within and dependency on international financial and commodity markets. It was the availability of cheap credit, the flow of international remittances, and the price of light-technology imports that made Yugoslav companies' production uncertain.

As I traced in Chapter 1, the Yugoslav economic system was unable to develop at the same pace as Western economies. In need of constant injections of hard currency, Yugoslav companies tried to manipulate currency restrictions and accounting rules. These elaborate ruses, however, were not successful at the systemic level and possibly decreased the overall solvency of the country during the 1960s and 1970s, as the international economy approached a global slowdown.

Macedonian policy makers were particularly concerned with "the problem of liquidity," both at the federal and republic level.[25] In April 1971, the Executive Government of the Socialist Republic of Macedonia noted that the global economic slowdown had reduced the liquidity of the Yugoslav state. As a consequence, Macedonia, part of the Yugoslav periphery, received fewer new federal investments than other Yugoslav republics (15 percent yearly increase against the average of 32 percent), often through programs that were "not secured with the necessary funds"[26] and that were disbursed with increasing delays.[27] The federal funds that did get to Macedonia tended to be tied up in the reconstruction of Skopje or to flow back to other countries in Yugoslavia, where the most technologically advanced companies were located.[28]

During interviews, former directors of socialist companies suggested that it was this reduction of Yugoslav investments that plunged companies and banks into illiquidity. Indeed, documents suggest that fluctuations in the SFRJ credit and investments affected banks' ability to fund payments between companies. Because banks could periodically run out of cash,[29] 22,000 Macedonian workers experienced problems with payments in 1970,[30] while in the first three months of 1971, 4,500 workers received reduced, minimal, or no income. Even major Macedonian companies such as Zelezara (6,300 workers), Metal Zavod Tito (1,800 workers), the chemical factory Ohis (2,800 workers), and the large factory Alumina Skopje paid workers' salaries with a delay of between two and fourteen days.

If banks were illiquid, however, the main cause was not a lack of federal funds and credit. Between 1965 and 1970, the amount of credit present in the Macedonian economy had almost doubled. Instead of being funneled toward productive investment, however, this money was utilized to cover the losses of Macedonian companies—paying workers' salaries or providing them with cheap consumer loans or mortgages.[31] These practices, needed to guarantee employment and a rising standard of living, crippled Macedonian companies' ability to pay their suppliers and invest in technological developments. Dependent on technologies from other republics, Macedonian firms continued to import more than they exported and had increasing difficulty in generating profits.[32] In 1969, one-fourth of Macedonian companies, largely agricultural firms, operated with some losses[33] and produced 8 percent of the losses of the entire SFRJ while contributing only 5 percent of its overall income.[34]

Unable to pay their debts, Macedonian companies had no choice but to grow increasingly indebted to one another, tying up a cascade of resources in unsold stock, unpaid buyers' claims, and losses. Zelezara, for instance, owed 180 million Dinars to suppliers, yet it was also owed 300 million Dinars by buyers. These mutual debts decelerated the circulation of assets in the Macedonian economy, which was the lowest among the republics (with an index of 3.5 against an average of 4.6),[35] and tended to decelerate further as companies resorted to bills of exchanges and *acceptni nalozi* (IOUs).[36]

In the assessments of Macedonian authorities, something needed to be done before the serious and possibly growing delay in payments[37] turned into a widespread "psychosis of illiquidity." To try and stop companies' cadres from wasting "a dozen days every month" finding ways to "secure funds to pay for workers' individual salaries,"[38] the communist leadership turned to an ingenious set of clearing agreements—what they called *multinateralna kompenzacija*. Because payments between enterprises were not processed by banks but transacted through the Public Accountancy Office (SOK),[39] Yugoslav leaders could identify chains of debts that started and ended with the same company—thus settling them centrally without the need for monetary payments.

While the Yugoslav state conceived of kompenzacija as a tool to keep production alive and workers employed,[40] individual managers I interviewed had quickly understood the potential for profit embedded in these clearing circles. When a new wave of kompenzacija was due, well-connected managers inflated their own claims and thereby ensured a windfall of not-so-socialist profits that helped pay off other debts or increased their own individual income.

When kompenzacija could not be done through a simple accounting mechanism, things could get messier. The case of the Metallurgic Kombinat Smederevo shows that, in some cases, the socialist state directly organized intricate schemes of in-kind payments between firms.[41] Like other, similar heavy industries, the Kombinat was supposed to receive technical upgrades that would transform it into an industrial gem of the Yugoslav production system. Meanwhile, the partially worked iron slabs it produced were sent to other Yugoslavian steelworks so that they could refine them and send them back for the final polish.

Unsurprisingly, this intricate exchange of goods between companies grew financially unsustainable. Banks (that were owned by public enterprises) started lending money at almost negative interest rates. When this again proved insufficient, the Socialist Republic of Serbia imposed agreements on other companies to buy even defective products or to compensate the Kombinat with materials, such as ore, spare parts, or hard currency—the only gateway to foreign technological fixes.

As the case of Smederevo shows, the socialist leadership utilized kompenzacija to redistribute risks and revenues in the economy. Profitable companies were called upon to offset the losses of unprofitable firms, either with money or goods. The assumption was that the total value of labor would not decrease and that the state would balance debts and credits accumulated by different companies. As directors of socialist companies liked to say, the state would "close the circle" of credits between companies and decouple salaries, wages, and even profits from the availability of money.[42]

Kompenzacija and Transition

The transition from socialism generated a peculiar kind of illiquidity: if, on the one hand, the dismantling of the productive system caused a nightmarish scenario for unemployed workers, on the other hand, the privatization process allowed managers to strip former state-owned companies of their assets. Faced with heightened expectations for consumption but a fragmented market, Macedonia saw a resurgence of kompenzacija as a form of exchange through which an emerging class of petty urban entrepreneurs could bank on gray cash and informal relations to accumulate capital.

> It was simple. My dad [a Macedonian entrepreneur] knew that he could very easily sell toilet seats here in Macedonia. But he did not have the money to buy them. So, what he did was to go to Serbia, where he found a company that sold toilet seats. This company was interested in getting door handles—so he went

around until he found another company who would sell him door handles on credit. He got the handles, went to the first company, exchanged the handles for the seats, brought them back to Macedonia, sold them, paid back the handles company . . . and so he became the King of Kompenzacija.

According to his son's account, the King of Kompenzacija was able to engage in in-kind private transactions precisely because of the dismantling of the SFRJ. In this case, two companies were interested in goods of different kinds but could not rely on the socialist infrastructure to exchange them. Entrepreneurs such as the King of Kompenzacija were able to match desired goods in different national markets to generate profit. This was particularly important in Macedonia, a country with an underdeveloped consumer industry. Because Macedonia had maintained a neutral position during the Balkan Wars and had reinforced its strong connections to Serbia in the aftermath of the Greek embargoes, kompenzacija flourished alongside other kinds of informal trade and smuggling that connected Skopje to Niš and Belgrade.

The fall of the socialist system was crucial to this new set of kompenzacija exchanges in another sense. As former socialist companies had been privatized and stripped of their assets by unscrupulous managers, workers were either laid off in droves or often paid with goods such as barrels of cheese, coupons for purchases in grocery stores, or knitwear. As more and more companies had their accounts blocked and stopped paying their suppliers or subcontractors,[43] many citizens, including most of Construx's workers, decided to keep stacks of cash, often converted into more stable foreign currencies such as the deutschmark—an extreme measure justified by the fear that some Macedonian banks might soon collapse. Kompenzacija thus re-emerged as a way to get by, whereby a fragmented economic system could convert goods into money through informal relations.

This kind of postsocialist kompenzacija ensured liquidity in the same way that barter did in other parts of Eastern Europe by matching desires and transferring values at a time of political fragmentation.[44] It also constituted a way for close businesses to help one another, extending credit through in-kind exchanges. Kompenzacija equivalences also relied on "differences," but not between different moral spheres of value and evaluation. They relied on different markets, on the different availability of supply and demand, or on the different monetary price paid for a good across newly established national boundaries.

Kompenzacija made possible the social rise of many small entrepreneurs who had no monetary or economic capital but were able and willing to engage in chains of non-monetary transactions that eventually let them join the ranks of petty capital owners. Through informal channels tolerated by the political elites, kompenzacija became a socially acceptable alternative to money that could generate profits in the absence of a functioning state.

Early 2000s: Kompenzacija and Precariousness

In the early 2000s, kompenzacija assumed a very different form. Rather than being a survival mechanism, kompenzacija became part of a centripetal push in Macedonia's economy. Under these conditions, kompenzacija signaled a series of forced credit relationships that became increasingly exploitative depending on a company's distance from the VMRO–DPMNE regime.

I met Marko the first day I arrived on the construction site. He was hanging around outside the elevated container where the supervisor's office was located. Over the next few days I would often see him coming and going, having been called in to solve some problems by Toni, the supervisor, or simply stopping by as a courtesy, his roaring voice filling the air. Most strikingly, he seemed to have a joke ready for everyone: all the other managers or directors of subcontracting firms spent time laughing with him and telling stories. Just below the elevated container, Bobi had a different opinion of Marko. "I worked for him about six months," he told me while anxiously smoking a cigarette, "and he never paid me. He promised me 500 euro per month, but he was never on time. 'I do not have the money,' he kept telling me. 'Here is an advance of 100 euro'—and it's been three months that I haven't gotten anything. I am not insured, nor do I claim taxes and social insurance. What am I supposed to do?"

Ultimately, Bobi left the company. He joined another firm working on the same site, along with seven of Marko's former employees. Reduced to only five operatives, Marko suddenly disappeared from the site, visiting only on occasion and unannounced. Instead, he intensified his virtual presence in the company's office to solve his kompenzacija issues. He was scheduled to receive an apartment for the work he had done on two different buildings. But as his main company was currently in financial trouble and the bank had blocked his account, he begged Construx (the contractor company) to pay him via a different account belonging to a subsidiary he owned.

For Marko, kompenzacija constituted a problem, although it was not as acute and urgent as it was for Bobi. On the one hand, he would become the owner of a relatively coveted and stable good, the apartment; on the other, it was unclear when, how, or if that would happen. Almost a year after that first encounter, I sat down with Marko as he hopelessly explained his difficult situation.

> You see, I was supposed to get money for the deal. Then they said, "Can we do kompenzacija?" I couldn't really say no, so I accepted. Now it turns out that the apartment is used as collateral from Construx, and I cannot get the official papers, so I cannot sell it! So I decided, no more kompenzacija. I could not keep my employees, I needed to restructure the whole company.

Kompenzacija jeopardized Marko's financial stability and strained his relationship with Bobi. His company had already performed half of the work when Construx offered to pay him with apartments. While he had a contract for a monetary amount he would not disclose, he agreed to Construx's terms. In part he felt he ought to support Construx, a company that had been very loyal to him in the past and had a good reputation. But this moral obligation also had darker roots: Marko knew very well that if he did not comply with Construx, he risked being cut out of the circle of preferred subcontractors. In a small country such as Macedonia with raging unemployment, falling outside of this circle could be the equivalent of business exile. Unsure about how else he could recover at least some of the money he was owed, Marko decided that kompenzacija was his best bet.

After all, kompenzacija was easy to do. Many interlocutors recalled deals done over dinner or drinks. Indeed, for many of them kompenzacija had a distinctly human flavor that corresponded to the informal and sometimes mutually beneficial deals they had struck so many times during the years of the transition from socialism. Accountants and lawyers agreed—from their perspective, kompenzacija simply meant balancing the contractor's debt with a transfer of ownership of an asset, generally an apartment, to the creditor.

And yet, in most of the accounts of kompenzacija I collected, there was a sobering point—a moment when convivial agreements turned sour. While a monetary payment would have been the end of a transaction, with kompenzacija it was only the beginning of a series of other conversions that often failed to materialize. Subcontractors had to wait for the company to finish building the apartments. Then they had to receive legal ownership, a complex and lengthy process, as the real estate registrar was in the middle of a digitalization process, and apartments had to be released by the banks, which generally had control over them since they were used as collateral for loans. Finally, subcontractors such as Marko had to sell the apartments in a market where housing prices were increasingly volatile.

Between 2007 and 2015, Macedonia's construction sector expanded dramatically. If one excludes civil engineering works, a sector that doubled in 2013 and tripled in 2015 when compared with 2010, Macedonia's housing sector in 2015 had productivity of about 180 percent of what it was in 2010—the exact opposite trajectory of other EU countries that were experiencing the implosion of the financial real estate bubble of the early 2000s.[45]

Macedonia's intense construction activity did not always translate into profits.[46] Early analyses[47] stress that the construction sector was increasingly indebted; sales of apartments were increasingly rare, pressing companies like Construx to rely on promotional discounts. The average price of apartments also decreased steadily. Despite the government's efforts to subsidize housing mortgages for young couples, buyers seemed unable to afford the nominal price of around 1,200 euro per square meter in a decently located, averagely constructed building.

In 2013, receiving an apartment as kompenzacija was a liability. This not only forced the subcontractor to spend increasing amounts of time and energy to sell the apartment, but its value was destined to decrease rapidly. Instead of an exchange of equal goods, kompenzacija was an exchange between one good (labor), the value of which was supposedly constant, and another (apartments), the value of which was shrinking. Kompenzacija promoted a new relationship between labor, goods, and money that generated losses in the absence of the political connections needed to unload goods quickly.

At worst, Marko's company, and most of the companies I examined throughout my research, could off-load the burden of kompenzacija onto workers. That meant firing workers—often hired without regular contracts anyway—or keeping them at work with the simple promise of future pay while providing them just enough money to survive and come to work. If, for company directors, kompenzacija meant exposing their businesses to the precariousness of a falling bubble market, workers experienced kompenzacija as an even greater mechanism of precarity—one through which they entirely lost control over the monetary value of their labor.

Krste and Bosko, both workers at Construx, were just a few of the many employees in the construction sector who directly experienced the effects of kompenzacija. For Bosko, kompenzacija was about a car:

I worked for an architectural firm that got a contract with an important politician. One day the manager of the company calls me: "Come out," he says. I go, and I see him with three black, medium-sized cars. "Choose one," he tells me, "it is yours." Instead of my fee, they turned up with those cars! Eventually I had to close down my own private activity because of kompenzacija!

Had he not accepted kompenzacija, he would have had no way to retrieve the money he was promised. Courts were simply unhelpful without the right political connections, and because his client was an important man, he was perfectly positioned to manipulate the legal system. Not only did Bosko stand no chance of fighting through institutions, but he was also afraid for his physical safety in going against a member of the VMRO–DPMNE regime. Unable to mobilize political support, Bosko was eventually stuck with property that he did not need and did not want, which eventually led him to the brink of personal bankruptcy.

In some cases, kompenzacija was embedded with more explicit forms of violence. At 1.60 meters tall, Krste was known throughout the construction site for his gentle manner. But after a year of begging his previous employer to pay him his six months of overdue salary, he had enough. He went to the company's office and sat in the sales room. "Every quarter you make today selling things, I will take it. And if you do not sell anything, I will take stuff from your store until the debt is repaid." His face turned red as he recalled the incident, and his body movements became increasingly nervous as he continued:

And then I started provoking my former employer. I insulted him and his family. And so he punched me in the chest. But then—**BAM**—I hit him straight in the face and he fell to the ground. His brother tried to stop me, and so he was able to flee. But I went after him, pushed him down in the street and then **BAM BAM**, I kept on kicking him until he was all covered in blood!

Eventually Krste got some money back—by transforming a labor relationship into violence, he was able to avoid the threat of kompenzacija and actually convert blood into money.

There is more violence embedded in kompenzacija than the (rare) physical assault or the (much more common) psychological and existential insecurity reported above. With temperatures as extreme as minus fifteen and plus forty-five degrees Celsius, workers operate on ten- to twelve-hour shifts in which they are required to complete physically demanding tasks with very rudimentary technological help. Despite the dangerous and unsafe conditions that they work in, health insurance comes only with a regular monetary wage—if a company does not fulfill its tax obligations, the state cuts all the workers' benefits, including insurance and pension payments.

Kompenzacija transfers the burdens of social security and safety from the employers onto workers' shoulders. Workers paid in kompenzacija or employed by a company that gets involved in it cannot access public health care, a service that they desperately need because of the risky nature of their labor. While the government has recently tightened controls over the construction sector, with the goal of reducing hazards to workers' health and combatting workplace accidents, it is clear that the main purpose is to collect fines from companies that employ undeclared labor or do not pay taxes regularly. Because almost every company is at fault in some of these areas, inspections became the main political weapon to hit entrepreneurs who were firm in their lack of support for the VMRO–DPMNE. Companies such as Construx were periodically inspected and lived with the constant fear of incurring charges and fines. Yet the deaths of construction workers that have occurred in major government-supported projects have been completely ignored.

Kompenzacija and the Global Financial Crisis

For most Macedonian construction companies, kompenzacija was a necessary evil that allowed them to access government contracts in a climate where few other sources of funding were available. Partly this was a consequence of Macedonian banks' hesitancy to lend money in a notoriously volatile economy. Since 1992, when accounts in hard currencies such as dollars or deutschmarks were confiscated by the Macedonian government to fund its reserves,[48] the country had experienced a proliferation of delinquent debts.[49] In 1994, bad loans amounted to 80 percent of the portfolio for Stopanska Banka, the largest bank in Macedonia, which was then owned by the state.[50] In 2000, 26 percent of total loans were overdue, while intercompany arrears "emphasized the problem of lack of liquidity" and totaled 32 billion MKD.[51] Around the turn of the century, several small banks defaulted, including Eksport-Import Banka, Rado Banka, and Almako Banka.

These fears lessened in the early 2000s, when European, especially Greek, financial institutions took over Macedonia's banking system. Between 2005 and 2008, credit grew an average of 40 percent each year.[52] And yet, at the first sign of global turmoil, the European financial institutions that owned Macedonian banks reevaluated the structural weaknesses of the Macedonian economy and decided to shift their lending toward customers that they considered safe—even if they had financed most credits from domestic deposits rather than junk derivatives and other risky financial products.[53] In 2013, credit to enterprises grew almost zero percent, while collateral requests soared to around 300 percent of the loan value.[54] Instead of crediting enterprises, Macedonian banks preferred purchasing public debt, increasing their portfolio from 3 percent in 2011 to 10 percent in 2015.[55]

At the precise moment when they needed financing, most independent construction companies began having problems getting loans. Companies that had a good reputation or enjoyed ties with the government, on the other hand, could repackage existing impaired loans as new loans—a move that circumvented reserve requirements for banks and stabilized non-performing loans (NPLs) at an unrealistic 11 percent of the total loans.[56] The same was true for individual citizens. Newly hired public employees told me that the most important benefit of their positions was the option of converting secure employment into a credential for private consumer loans or mortgages. Individual loans were even more important for those who, before being awarded a permanent contract in a public institution, were asked to volunteer without pay for extended periods of time—sometimes even years.[57]

While the global financial crisis drastically reduced the credit available to private enterprises, it became a boon for Macedonia's public finances. Since 2008, regulators, central banks, and international organizations grew increasingly weary of the repercussions of credit freezes on public debt. Faced with the specter of multiple public debt defaults, Mario Draghi, director of the ECB, announced his commitment to buy public debt from European countries under speculative attacks—the famous "whatever it takes" speech that, together with the quantitative-easing policies of other central banks, made cheap money available to global markets and encouraged investments in long-term public debt.[58]

Paradoxically, this geopolitical context, plagued by uncertain global credit and potential public defaults, offered Gruevski the opportunity to access and monopolize international credit and turn kompenzacija into a political tool. Until 2007, Gruevski had been rather reluctant to engage with international financial institutions, continuing instead with austerity policies and neoliberal reforms. In 2008, the collapse of foreign investments, European remittances, and a worsening trade balance forced Macedonian regulators to burn through their reserves and replenish them with external borrowing to maintain the

Macedonian denar pegged to the euro.[59] By early 2010, as the global financial crisis was increasingly affecting European economies, the IMF and other European institutions grew increasingly preoccupied with the regional stability of the Balkans and offered Gruevski economic support. In 2011, Gruevski signed a Precautionary Credit Line (PCL) with the IMF worth 480 million euro with the explicit goal of off-setting potential spillovers from the Greek debt crisis—a scenario not so remote given that major Macedonian banks and strategic companies, including the country's main refinery, were owned by Greek investors.

In the IMF's plans, the PCL constituted a mechanism of last resort in case of economic catastrophe, destined to help Macedonia reassure markets and investors. In March 2011, only two months after signing the agreements, Gruevski called for snap elections and drew 220 million euro from the PCL. Officially, the money was used to face the challenges of political instability that came with the election. In practice, it helped finance parts of the Skopje 2014 project—together with a further 130 million euro, partially guaranteed by the World Bank, which Gruevski raised in November 2011 from Deutsche Bank and Citibank.[60]

Suddenly, international private investors began to be interested in Macedonia's public debt, which offered higher returns and relatively low risk in a global climate of extremely low interest rates. By 2015, the government embarked on routine road shows and held meetings with major investors to place treasury bills and euro obligations on international markets—managing to triple the country's debt in absolute terms from 1.3 billion euro (20 percent of GDP) in 2008 to 4.36 billion euro (47.9 percent of GDP) in 2015.[61]

While the global financial crisis facilitated the honeymoon enjoyed by the VMRO–DPMNE and international investors, average Macedonians found themselves in a rather different situation. Salaries stagnated at around 350 euro per month; inflation remained relatively low; and savings continued to be negative, with a low of 15.4 percent in 2007.[62] With the notable exception of construction, pensions, and hiring in public administration, the Gruevski government did not invest much in social welfare and froze funds allocated in the budget.

The Macedonian government could not spend all the money it raised on international markets. To fuel the extractive schemes that enriched oligarchs through unproductive real estate (see Chapter 1), Gruevski had to earmark the remaining money for debt servicing. This led to significant government

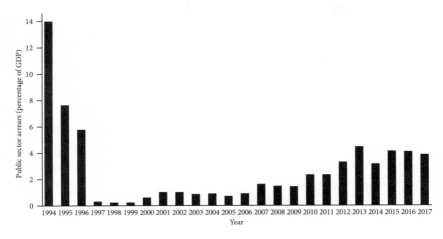

Figure 10. Public-sector arrears as a percentage of GDP for Macedonia. Source: World Bank, International Debt Statistics, NBRM. Courtesy of Gani Ramadani

arrears, including VAT refunds, which the IMF estimated at 2 percent of GDP in 2014,[63] but, when also including payments for public contracts, were undoubtedly higher (see figure 10 for estimates from a combination of other sources). Even construction giants such as Beton and Granit that were controlled by businessmen close to the government experienced significant delays in government payments. Smaller companies such as Construx waited more than twelve months to be paid or to receive their VAT refunds. In 2012, the problem escalated to involve international contractors, with diplomatic tensions surfacing in the IMF's yearly report, when a conservative estimate of government arrears listed them at 5.6 billion MKD.[64]

By 2014, contractors with limited access to bank credit quickly ran out of money whenever public investments stopped, propelling toxic circles of inter-company debts.[65] "We're stuck—it's like they turned off the faucet," the director of another construction enterprise told me. There was a veritable struggle to turn on the government's faucet and enter the circle of contractors that worked with government institutions. Companies knew very well that a fixed bribe of 10 percent of the gross value of the project was needed to win major tenders. But there were other burdensome financial constraints needed to intercept public investments, which often included forced credit, delayed payments, and forced donations of infrastructure or public installations.

In the right-wing, ethnically Macedonian municipality of Aerodrom in

Skopje, such payments have taken a surprising form: the donation of churches. As one of the fastest growing neighborhoods, Aerodrom has been the destination for many investments from both local government offices and private investors. Recently, a Turkish holding called Cevahir erected the first of four 40-story towers—a record in seismically cautious Skopje. Immediately afterward, the municipality sped up the installation of Christian symbols—including a 20-meter-high iron cross—in order to discourage Muslim buyers and maintain the ethnic primacy of Slavic-speaking, orthodox Macedonians in the municipality. Meanwhile, private developers and construction companies have started to build churches. In an area of about one square kilometer, construction companies have "donated" eight churches over the past ten years.[66]

"*Mito* (bribery)—that's what it is," commented the director of Construx, who, like many other professionals in the sector, had no doubt about how to interpret these donations. He himself had been forced into building a church in a different neighborhood. "It was either that, or money. But at least a church is useful for people," another employee at Construx clarified. Donating a church was compensated by favors from the local and central governments, which included receiving tenders or being able to buy denationalized land at a lower price. But more important, a church could directly appeal to prospective ethnic Macedonian buyers interested in the newly developed complexes.

Pyramids of Forced Credit

Oligarchs who tolerated the regime's conditions were in turn allowed to exploit subcontractors by imposing kompenzacija and other dubious deals without legal consequences. In one of the many examples I came across, the supervisor of a project that formed part of the Skopje 2014 plan explained how hard it was for a subcontracting company to do business with an investor close to the government.

> The deal is for 100,000 euro, and it is 70 percent kompenzacija. Some of the apartments that the subcontractor will receive are already built close to Vodno [the mountain that overlooks the city], the rest are still to be built. But here is the catch: the elevators are from Germany, and the factory there would not take kompenzacija. The subcontractor has to take out a loan using the kompenzacija apartments as collateral, and then he has to use this cash to start paying for the elevators, waiting and hoping that the rest of the money will come in time to pay back the loan.

Because of the possibility, or illusion, of receiving at least some cash, companies were willing to take on significant risk. Businessmen I worked with quickly dismissed the idea that the kompenzacija they were experiencing was akin to older, win-win forms of barter exchange. Instead, they suggested that the "mafia-state"[67] was strangling them through these extractive deals. Rather than being an "informal," moral[68] way to get by and create some of the interstitial structures observed in Serbia[69] or in Bosnia,[70] kompenzacija forced contractors or subcontractors to provide credit to companies closer to the government that could save their monetary resources for other investments.

In the elevator deal, the subcontractor took the financial risk by leveraging the apartments he received as kompenzacija. The contractor, an oligarch close to the VMRO–DPMNE, unloaded his portfolio of hard-to-place apartments[71] and kept most of his money as proverbial bait for other desperate subcontractors. Unsurprisingly, the proliferation of kompenzacija was one of the reasons the top 1 percent of earners increased their share of wealth from 6.8 percent in 2007 to over 12 percent in 2014, the highest in Europe.[72]

Even building companies opposed to the VMRO–DPMNE, such as Construx, participated in such exploitative practices. As a company that could access cash by selling apartments, Construx could impose kompenzacija on other subcontractors.[73] "We offer them kompenzacija," one of the managers of Construx told me. "If they do not accept . . . well, do you think they have a choice?"

As I exited the restaurant where I had been conversing with Construx's managers, I remembered a conversation I had had a few months earlier with the director of a different, successful construction company. Sitting at a café, he looked at me with glassy eyes, wary of sharing details about his business. The kinds of questions I was asking, focused on finance, were suspicious. His fears were understandable. While I was not a spy, an undercover agent, or a member of the SDSM opposition party, he owed his fortune to the regime, from whom he had received substantial investments. For him, the global financial crisis did not exist. Concerned that I would not get an actual answer, I made a passing comment about the housing market being prone to bubbles. "The market?" he started laughing. "Do you think I am crazy? I would never invest in a free market!"

That sentence captured a common feeling in Skopje. Most businessmen refused the idea that the urban real estate market could behave independently from the government. Macedonian interlocutors of different political sides

agreed: Skopje was dominated by "an urban mafia," "an octopus that stran-
gles you," or "a system that drags you down." Indeed, the multiple layers of violence and oppression found in kompenzacija show that businessmen's inter-
pretations were rooted in actual experiences of dispossession promoted by the
Gruevski regime. And yet buying into poisonous kompenzacija deals and rep-
licating them further was not always a necessity—nor always Gruevski's fault.

Many of the issues that framed Macedonia's illiquidity predated the
VMRO–DPMNE regime. Since socialism, the Macedonian economy had
been peripheral in both the global capitalist system and Yugoslavia. Macedonia had then been devastated by the postsocialist transition in the 1990s
and unsettled by a succession of economic and political emergencies until
the global financial crisis. Because of this larger historical context, Gruevski
could take advantage of the sudden freeze of international loans available to
companies and the sudden availability of funds for governments and consumers. With projects such as Skopje 2014, his regime could conjure a mirage of
profit before a business sector in crisis and normalize the kinds of exploitation
that ensued once the specter vanished.

In this subtler sense, kompenzacija did more for the Gruevski regime than
simply siphon value away from the periphery of the Macedonian political
economy and toward his allies and relatives. As this "psychosis of illiquidity" spread, companies that could have paid in cash tended to resort to kompenzacija and force subcontractors to accept toxic deals. Blaming the government for reciprocal forms of exploitation, Macedonian companies found
themselves increasingly interconnected in new financial binds, sometimes
as victims but often as perpetrators of forced credit relationships—a rather
stark departure from other financializing economies, where loans were offered rather than imposed.[74]

Unlike the early days of the transition from socialism, by 2013 citizens
could not pay bills, taxes, or groceries with kompenzacija. Macedonians still
needed money as a means of payment for most of their daily transactions—
no one wanted to be an outlier stuck with unwanted goods. As recipients of
kompenzacija tried to force others into similar deals, Macedonians' illiquid financialization recalled pyramid schemes in which investors received profits
based on new entrants' quotas rather than actual returns from their capital.[75]
To keep the scheme running, companies sometimes increased their prices 20,
30, or even 40 percent. Keeping costs high for building companies, subcontractors ignited an upward spiral of virtual prices that created further problems for vulnerable construction companies.

And yet kompenzacija was a much more dangerous pyramid compared with other speculative endeavors such as Ponzi schemes. The failure of a Ponzi scheme is typically dictated by its inability to produce profits and generally leads the entire pyramid to collapse once no new members can be found. Kompenzacija, instead, thrived in the absence of profits. Because the global financial crisis made construction-sector financing and profits increasingly hard to achieve, companies were stuck with unwanted credit. But because it was rooted in labor exploitation rather than fictive investments of financial capital, kompenzacija did not have an obvious breaking point. As long as workers and businessmen could eat and were convinced that there was no alternative to the VMRO–DPMNE regime, their labor could be continuously mobilized to provide additional credit to politically connected companies. And in a world that was increasingly seen as completely saturated by Gruevski's tentacular regime, it did not make much sense to try and look for alternatives.

Forced Credit and Power

When I asked the son of the King of Kompenzacija what his plans were for the future, he sipped his imported beer and looked out the window for a moment. Then he answered:

> I tried to work with my dad. But it is impossible. He does not realize that he's just losing money. We now have three apartments that we do not know how to use, and we can't sell them to anybody. And look, you see my black [Volkswagen] Golf car parked outside? That was also kompenzacija. He got it because he knew the guy would never pay him back. I tried to stop him from doing more kompenzacija; he did not realize that all his work, all his capital spread around, all his energy spent not sleeping at night and spinning around has a cost. You work more, and you barely break even.

These words sum up the role that kompenzacija played in Gruevski's Macedonia. It constituted an agent of a specific kind of illiquidity whereby a powerful authoritarian state intercepted international flows of capital and turned them into forced credit. In-kind payments as conducted through kompenzacija configured a relationship whereby more and more input had to be provided in order to generate some kind of output.

In such a system, the conversion of labor into money via goods follows unequal rates. Many realized the nefarious effects of kompenzacija only too late, when they accumulated an overwhelming amount of monetary credit, which would be paid in goods they could not sell. Until then, kompenzacija had a dream-like quality; like a future derivative, it was just a sign on paper that balanced a column of minuses with a single plus, a handshake with a smile, or a disquieting afterthought with a witty joke. After the deal was in place, however, kompenzacija transformed labor into cars, apartments, and churches—past testimonies of success and status that, during the regime, hid dramas of monetary loss and forced labor.

Companies literally fought to get into poisonous kompenzacija deals that carried some mirage of money. In this sense, kompenzacija signaled not a fragmentation and proliferation of different and smaller political authorities, as most of the literature on postsocialist exchanges has suggested,[76] but the reconstitution of a party-state-like structure that dominated Macedonian life economically and politically. Built upon the emotive and material legacies of socialist in-kind payment systems, this new political economy was a hybrid combination of socialist and neoliberal techniques of power whereby in-kind exchanges wove financial flows into the Macedonian fabric.

Rooted in some collective expectations of state paternalism without hopes of equality, kompenzacija anchored a quasi-pyramid construction expansion to labor exploitation and political patronage. For some, this was a relief. The director of a company close to the VMRO–DPMNE commented aptly that only fools rely on the market. He, and many others, chose political domination over illiquidity. For others, it became a useful expedient. Construx was no "fool," but it had been pushed further and further away from the political-economic center. Faced with a difficult market, Construx tended to rely more and more on kompenzacija. After all, if the government was preying on them, why should they not do the same to their subcontractors? The result was a cascade of risks, uncertainty, and unwanted goods that fell on the shoulders of those who found themselves at the bottom of the political and economic pyramid.

When my interlocutors were faced with kompenzacija, they felt powerless. Most of them knew, or figured out quite early, that kompenzacija would force them to lose money and time. They also felt they had no other choice. Kompenzacija threw businessmen against the proverbial wall, where they were face to face with the specter of financial collapse. As Construx's director put it, his subcontractors had already de facto invested in the company by working or providing materials for future pay—if they did not accept kompenzacija, they faced the risks of financialization alone. If they did accept kompenzacija, on the other hand, they became directly involved in the destiny of the company—a Faustian bargain that could lead to even further economic disaster, but that companies such as his could leverage while blaming their bad choices on the government.

This constant and exaggerated reference to Gruevski's capacity to force cycles of kompenzacija played into the hands of the VMRO–DPMNE government. Convinced that the economy was completely controlled by the regime, entrepreneurs joined the VMRO–DPMNE's pyramidal system for reasons that went beyond economic opportunism. It became a way to find an existential footing against the tidal wave of illiquidity and financialization, even if it was precisely the VMRO–DPMNE system that made it so threatening. As the director of Construx put it, "There's no way to survive outside of [the system]. But once you're in it, God help you."

4 Illiquid Times

ON MACEDONIAN CONSTRUCTION SITES, few moments are as enjoyable as October afternoons. Warm sunlight paints in earthly tones the glittering swirls of dust that adorn workers' silhouettes. An aeration unit waits, silently, to be painted over with a new coat of leftover red—close, but not quite the same as its original tone. Gorast appears carrying a once-yellow ladder kept together by far too many metal nails and patches—practically a cyborg, as far as ladders go. "You see, this," panted Gorast, picking up a hammer from the toolbox, "should have been thrown away years ago. But no, here I am fixing it once again." Then he stopped, a moment of gravity amid the surreal quiet of the site. "This, my friend, is what Macedonia *is*."

Macedonia, a broken ladder. Gorast's diagnosis was witty, funny, and yet deeply caustic. A ladder that keeps on breaking conveys a distinct despair about the future, a sense that small acts of care, such as repairing defects or retouching details, are doomed to fail and to become detrimental to one's social and individual growth. Instead of being tools for building the future, broken ladders immobilized workers in the present—consuming their energy in attempts to fix a wrecked environment that was becoming progressively more fragile.

Damaged ladders, leftover paint, and other similar failures infused the workplace with an atmosphere of futility—a sense of disarticulation between workers' actions and their consequences, between their existential aspirations and the political and economic conjuncture they lived in. By October 2013, several Macedonian construction firms found themselves entangled in a web of financial debts and were focused on fighting against the credit squeeze and political pressures of Gruevski's government. Instead of purchasing materials and paying subcontractors, companies like Construx dedicated their resources to finding new buyers—even if that meant stalling the current construction projects or delaying all other payments. Gradually, funds dried up, bringing construction sites to a slow, painful halt. Workers who had prided themselves on being productive citizens, capable of transforming inert materials into hospitable homes, found themselves completing menial tasks or altogether idle—waiting for money, for materials, for an explanation—anything that could help them decipher their future.

Isolated on the construction site, workers felt increasingly useless—not only because they were unable to complete any job properly but also because whatever they did seemed to have little effect on Construx's direction. Stuck between a desire to quit and a fear of finding worse conditions elsewhere, workers wondered whether their entire existence was plunging into a sort of nothingness, a melancholic phenomenological condition "of mourning, grief, and loss" unleashed by their structural inability to patch together present action and future outcomes.[1] In that gray, uncertain place their dusty lives felt like a trap—outcasts stranded in a bubble of anomalous slothfulness while the world around them ran after dreams of financial speculation.

Localized and circumscribed, the sense of nothingness of October 2013 felt very different compared with other moments of disruption that had been common in socialist and postsocialist working places. Since World War II, Macedonian companies had been known for fluctuating production rhythms that affected their exports' quality and cashflow. Occasionally, salaries and promotions would also be held up—delays that caused significant individual problems and yet were not powerful enough to disrupt the overall sense of forward motion of social life (see Chapters 1 and 3). That correspondence between the rhythms of the workplace and the direction of the wider society had continued even during the hyperinflation of the 1980s and the economic collapse of the early 1990s, when Macedonian workers had faced a more radical sense of uncertainty.

With the disintegration of socialist Yugoslavia, the Macedonian productive system fell apart. Without markets, without resources, without credit, socialist companies closed, stopped paying salaries, and went into disrepair—often after being privatized for pennies on the dollar. Faced with rapidly spreading deindustrialized workplaces, workers found that the path toward a liberal, progressive society had been washed away by a deluge of botched free-market reforms. Macedonia now resembled a muddy wasteland with no way in or out.

Unlike Gruevski's illiquidity, the stagnation that followed the transition had been a collective experience characterized by a sense of overwhelming change rather than individualized passivity. Rather than feeling like an "end to life," an existential condition where working-class professions and lifestyles had lost all meanings,[2] the collapse of factories had pushed workers to mobilize—first as workers, then as ethnic groups, then through kinship networks. Contesting their uncertain working conditions and the loss of a better future, workers experienced factory floors and construction sites as spaces of social articulation. Through belligerent mobilization, first, and later through more private complaints, workers and citizens often took time off work, creating complex entanglements that elaborated the transition as a collective experience—one that had trapped the entire country in a hole.[3]

In 2013, the crises I observed at Construx (and other) workplaces felt very different. Gruevski's investments in real estate had prompted a selective revival of construction activities and working-class identities. Companies with the right connections profited enormously from the climate of uncertain payments made possible by the regime's ability to manipulate global credit during the financial crisis. Throughout Skopje, buildings mushroomed; crews of masons transformed bricks into homes and sweat into money—scattered patches of hope of progress and wealth that had suddenly sprung to life.

But not at Construx. Construx workers wondered, Why were *they* stuck? In the 1990s, being idle when *everyone* was struggling was difficult. But being frozen, physically and economically, while others seemed to be able to move forward, called into question their individual ability to leave a mark on the world—a literal crisis of presence that left workers feeling disconnected without a clear sense of what had happened and what could be done to fix it. Was it Gruevski and his regime who plunged Construx into a financial hole? Or was it the company that had made investment mistakes? Should they blame the global financial crisis or the greed of bankers that starved Construx of needed credit? Questions without answers were fuel for the sticky, corrosive nothingness that crept slowly into their lives.

In October 2013, Construx workers had started a low-intensity, pervasive, and yet invisible fight to contain their growing feeling of futility—and it is those struggles that I chronicle in this chapter. To reinvent a semblance of practical and individual normality in uncertain times, workers manipulated one of the few resources they could control—their time. Adjusting the pace of their work helped them feel in control of their own working rhythms and interrupt the sequence of constant worries about their future and that of their families. Slowing down, stalling, or speeding up the tempo of their social interactions allowed workers to take ownership of uncertain moments and to transform them into spaces of potentiality and empathy. Their temporal craftiness constituted a "woven time," a temporal space that not only threaded different kinds of "activities together into a single tapestry of the everyday" but also reaffirmed workers' creativity in the material and relational world.[4]

Weaving time expressed a "creative impulse . . . in a waiting arena."[5] Through these rhetorical and agential strategies, workers found ways of acting even amid uncertain prospects—a hard thing in post-Fordist workplaces[6]— that helped minimize the most serious psychological damage associated with precarious workplaces.[7] Yet it also generated more uncertainty, which worsened their tentative working conditions. Cracking a witty joke at the right moment could amuse a disgruntled buyer enough to prevent a lawsuit—until the next delay. Reminiscing and daydreaming allowed workers to feel in control of their own working lives—but not of the building, whose completion inevitably slowed down even more, breeding more resentful buyers.[8]

Perhaps, had they not been manual workers but financial investors, weaving time could have turned uncertainty into profit—creating opportunities for hedging risk against future rewards.[9] In their current predicament, however, gentle temporal tricks only exacerbated the asynchronies of finance, life, and work that already plagued their working days. Then weaving time took a darker turn. As workers felt themselves slipping into nothingness, their temporal tinkering shifted from creative acts to nihilistic gestures, where agency became synonymous with political submission.

Incongruities Explained: Temporal Cycles Falling Apart

The first time I set foot on a Macedonian construction site, I was struck by its liminal beauty. Everywhere lay iron, bricks, and sand—materials waiting to become something else. For most of my middle-class interlocutors, however, the idea of visiting construction sites and dealing every day with workers was rather unappealing. Unfinished plots of not-yetness unveiled the messy underbelly of their own fragile social ascent—as if the very view of the site, especially of construction workers, fractured the illusion of having, finally, moved on from the alienation of their postsocialist condition.

Unsurprisingly, construction workers did not like being examined and appraised by urbanites. The mere sight of "civilians" plunged even warm October days into a glacial silence accompanied by heavy and suspicious stares. And yet this chilly welcome could melt into vigorous handshakes and thundering laughter when visitors recognized the workers' creative presence. Laboring with bricks instead of massaging data, construction workers had embodied Macedonia's hopes to literally build a better future. But that dream had evaporated in the 1990s with the collapse of socialism. By 2013, in a country that was trying to reinvent itself as a land of internet technologies and digital experts, being a construction worker looked increasingly out of place.

Being liminal, however, had its advantages. Workers could appropriate the construction site as *their* place—performing short stories, songs, or limericks that suspended the "normal" order of things and celebrated through ridicule their peculiar looks and smells. At Construx, that indulgent out-of-placeness even produced a fictive language, "the construction speech," a mocking, improvised idiom that workers hammered and crafted from their own northeastern dialects. An unfinished language, for those who dwelled on the unfinished.

Unlike middle-class citizens, accustomed to consuming objects and spaces already completed, Construx's workers identified themselves with *the process* of building—a transformative mastery of the built environment that inscribed their own grind in a long history of masons, master craftsmen, and artisans. For half of these workers, the legacy was both a gift and a curse, passed on from father to son for several generations, as their families had moved from villages in the eastern and northern parts of the country and made the periphery of Skopje their new home—the last migrants since the 1950s to claim a land made vacant by the (more or less forced) departure of Yugoslav Turks.

Expressing their control over the not-yetness, the process of building made workers proud—not an aggressive pride but a fulfilling centeredness, a way to reclaim their place in history and society, infusing sweat and drudgery with dignity and gravitas. The ability to subdue matter and themselves through a transformative discipline helped them justify their liminal existence as a foundation of society—a process that workers loved to recall in its relentless rhythms. The taxing pace of life that disciplined their physical tasks as early as 5:00 a.m.[10] became, by itself, the key to their existential realignment with "civilian life," even when it was precisely this temporal discipline that forced them to miss so much of what happened beyond the workplace.

Confined to their workplaces and disciplined by a rigid temporal schedule, workers found other ways to embed their days, and especially their breaks, within the seasonal life cycles of the country. During the summer, workers supplied the 11:00 a.m. lunch break with tomatoes, zucchini, and peppers. In the fall, they brought homemade wine or rakija that most of them distilled during weekends, eliciting lunchtime stories of camaraderie in rhythm with the season. During the winter, chestnuts, pickled cabbage, or even pork rinds appeared as early as 7:00 a.m.—especially in the exciting days that followed the slaughter of domestic pigs.

These incursions of social time into their working routines attenuated the cold darkness or savage sun that accompanied their duties. Managers encouraged, or at least tolerated, occasional breaks to have a drink and celebrate ritual occasions and household saints (*slavi*). Almost every week, a few boxes of *napolitanki* (wafers filled with cream) or peanuts from the discount store celebrated someone's birthday or a household event—markers of time that gave depth to workers' liminality and reconciled their work life to their social world.

"It came through? IT CAME THROUGH! YESSSS! HOORRAAAY!" With that scream, the sleepy atmosphere of the October's afternoon shattered like a cloud broken by a single ray of sunshine. Workers anxiously emerged from their hiding places, almost trotting to hear from Folco, getting hugged and shaken in the process. Infected with the euphoria, a couple of comrades ran to the local discount store and bought juice, wine, and cookies (see figure 11). When they returned, a dusty plank and a wheelbarrow had been arranged— an improvised altar around which workers sang and danced the Oro, arms locked and feet oscillating a few steps ahead and a few steps behind.

Folco's impromptu celebration had been triggered by one simple word: *plata*—salary—a word that they had been anxiously awaiting. For the previous two months, workers had called almost daily to find out whether their company, Construx, had paid their salaries. *Ima Nešto?* (Is there something?), they asked on the phone and then to each other. *Ništo* (nothing), they were told—a painful avowal that echoed throughout the silent site as a whispering cloud of corrosive anxiety.

Without money, workers had begun to economize on little things. Cookies, wine, and drinks had been the first to succumb. And yet, over time, the nothingness had expanded. Two months into the delay, celebrating *slavi* or

Figure 11. Workers celebrate the payment of their salary. Photo: Author

other festive occasions had begun to feel out of place or had become too expensive. When six months of irregular funds disrupted the supply of building materials, workers started to feel caged—in a workplace that neither paid
them nor allowed them to work properly. Eight months into the delay, *ništo*
had taken on a heavy connotation that threatened their own families, their
own future, and the very meaning of their lives. With tears in his eyes, Nico
recalled the sense of humiliation that encompassed the workplace. "I always
buy myself a new shirt for Easter. That is not much, but I do it every year.
This year . . . this year I could not afford it." The low hum of defeat inhabited
the silence that followed. "And this weekend is my daughter's birthday. What
am I supposed to do? You know, a cake costs money. What can I get her? Not
to mention a party! But she's a kid, how can she understand that I have no
money?"

In the empty time that punctuated their days, workers obsessed over that
question. How could the rest of the world understand them—now that they
had no money to justify their liminal work life or their prolonged absences
from their families? How would their friends and relatives accept their sudden withdrawal from festivities or marriage celebrations? How could they, the
workers, accept working on small, menial tasks without pay—when all around
them construction sites buzzed with activity? *Ništo*, they repeatedly answered

to each other. There was nothing they could explain or do, an admission of financial powerlessness that corroded other aspects of their lives—a painful, slow nothingness that threatened to swallow them alive.

Finance and Clock Time

The protracted emptying of meaning and activities from construction work constituted a temporal manifestation of Gruevski's illiquidity—a temporality "suspended between everyday survivalism and the far horizons of a millenarian future" that had taken by storm even prudent and solid companies such as Construx.[11]

Founded in 1991 by two friends who, according to the director, "met in a dark basement, with two broken chairs and a bucket," the company had been for almost twenty years a model of slow and constant growth. In the 1990s, the company had designed small projects, working mostly as a design studio and hiring external crews. That work had led to larger deals for local banks and foreign embassies, which convinced the managers to hire a permanent team of workers before launching into self-funded multi-dwelling units and infrastructural work in one of Skopje's fastest growing municipalities.

With Gruevski's rise to power, Construx faced a dilemma. Unwilling to support the regime, the company received fewer public contracts and less advantageous conditions from creditors. At the same time, the seemingly massive construction spree launched by the VMRO–DPMNE government had galvanized the expectations of builders all around the country. Every day, investors with no experience in the sector created new companies and started new (more or less legal) housing projects, hoping to capture either public funds or buyers with access to first-homeowners' loans (see Chapter 3). That left Construx with few alternatives. With so many new competitors and excited buyers, its managers considered that their best hope for survival was to go all in and ride the construction boom—rather than being overwhelmed by a wave of low-quality but cheap apartments. In 2011, after rising to the attention of the Macedonian public as the fourth-fastest-growing and most successful construction company in Macedonia, Construx abandoned long-term contracts from international investors to develop more lucrative residential buildings for the local housing market.

By October 2013, the company had built several nine-story buildings and had three more under construction, for which they hired thirteen new high-level workers (four engineers, three land surveyors, one architect, two financial experts, and three planners)—effectively doubling its administrative cadre. The "Den," in Skopje's newest residential neighborhood, was receiving the finishing touches; the "Pool," located in one of Skopje's historic neighborhoods, was expected to be completed shortly; the "Nest," a continuation of an older eight-story building, was scheduled for completion during the summer of 2014 but was only finished in late 2016. With so many "fronts" on which to operate at once, Construx decided to shift its policy of hiring contractors only for specialized phases such as electrical, plumbing, or steelworks. If it wanted to stay ahead of the competition, Construx had to be fast—hiring more subcontractors, including companies with a friendlier position vis-à-vis the Gruevski government but still run by relatives of Construx's directors.

To support this heightened pace of investment, the company decided to increase its credit lines and rely more heavily on banks. Thanks to building plots bought cheaply at the onset of the global financial crisis, Construx had no problem obtaining loans and beginning construction. But as the crisis deepened and international investors who owned the Macedonian banking sector grew stricter with deadlines and less flexible with payments,[12] this exposure turned into a liability. Alpha Bank, one of Construx's major partners, almost ceased to finance the company's operations. Stopanska Banka, one of the largest banks in the country, increased the required collateral and forced Construx to offer an ample portion of the buildings under construction as collateral. Under these new arrangements, proceeds from sales of apartments first went toward paying back Construx's loans, which deprived the company of liquidity and income in the early phases of the construction process.

By the end of 2013 the situation was increasingly dire. Construx had very few cash reserves, three buildings to complete, and significant competitors supported directly or indirectly by the government.[13] Forced to privilege debt repayment over investment, the company began to saddle subcontractors, suppliers, and even workers with their accumulating arrears. With time, subcontractors stopped working or became so sloppy that they could not complete their tasks without jeopardizing Construx's reputation for quality building. Suddenly, the company's "near future" looked evanescent—disappearing into the trap of Gruevski's illiquidity.[14]

So the company turned to its own workers. Forced to abide by the tight schedule of loan repayment, Construx hoped that it could get its own *maistori* (masons) to speed up the completion of the buildings, asking them to work longer hours than usual. But without the financial infrastructure to compensate for their labor or procure materials, these efforts were fruitless. During the winter of 2013 and the early months of 2014, Construx became less and less able to coordinate the timing of its own work and that of its financial obligations—completely upsetting the temporal horizon that regulated the construction site. The more the pressure of repaying financial obligations oriented Construx toward the progressive goal of skimming money, marketing, or paying penalties (or interests) for their delays, the more erratic its work schedule became.

Uncertain Waiting

On the construction site, an increasingly fuzzy near-term future was replaced with a series of emergencies, disruptions, and delays that filled the workers' waiting with peculiar, if opposed, challenges. At first glance, the illiquid workplace appeared empty—emptied of time and meaningful tasks, an island of eerie silence in Skopje's construction bubble. And yet this nothingness was also full—of doubts, of rumors, of problems to solve without certainties to rely on.

The immediate problem was that most workers had debts—generally small consumer loans or house improvement loans, with a few larger debts for health-related issues.[15] In all but two cases in which workers had been forced to use their houses as collateral, these loans had been conditional on their stable employment and Construx's own reputation. Now that the company was facing financial challenges and workers needed credit more than ever, banks started to harass them with daily calls inquiring about the repayments they had missed. Insisting and disparaging, calls and letters from credit institutions or telephone providers made workers feel personally guilty for something they had no control over—yet another proof that, in financialized Macedonia, postsocialist survival strategies, such as accumulating unpaid bills and keeping a small plot with produce, chickens, or pigs, were not enough to survive.

To appease creditors, workers cut back on every expense not directly needed for survival. They eliminated presents for their young children, negotiated the purchase of university supplies, and stopped buying clothes, although they tried to keep some pocket change for weekly bets on soccer results. When these measures became insufficient, workers started to take on private side jobs, something that they had done in the past but had dropped during the recent construction boom. Long days and weekend shifts with Construx became not only meaningless but also real impediments, a nothingness that chained workers and caused them to lose tangible income.

Matei provides a case in point. Without a father and with a retired mother, he needed extra income to support the family now that he was not being paid regularly. He tried to make a living out of betting on sports events—especially soccer. But that did not go as well as planned, and after a few months he lost count of his own profits or losses. Then he started waiting tables at a local restaurant specializing in weddings and other celebrations; this meant he had to work until two or three in the morning on Fridays, Saturdays, and Sundays. Working at Construx seven days a week with shifts of ten hours a day (eight hours on the weekends), for the whole summer and for a good part of the winter of 2013, he was exhausted.

Matei slept only two or three hours per night. Yet he was never late. He did not complain, nor did he cease gliding around the workplace with the quickness and dexterity of a cruise ship waiter. But not everyone was able to maintain such high morale, and over time the preoccupation with money affected workers' productivity. Inevitably, workers ended up pacing their shifts of labor-intensive activities increasingly far apart in order to save the core of their energy for their free time, when they would actually be paid for their efforts. "We work, but let's be honest, we do not really work," one of the workers admitted, as they all discussed the option of going on strike.

Saving energy during the workday to invest in after-shift private jobs was a common temporal tactic in the Macedonian construction industry, especially among ethnic Macedonians. Most of the big, formerly socialist companies such as Beton or Granit paid skilled workers as little as 150 euro per month (9,000 MKD) for eight- or nine-hour shifts without any additional money to cover lunches or transportation. Workers suggested that a family of four needed about 500 euro per month (30,000 MKD) to survive. The reason they kept these jobs was, as they told me, that they granted health insurance and pensions, while the side jobs paid for their survival.

Workers could have left Construx and tried their luck with a successful company such as the one that I will call "Imagine." "I thought about it, I asked around, you know," confided Marko to me on a cold night in January. "But there you do not count for anything, the owner bullies you, you have no machine to help you bring heavy weight up and down. There, you're just a piece of meat that moves." In a climate of financial uncertainty, managers of companies who did have access to money gained tremendous power over their workers. Imagine, for instance, was known for its brutal working conditions (see figure 12). On a new construction site, their work began at 5:00 a.m. and

Figure 12. Workers without harnesses stand on scaffolds while they lower materials manually at a work site of one of Construx's competitors. Photo: Author

continued without interruption until late in the afternoon, even when temperatures skyrocketed over forty-five degrees Celsius. When the owner showed up, an Imagine worker confided, he shouted orders and insults at workers, pushing them to work faster—or to hide, afraid, in a dark corner.

Most of these companies combined legal and illegal work. Many of their workers had no contracts, benefits, vacation leave, or insurance. Some employers declared only part of their workers' income to tax agencies. Typically, whatever exceeded the minimum wage of 9,000 MKD was paid in cash. While such an arrangement would have solved some of Construx's workers' immediate problems, it would have created additional problems further down the line, as the undeclared salary would have cut into their pensions or made them ineligible for health insurance.

Compared with working at these companies, working at Construx was like being in paradise. Until 2013, the company had paid workers handsomely, at least by Macedonian standards; unskilled workers made 300 euro per month, while skilled maistori had salaries up to 500 euro per month. More important, the company declared the whole salary for tax purposes, which meant that workers received welfare benefits based on the 500 euro once they retired. Even when workers lost their health insurance,[16] Construx offered to reimburse their health expenses and kept paying dues for their pensions.

This specific context added to the many doubts that had invaded the uncertain days of Construx's workers. On the one hand, they felt attached to the company, which had been until that point very honest with them, led by an owner they respected. And yet, on the other hand, they could not ignore the repeated signs of obvious decline. Stuck in a schizophrenic wait, with no information and filled with anxiety, the workers' outlook changed daily. At times they seemed convinced that it was best to keep their current jobs, where they felt unappreciated but could save their energy for private work. At others, they seemed ready to join successful companies, where decent salaries and recognition for their skills would entail brutal working conditions and cost them their future pensions.

Pushed by financial uncertainty and ready to trade heightened exploitation for ready money, some younger workers chose to try their luck on the job market. Without retirement in sight, they felt they had nothing to lose and found it untenable to sacrifice their present for an uncertain future. After dealing with increasingly delayed wages for six months between April 2014 and April 2015, seven of the youngest workers resigned. One found work as a truck driver, another in a gas station, two migrated to Germany and Slovenia, and one found a job in a foreign-owned company that produces vehicles. Two more, however, changed their minds and went back to Construx one day later. They resigned again in the fall of 2015 but were back to working with Construx in the summer of 2016. In contrast, older workers who could envision retiring in their (not-so-distant) futures decided to stay and "wait out" the crisis[17] in pursuit of a safe pension—a necessary anchor to traverse the dark and uncertain future ahead, even if that meant working additional side jobs in the present.[18]

Bending the Present and Weaving the Future

Workers who decided to stay at Construx remained troubled by their medium-term building failures and tormented by doubts about what to do in the long run. Day after day, their time spent on the construction site was filled with trivial emergencies that diverted their energies from more important construction tasks—a "chronic impermanence"[19] that short-circuited their aspirations and turned their work into empty performances—*mock-work*, in Rajkovic's brilliant definition.[20] As delays continued, workers felt they were drowning in an existential nothingness, a muddy uncertainty that halted any forward progress in their work, emptying their physical tasks of meaning and purpose.

In this context, small acts of ordering the world around them, giving it a density or direction, took on deeper meaning. Meal-time rituals allowed workers to embed a degree of normalcy in their working schedules. Manipulating breaks, suspending work, and pacing it to their moods granted some degree of control—if only over the ability to conjure alternative futures without fear of being erased by financial consideration.

Despite its warm colors, by autumn 2013 the Pool had become a deeply disquieting building, especially at sunset, when its shadow expanded like a monument to Construx's own powerlessness. It had been weeks since Construx's management had assured buyers, managers, and workers that the building was done. Almost everything was there—roof, air systems, cabling, even façades and air conditioning—it was all ready. What it did not have were a few crucial services such as running water, electricity, and waste disposal pipes—invisible systems whose absence made the majestic building completely uninhabitable. Every day, workers turned away angry buyers who could not understand why they were fixing small details instead of addressing the structural problems that prevented over sixty families from taking possession of the apartments they had purchased.

Inside the building the atmosphere was not much better. Dusty and silent, the only sign of life was the stale smell of cigarettes, tangible proof that somewhere a worker was taking a break. In an entrance several floors up, Folco, the team leader, was lying down, his eyes closed, while his partner Dino lingered on a nearby balcony ruminating about his own misfortune. For a while nobody spoke. Finally, voices from the outside broke through the clouded atmosphere, bringing them back to the tedious task of placing laths on fissures between wooden floorboards and on other surfaces. Folco, the more experienced of the two, measured sizes and angles; Dino molded lath with his circular saw, cursing the building and everyone who worked on it for its poor floor leveling, which forced them to cut, shape, and sculpt each piece countless times.

Like a silent ghost, Aleksandar appeared suddenly behind our backs. For a good half an hour, we talked about Dylan Dog, Corto Maltese, and other comics he read and published in Macedonia, digressing to his work as an author and his past as an unlucky hotel manager. I felt a bit uneasy chatting for so long, but Alex reassured me. Unless Construx had the money to hire plumbers and electricians and get the municipality to move forward, these pauses would not make any difference.

By 10:40 a.m., I joined the other seven manual workers present on site in the small, bare shop that served as both changing and eating room. There, exposed bricks and handmade wooden coat hangers framed a worn table carved by cohorts of workers and a multitude of makeshift places to sit. Overturned plastic buckets, wooden benches, or old chairs covered with rust; a stack of tiles or parquet flooring, a stone, a step—anything could serve as a seat as long as it was covered in plastic. Putting a piece of PVC or plastic under our buttocks, workers told me, was the only way to shield us from dust—the workplace's natural pest. But like efforts to take control of time, keeping the pernicious particles at bay was a failed endeavor. Food, clothes, fingernails—everything tasted and smelled like dust, a distinct staleness that could not be washed away but only pushed out of one's mind.

Matei, the deputy warehouseman, organized the meal, taking most minds off musty thoughts and feelings. A cinnamon box filled with salt, vegetables from someone's garden, and white plastic food containers appear together on the table, moving around accompanied by jokes and frivolous observations. Methodically, we unwrap our food. Someone, usually Alex, fills everyone's cups with a round of unbranded soda regardless of what people paid for—it's hard when some can't afford to pay for drinks, but it's harder when some drink and others don't.

Eating lunch imparts order and direction to the working day, a revelation celebrated with a dedicated swish of wrappers and the occasional grunt accompanying a *kebapčinja's* (ground meat stick) fall to the floor. Those who eat soup break their bread with self-deprecating gravity, while those who ordered cheap cold cuts dip into the sour cream. Soon the meal is done: we look at each other, relieved. Sometimes there is homemade wine or rakija from last year, although many have already bought grapes for this season. It is easier to talk after a glass, and the conversation pivots to politics, sports, or the old days. Sometimes Igor, an older man who used to be a professional waiter, tells of his time in Tito's guard. Regardless, Matei always has the last word. First, he shares sporting bets results, then he calls our names to collect the money we owe him for the meal, with a special eye for Igor, who can't write and read properly. Often, Dino lies on the bench, pretending with admirable determination to rest or sleep. Sometimes he is so determined that he snores—only to wake up abruptly as the final political argument descends into thunderous laughter.

After the dense sociality of lunch, walking out of the nurturing space of the "office" and stepping up into granite halls feels alienating. Empty, white apartments seem to reject workers' presence—they can neither afford them nor complete them. Sometimes, in partly furnished rooms, strange imaginary dialogues ensue. That afternoon, Folco and Dino could not understand why the owners decided to build a closet over the doorbell. Pondering the situation, Folco sits on a chair and looks around. "No sense in having the table here," he says. "Well," answers his partner Dino, "it depends on where the TV is—see, if you put it there"—he moves to where the TV should be—"then . . . No, you can't really see it. So stupid." They wander around and touch everything in that apartment that they could never afford. "Sit," Folco tells me. "It does not matter what we do. It is useless now."

I sit, wondering how much human energy, time, and life has been infused into those empty apartments. Unlike customers who see these spaces as empty, workers know their history and can recognize signs of their own presence—marks that will need to be erased in order for the apartment to begin its destined life. And yet, in these suspended moments, sitting on plastic-wrapped chairs, Dino and Folco cannot stop wondering—what if they were owners rather than workers? They embrace the stillness of the moment to tinker with this image of themselves and ponder alternate existences rooted in something more than empty time and plastic containers. Dino seems to enjoy it so much that he loses all interest in work. Folco eventually turns back to the floorboards and speaks out loud some new lath measurements. Dino insists: "No." He throws a piece of lath on the floor, now shouting, "NOOO!" Folco stands up and grabs him by the ear, beginning a mock fight. "Come on, don't be stupid, it is late. Where were we? 176, 170. Come on now." Dino laughs and turns on the saw. Back to "real" time.

Like Dino, other workers enjoyed manipulating their time, weaving imaginary futures into their working routines or holding on to the present with an additional joke or an extra cigarette. Deprived of the possibility of identifying with their work, their capacity to slow their productivity and dictate their own tempo became an expression of their own agency—a space for claiming meaning for themselves. Stretching time and deviating from the "normal" flow of work meant embracing the uncertain temporality created by the discrepancies between construction and financial times. The deep care given to their ceremonial meals and their constant attempts to sit on "clean" plastic surfaces are a testament to their attempts to impose a new temporal horizon by directing the flow of time toward new social goals or by letting their dreams, fears, and presence fill the emptiness of the space around them—a literal reversal of the "crisis of presence" engendered by financial uncertainty.[21]

Weaving Time, Weaving Relations

Temporal strategies that expanded, contracted, or redirected the flow of events did not mediate only the relationships between workers, their surroundings, and their future selves. Weaving time was also utilized in more interactive settings such as conversations. When buyers or subcontractors arrived angry and threatened to sue the company, workers tried to defuse the emergency by manipulating the timing that regulated their interactions. Paradoxically, changing the tempo of their chats and connecting future hopes and past experiences resulted in an acceptance of uncertainty, in which buyers, workers, and subcontractors shared a mutual horizon of possibility.

Both Toni and I were still shaking. When we first saw the middle-aged woman enter the site, we assumed she was one of the many buyers concerned about their apartment. But when we realized that there was no hesitancy in her step as she marched into Toni's elevated office, we felt queasy. She was an inspector sent by Stopanska Banka to verify the conditions on the work site and confirm that the work was proceeding according to plan. Based on her report, the bank would approve or deny the release of the last tier of the credit that Construx relied upon to continue its activities. Given its recent troubles, Construx could not afford to be behind schedule and miss this much-needed injection of cash. But they *were* behind, and when the inspector called her boss to confirm that everything was fine, it seemed that Toni had performed a miracle.

The building had neither electricity nor running water, partially owing to Construx's own delay but mostly as a consequence of the uncertainty that hovered over how and where the infrastructure would be dug, and by whom. The paperwork and plans that described where the existing systems were located had been lost in the 1990s. While Construx and other investors in that area had paid the infrastructural tax[22] and used a plan approved by the municipality, the mapped designs did not match what was found on the ground. In the following weeks, the municipality's engineers and planners would ask us what they were supposed to build. To everyone's dismay, they had no idea how to connect Construx's building to the existing street network or even where the infrastructure should be located. When they ultimately found some sort of solution, the pipeline they built was placed at the wrong level. Buildings on the south side of the street were unable to connect their canalization because their pipes were too low, while buildings on the north site had pipes built too high. Now Toni, the Pool's site manager, was forced to come up with a solution.

With all the financial constraints that Construx was experiencing, acceptable solutions were hard to find. I would often see Toni sitting at his desk, slowly smoking a cigarette with a blank stare. Suddenly, he would discuss an idea or a joke—as if those words would dispel the numbing atmosphere of nothingness that had crept into the room. For those buyers who had already sold their former homes and had nowhere else to go, Toni had cobbled together makeshift electric and water arrangements—a quite literal temporal bubble which allowed some "lucky" (or desperate) buyers to find themselves in furnished living rooms while everywhere else the building lagged behind schedule. It was one of these time-warped apartments, which resounded with chatter and the aroma of homemade dishes, that Toni and I visited with the inspector—knowing full well that if she poked her head into any of the adjacent units, it was "game over."

> Inspector (I): So what about the lights?
> Toni (site director) (T): As you saw, there's electricity in the apartments.
> I: But there was no electricity in the hall—are there lights in the hall?
> T: I don't know, maybe something happened to the fuse.
> I: What about in the other halls? If I go, will I find electricity there? Let me go to the next door and see [*starting to move*].
> T: I don't know, I don't know much about the electricity, but there might be no light.

I: So there's no electricity in the halls or apartments, right? You didn't *provide* electricity there?

T: We didn't *provide* electricity there.

I: But there is electricity in the apartments that are inhabited.

T: That's right, we only provided electricity to the apartments that are inhabited.

I: So, how many are those?

T: I don't know.

I: Just give me a number so I can tell them . . . some [*nekolku*]?

T: Some.

I: Ok, so then let me go now . . . Oh, give me your number.

T: Here it is . . .

I: Not you, him [*pointing at the anthropologist*].

Fabio (F): Oh, ok, so it is . . .

I: So ok, so if I contact you then . . . you're together, right?

T: Yes, he's my right-hand man. I don't want him to leave Macedonia, I'll never let him leave!

As the inspector left, we paused for a second, sweating in some sort of ecstatic trance. Suddenly, Toni turned to me and crossed himself, his eyes to the ceiling. "I lie, how much I lie . . . let me cross myself again. Oh my God, I can't lie, I don't know how to lie . . . and you helped me! Just so you know, you helped me a lot, talking about Italy—how she could contact you to help her niece who's studying there. . . . I was thinking, okay, let them talk about Italy!"

Toni structured the entire conversation as a desperate attempt to stretch, shorten, and connect the temporality of the exchange to turn the interaction away from the empty apartments and toward a mutually beneficial future. For Toni, this meant weaving three temporal dimensions at once. First, he manipulated the tempo of the dialogue. This included changing topics, conjuring personal and intimate temporalities, and shortening or lengthening the time that the inspector had to request more information. Second, he isolated or connected past and present, rediscovering promises long forgotten or instead confining them to the remote time of history while evoking a future full of possibilities. Third, he produced a shared space of uncertainty, which both he and the inspector could uncomfortably inhabit in the realization that its undisclosed potential was better than its (potentially?) catastrophic reality.

In the first instance, Toni wove the tempo of the conversation to prevent the inspector from wandering into other rooms, dark and waterless. He used his powerful laughter as a way to interrupt the professional examination of the building and jumped on any reference to personal topics that could lighten our exchanges and shorten the inspector's window of opportunity to ask questions. As soon as he learned that she had a niece studying in Milan, he introduced me into the conversation, asking me questions to showcase my usefulness as an Italian academic.

Then he tried to co-opt the inspector's own language and reservations to make her complicit in the exchange. With a calculated reluctance, Toni admitted that "they did not *provide* electricity" to the halls, a partial admission of negligence that appeased the inspector's curiosity while preventing her from discovering that they *had* no electricity at all. The end of the conversation is indicative of woven time's results in Macedonia: both parties settled on an (un)comfortable middle ground of uncertainty. Not all the apartments have light. But *some* do. The reasons are unclear and they'll both leave it at that.

On the way out, Toni eavesdropped on the inspector's phone call in which she mentioned a restaurant she planned to go to for dinner. As soon as she finished, he praised the establishment: "Oh, that one? It is a great place to eat frogs' legs. You should go there right away—you know, you can't waste any more time here, frogs' legs can't wait." Conjuring the intimate and personal temporality of a relaxed family dinner with an admiring and almost jealous voice, Toni wove the inspector's future into our present and gave her a good reason to leave the site without additional inquiries.

Toni's skillful intertwining of multiple temporal directions was the most seamless of many instances where workers or managers who were asked to deal with precarious working relationships fell back on uncertainty as a rhetorical process of coproduction. Subcontractors waited for hours in front of the Construx director's door without being told if the director was going to receive them or even if he was actually there. When they met, the director offered vague answers to their pleas for payment. Buyers, uncertain about the status of their apartments, presented themselves at the construction site with Turkish delight (*lokum*), coffee, and sodas. Toni joked and talked about the old days and the weather, about anything except for what they wanted to know.

I was surprised to learn that, in most cases, strategies that postponed confrontations or professed ignorance were effective. Claiming not to know was concurrently unrealistic (in Toni's case, he *was* the construction site's director) but also morally acceptable. Reminiscent of earlier socialist times as well as postsocialist uncertainty, "I don't know" (*ne znam*) could be used as a last resort to demonstrate one's powerlessness within the company's hierarchy. It evoked a shared sense of nothingness that opened a window of empathy between the two parties built on practices rather than official policies (even though Construx's internal policy *was* to refer every question up the chain of command).[23]

But why would anyone accept uncertainty? If it was clear why Construx used uncertainty to keep its creditors at bay, why did creditors buy into it? Why would the inspector accept uncertain answers when her interests were certain? On her way out, she pressed questions that, without a doubt, she had had since the beginning. But she raised them only when it was too late to get complete answers. Toni mobilized uncertainty as a discursive trope again, claiming not to know enough about electricity. At that point, it became clear to me and Toni that the inspector had understood our ruse, but instead of pushing it further, she offered Toni a way out, as she did when suggesting that "some" of the apartments had lights. She preferred the (un)comfortable and uncertain middle ground in the form of an Italian contact for her niece to backing Toni against the proverbial wall. Weaving time bought Construx some breathing space while providing the inspector with some potential future benefits—a moment of mutual recognition that temporarily dispelled the sense of nothingness generated by financial troubles.

I witnessed many other construction managers trying their luck in similar fashion. They would stalk Construx's managers at the office or at their favorite restaurant and talk to them for hours. The conversations often developed as I expected. Construx's director led them round and round, while the inquirer seconded him until he or she found a way to present his or her requests. Yet these inquiries sometimes succeeded. I saw Mr. Construx pick up the phone to authorize payments for at least some of the sums requested. Weaving time together, interlocutors in Macedonia conducted elaborate negotiations in which both partners participated in the production of uncertainty, albeit with different agendas and interests. Construx's director gave in to some of these cunning rhetorical plays, evocations of a shared past or promises of future joint ventures. In the same way, the inspector accepted a vague answer, took my number, and set off to eat frogs' legs. Weaving time is "what you do," confirmed a director of another company. "You go there, pray, cry, and they might give you something."

I suspect that there was something else in the inspector's decision to accept uncertain answers. Perhaps the inspector recognized Toni's desperate attempt to weave time as a symptom of an increasingly oppressive political and economic conjuncture. Neither Toni nor the inspector was at ease with uncertain terrain; yet they recognized their common interest and vulnerability in *weaving time*—a transformative and generative space that, perhaps, allowed common citizens to navigate the increasingly exploitative and unequal landscape of financial obligations promoted by Gruevski's regime if they cut each other some slack.

The Unexpected Consequences of Weaving Time

Holding on to moments, taking extensive breaks, and manipulating the tempo of conversations constituted attempts to weave uncertainty within relationships and provide existential repair through new spaces of potential empathy. Despite their best intentions, however, weaving time failed to alter workers' structural dependencies, their company's obligations, or the feeling of decay that accompanied their empty working days. In fact, weaving time even posed new moral challenges.

Take Toni, for instance. A sixty-four-year-old engineer, one of eight children of an Orthodox priest, Tony struggled to justify his own behavior with buyers, subcontractors, and even the inspector. He placed a high value on work, and he genuinely enjoyed discussing the technical difficulties he had faced in the course of his long career. The way he saw it, what he did at Construx differed greatly from the fixes he had deployed to solve urgent problems in socialist construction companies. Alternative solutions under socialism aimed at making a progressive system work. In present-day Macedonia, his fixes replicated a landscape of exploitation to which there was no solution. More important, solving an immediate problem did not reconcile the imperatives of financial profit with that of work. Today's gimmicks cheated buyers or workers—lies, as he called them after the inspector left. And he did not like lying.

Other workers faced similar issues. Makeshift rituals of sociality, from sequencing meals to imagining ownership of empty apartments, went only so far in imposing a temporary structure of meaning on their everyday activities. When their tools broke and they had to fix them yet again or when they begged to know more about the company's predicament and were told to shut up and work, their faces darkened with a brewing sense of humiliation. Instead of centering them within a larger social world, the financialized workplace shattered their illusions and revealed their own superfluousness.

Being trapped by economic forces they could not control is how financial-ization, under Gruevski, impacted the lives of construction workers. These feelings reflected structural changes brought about by the regime. Lack of po-litical connections translated into financial hardship, which forced companies such as Construx to prioritize financial considerations over productive ones. As their working days became more erratic and meaningless, workers faced very hard choices regarding their future. Unable to change their predicament or to make truly informed future decisions, they were left with clever solu-tions, rhetorical sleights of hand, and other temporary arrangements—that is, uncertainty as a space of action.

Paradoxically, these arrangements resulted in an increase in uncertainty. To counter the sense of nothingness that was fostered by macroeconomic re-structuring and illiquidity, workers utilized temporal tactics reminiscent of socialist and postsocialist times[24] that aimed at domesticating uncertainty. They took breaks, professed ignorance, worked two jobs, and adapted to ex-tended work time when needed—expressing a level of agency and meaning in a temporally schizophrenic landscape.

It was not always clear how two interlocutors evaluated their attempts to produce and domesticate uncertainty. Trapped between the negative conno-tation of opportunism and the positive one of getting the job done, weaving time generated a suspicious space of potential collaboration whereby individ-uals could manipulate empathy. Rather than falling prey to the vagaries of fi-nancial markets or other impediments to action,[25] Macedonian workers tried to infuse uncertainty with existential and relational dimensions and turn it into a new temporal dimension—a woven time that gave meaning to work both inside and outside of Gruevski's regime through acts of improvisation.[26]

From the perspective of woven time, uncertainty was not the opposite of action. It did not negate the past or make the future impossible. Rather, un-certainty was produced by an intersubjective act of connecting past and pres-ent and prefiguring action in new forms that defied the expectations of lin-ear progress, a phenomenon observed in other societies plagued by financial crises.[27] When workers wove their time on the construction site where I con-ducted research, they often crafted holes in it—carefully including ambiguity in their time continuum. Uncertainty provided room to maneuver and to re-claim their value as persons and agents, a value they had lost in Macedonia's increasingly rigid and hierarchical political-economic scenario.

Uncertainty and woven time were effective in creating temporary spaces

of empathy that acted as existential defenses against the increasing useless-
ness of work under authoritarian financialization. Yet they failed in a material
sense to help individuals or their companies regain a healthier position in the
financialization process. Financial obligations stipulate a very clear schedule
of repayment, and while uncertainty might postpone the inspector's negative
report or a worker's demand, it did not lead to substantial debt restructuring.
Toni was successful in deploying uncertainty on this occasion, but financial
constraints were not amenable to being undone by means of uncertainty; in
the long run, Construx was obliged to increase the amount of resources designated for paying back financial obligations.

Deprived of more and more liquidity, workers continued to experience uncertainty in the absence of its potentiality. While weaving time created spaces
of action and meaning, the even slower rhythm of work did not help Construx's overall situation. Uncertainty began to look more and more like precariousness, a labor relation of intense economic deprivation that oppressed
workers well beyond the potential opportunity it presented. Failing to change
their condition over time, weaving time came to embody yet another existential failure, proof that workers were doomed, inherently flawed, and unable to
resolve their issues without the help of an external force.[28] That external force,
all-powerful and encompassing, was the VMRO–DPMNE.

Providing an appearance of existential meaning and control, weaving time directed one's activity toward unproductive actions that exhausted
people's energies in attempts to postpone catastrophe rather than prevent it.
When the temporary space of empathy dissolved, workers found themselves
increasingly drowning in the nothingness of the construction site—ready to
do anything to change and closer to the ideology of the VMRO–DPMNE regime, which had made opportunism and lack of productivity the hallmark of
its administration. Instead of directing workers to seek radical change, weaving time "worked both ways . . . as a strategy for social betterment [and] as [a]
process of co-optation for maintaining power."[29] The more workers relied on
weaving time, the harder they found it to think of their suspended temporality as a space for solidarity or alliances.[30] Instead of opening spaces for questioning their condition, the illusory nature of weaving time pushed workers to
embrace Gruevski's authoritarian ideology. After all, was there much difference between submitting to a regime and drowning in nothingness?

5 Speculative Masculinity

PERHAPS IT WAS THE DUST. Perhaps it was the endless repetition of meaningless gestures. Perhaps it was a nostalgic pull of their youth, when life was hard but endowed with a sense of social progress. The more workers felt they were losing control over their working days, the more they daydreamed—imagining a glass of rakija in their hands while sitting on the porch on one of Skopje's famously warm evenings. These imaginary escapades offered a sense of fulfillment and *ubavina* (literally, "beauty") that seemed to put workers back in the center of a social world—*their* social world—inhabited by male friends and comrades. *Ubavina* was embodied in a symphony of roaring, baritone laughs—a sense of untamed presence—accompanied by the aromas of freshly cooked food and the tinkling of (empty) bottles being tidied in the background by their industrious wives.

That male-centric world and its convivial plenitude felt miles away on the night I visited Krste in his new role as Construx's night watchman. It was not a hard job, he contended. Yes, he had to stay awake all night, but its odd timing allowed him to take on extra "private" contracts during the day. In his little makeshift cabin, the crackling sound of a discolored Turkish TV program kept him more or less awake. And when he did doze off, he told me, he could curl up on his uncomfortable plastic chair, which he had made less so with a small cushion and an old rug.

Krste really needed that private gig and the extra money it generated. He and his wife had been trying to conceive a child for years, and they wanted to talk to new doctors to understand why it was taking them so long. "The stress at work does not help," he admitted, lowering his voice and eyes, perhaps ashamed of his multiple failures—at generating work, value, and life. "Regarding the delay with the salary, all my colleagues do is talk. They don't do anything—no strike, no action, nothing. But if you disagree, you've seen them, they treat you like a dog." Flustered and frustrated, Krste's words echoed off the exposed bricks and bare steps that led to the building's upper floors. Slowly, we let them fade away in the dark night.

When Krste was chosen as the new night watchman of the Nest, most of his colleagues turned against him. Suddenly, the shared meals and social rituals that workers relied on to endow their uncertain lives with a sense of meaning were torn apart by barely concealed masculine frustration—a diffuse and disruptive hostility I had sensed before but never with such an intensity. As Construx's crisis deepened, however, workers' moments of friendliness became rarer and were increasingly interspersed with subterranean suspicions that fractured their longed-for male-centric plenitude into myriad covert confrontations.

This chapter reflects on the gender paradoxes that permeated Macedonia's workplaces as finance (and Gruevski's regime) expanded, focusing on the difficult choices that workers faced trying to be "men" in a hostile economic and political landscape. As financial considerations gained precedence over physically demanding tasks and manual labor, male construction workers found their masculinity eroded. In this illiquid climate, workers' expectations of benign patriarchy were challenged by female colleagues who appeared primed for prominent roles, by ethnic Albanians who had an ascendant economic trajectory, and by their very own directors. The cause of and solution to these anxieties, which workers interpreted as a societal push to transform them into queer subjects,[1] was the regime—whose ethnomasculine politics seemed an anchor for working-class men amid a chaotic landscape of existential and (failed) economic speculation.

Construx's case reflected an overall trend in contemporary economies in which the expansion of finance reconfigured not only work regimes but also gender ideologies.[2] Until the late 1960s, the gender hierarchies in both Western and socialist states were articulated on the Fordist model of large-scale, vertically integrated industries geared toward mass production.[3] While its actual characteristics and social relevance in society are debated,[4] it is widely accepted that, ideologically, Fordism "created a labour force that was highly segmented by gender,"[5] naturalizing the hegemonic position of men as breadwinners and obscuring the crucial contribution that female workers made to economic and social progress.[6] Fordist workplaces, in other words, reserved unionized and relatively stable jobs for men, while women found themselves relegated to lower-paid, unskilled positions or to the domestic economy.

This gendered hierarchy started to shift with the acceleration of technological innovation. Beginning in the early 1970s, manufacturers moved their factories to the periphery of the global world system and started automating the most mechanical parts of their production processes. Physically demanding jobs evaporated in large parts of North America and Europe, replaced by careers in the service sector or precision-oriented tasks, which, because of their grueling working conditions or more precarious nature, were generally offered to women.[7] The boardrooms of these "innovation"-driven sectors, however, remained dominated by male managers who were increasingly attracted by speculative rather than productive opportunities. Connected to lawmakers and corporations through personal ties and lending relationships, a growing class of male financiers with their aggressive, risk-taking ethos emerged as the hegemonic figures of the early twenty-first century—popularizing a new kind of gender ideology that affirmed finance as a new, partially disguised medium for masculine domination.

With its insistence on microcredit and a new array of products and careers directed precisely toward women, financialized capitalism seemed to promise new opportunities for gender equality through access to credit and entrepreneurship for the female workforce. Yet beneath its inclusive veneer, the empowerment provided by financialization was generally "configured so that it [did] not threaten men's position of authority."[8] In financialized economies, women appeared as subjects of financial exploitation[9] or as stewards of "caring" or "emotional" speculations[10] unable to significantly benefit from global speculative opportunities. This increased visibility of women, and the occasional success of some upper- or middle-class women or non-heterosexual males who, against all odds, had managed to attain prominent positions, generated widespread anxiety for those working-class heterosexual males marginalized by financial expansion. Unable to progress and yet embedded in ideologies of masculine hegemony,[11] many working-class men perceived financialization as a reversal of gender roles—a downfall in which they felt robbed of well-deserved privileges and forced to become passive, feminized, or queer subjects.[12]

This gendered resentment is often identified as one of the "cultural" factors that led a disgruntled working class to develop a visceral aversion toward

Figure 13. A worker, preoccupied, considers his future. Photo: Author

Western, urban elites and their financial and queer values.[13] Indeed, in dein-dustrializing Macedonia, the contradictions between the hegemonic expec-tations and dispossessed realities of male, blue-collar workers provided fer-tile ground for authoritarian politics. While internationally Gruevski painted his regime as meritocratic, pointing at high-profile female political figures or gender-sensitive legislation, his domestic policies were directly targeted at a revanchist male audience. Under the VMRO–DPMNE government, millions of euro were devoted to construction projects that glorified the masculine roots of Macedonia—populating the center of Skopje with dozens of statues of male heroes, warriors, and priests.

And yet it would be misguided to understand the regime's appeal among male Macedonian workers as a form of "cultural backlash" in which aggres-sive forms of financial masculinities translated into simple ethnic and gen-der boundaries. If anything, Gruevski's gender ideology did not reduce the contradictions of working-class men to simple epistemological dichotomies but amplified them. Instead of reconstructing a simpler social world, cen-tered on workers, Gruevski imposed a model of patriarchal domination that most workers could not embrace *because* of the regime's financial schemes. Without pay or jobs—in a context where female colleagues had been forced to stop curating workers' relationships—male construction workers found their manhood eroded, transformed into an empty signifier, which they tried to fill by speculating not about future gain but about who was to blame for their failure.[14] In this increasingly tense landscape, manhood began to generate rather than solve paradoxes—a schizophrenic relational space that, instead of enabling men to engage in counter-hegemonic solidarities,[15] allowed the regime to live off the social contradictions it had helped create.

More Equal Than Others? Manhood During and After Socialism

In a major speech delivered on January 31, 2015, Prime Minister Nikola Gruevski publicly denounced Zoran Zaev, the leader of the main opposition party, as a traitor. According to Gruevski, Zaev had conspired with foreign intelligence agencies to obtain or forge recordings of phone conversations that damaged government officials. Gruevski painted Zaev as an immoral coward who had resorted to blackmail when he realized he could not beat Gruevski in the open terrain of political elections. The VMRO government would never stoop to such plots, concluded Gruevski: "Because we are Macedonians, not little Macedonians" [nie sme Makedonci, ne Makedoncinja].

Gruevski's insistence on his true Macedonian spirit reflected the fragile geopolitical history of the country and its multicultural character—a circumstance of great anxiety for Macedonians forced every day to confront the arbitrariness of their own national belonging. In 2006, the VMRO came to power pledging to restore dignity to Macedonia and its people against the claim of any neighboring country.[16] With his urban renewal projects, Gruevski renewed political tensions with Greece and provided a clear, visual narrative of who the "real" Macedonians were. Like Alexander the Great, Macedonians were masculine, aggressive warriors who fought their enemies and protected their defenseless motherland—represented by a few statues of female characters, mostly in nurturing poses.

This is the image that Gruevski evoked in his televised speech. In the VMRO–DPMNE camp stood the true Macedonian patriots, ready to fall into rank side by side with their leader and fight the nation's enemies. Zaev, on the contrary, was a "little" Macedonian, an emasculated subject who secretly plotted to subvert the political order chosen by the people—with the help of foreign powers. A little scoundrel like Zaev, in short, was not a Macedonian, and by extension not a man at all—a fact that VMRO members and sympathizers ascribed to his socialist roots, as if being a leftist necessarily meant disavowing one's masculinity.

Indeed, critiques that questioned how masculinity was embodied by so-cialist subjects were hardly unheard of in Macedonia, even prior to the 1990s. In the SFRJ, intellectuals, and even their semisatirical representations such as those in the film series *Tesna Koža*, suggested that the bureaucratic praxis of Yugoslav socialism betrayed the goals of gender (and economic) equality, forcing certain men to assume feminine, dependent roles. At a deeper level, however, these analyses suggested that socialist discourses of gender equal-ity, often framed as issues of women's emancipation, implied a subordina-tion of women throughout society. In the more or less explicit critiques that were voiced during the 1968 protests, students and Yugoslav feminists argued that the country's patriarchal structure made it "ideologically impossible for women to achieve real equality."[17] Indeed, the responsibility for domestic life was left almost entirely to women, yet they were also encouraged to take part in the workforce, where they were hired in the lowest-paid professions (such as textile work).[18]

Despite these gendered hierarchies, socialist rhetoric and rights were not just a façade. Women had access to political and economic rights, including childcare and paid leave, that were comparable to if not more substantial than those available in the "first world."[19] If gendered hierarchies allowed men to maintain control over women's public life, this was often justified on the ba-sis of socialist equality and morality—supposedly a blank slate that welcomed all identities into a transformative process toward a new kind of (wo)man. In films, leaflets, parades, and even sporting events, Yugoslav propaganda cele-brated male and female athletes, both professional and amateur, whose bod-ies were considered not as sexual subjects but as mechanical harbingers of so-cialist progress.[20]

Not all men and women, however, were celebrated at the same level by the SFRJ. Socialist men and women attracted varying degrees of scrutiny and op-portunity based on their ethnic identification. Rural Muslim women, for in-stance, were particularly encouraged to take part in amateur sports because their double markers of "marginality" needed to be "integrated" into the Yu-goslav socialist project. Macedonian male workers, symbols of a contested but geopolitically important country, enjoyed instead a central position within the boundaries of a Pan-Slavic and socialist brotherhood.[21]

The treatment of citizens who expressed different gender and ethnic iden-tities reflected a crucial component of the SFRJ's governance. Even more ex-tensively than in other Eastern European countries,[22] the decentralized struc-ture of Yugoslav socialism affirmed (but also limited) identities that were

generally ethnic and gendered in nature. That continuous balancing act between socialist equality and ethnic and gender hierarchies was synthesized in
the slogan *Bratsvo i Jedinstvo* (brotherhood and unity)—a recognition of ethnic differences subsumed in unity.[23]

By proclaiming equality and unity, brotherhood, rather than sisterhood,
identified a hegemonic position and verified the predominance of (certain)
male ethnicities in the very fabric of collective progress. For those male,
Slavic, industrial workers, Yugoslav socialism was not only a space of privilege but also a space of altruism. Macedonian male workers could think of
themselves as abstract socialist subjects, united by brotherhood and unen-
cumbered by gendered or ethnic identities, while also maintaining a degree of
symbolic superiority over women and members of the other ethnic groups—
precisely because of their symbolic commitment to a system that, in part,
aimed at creating collective progress. The camaraderie they felt was symbolic
as well as practical; as many of Construx's older workers suggested, it encompassed both comrade Tito and their unskilled (male and Macedonian) colleagues. It was this feeling that was evoked again and again in those moments
of *ubavina*—a "just" and "progressive" order, where workers' sociality was being nurtured by a paternalistic state and the caring attention of their wives.

Postsocialist Challenges

The financial crisis of the 1980s in Yugoslavia brought to the surface older ethnic tensions, tearing apart the feeling of hegemonic harmony that had characterized the experience of male Yugoslav workers. Instead of abstract subjects who were custodians of the collective progress, male workers had to face
mass unemployment, sanctions, and ultimately, bloody wars. Unable to claim
their manhood through work and overwhelmed by ethnic conflicts, men
came to think of their masculinity in exclusionary ethnic terms. Understood
as their ability to protect or violate the feminine body of the nation against
ethnic others, the hegemonic masculinity of postsocialist Yugoslavia abandoned any pretense of social progress and relegated women to objects of sexual fantasies.[24]

That masculinity had become increasingly intertwined with ethnic concerns was clear also in Macedonia, a country that had avoided the worst of
the Balkan conflicts. The chaotic economic context of the 1990s allowed marginalized subjects such as Albanian men to leverage earlier survival strategies
such as their vast international network of émigré relatives to gain political

and economic power. The result was that, while most Macedonian males were experiencing acute bouts of illiquidity and severe unemployment, foreign remittances allowed Albanian men to increase their level of consumption, start their own companies, and become investors beyond the ethnic niche—a relative economic mobility that made Macedonian men look and feel like "little Macedonians."[25]

"You know, I feel sorry for Macedonian men," Gani told me in 2014 while driving to Skopje from western Macedonia. An Albanian businessman, Gani had worked abroad for twenty years, starting as a dishwasher and ultimately buying a property in the early 2000s. Forced to return to the Macedonian Albanian community by the crash of the European real estate market, he felt that business opportunities were blooming all around him.

> Here, people have money. See that guy? He has 10,000 euro in his pockets right now. If I need cash, I just need to ask. It is not always legal money, but we will put it down for each other if there is a good idea. Thirty years ago, we were poor, we had no running water. Now we can build a new future.

After several years of dealing with foreign companies that produced construction materials, Gani had decided to produce his own products in Macedonia with an initial lump sum investment that was significantly larger than most Macedonian businessmen I knew could hope to gather over several years. He could not understand why Macedonian men were so angry with their Albanian counterparts. Successful Albanian entrepreneurs such as himself cared more about money than nationality—sure, he admitted, they did not always operate by the book, but neither did their Macedonian partners. What was the point of hating them?

After that question, he paused for a second, watching the road in silence. "Imagine that their girls, you know, twenty, twenty-one years old, they go with me, a fifty-year-old Albanian, just for 2,000 MKD (35 euro). I can basically fuck any young Macedonian girl, if I want to." I must have displayed a shocked or skeptical face because Gani pulled out a phone, connected it to the car speakers, and flipped through his contacts. Soon, a Macedonian female voice answered. Gesturing at me to be quiet, Gani excused himself for not having called her recently but promised that they would meet over the weekend. Then he said, "But you have to tell me that you like me more than all of the others." After the woman answered that she did, Gani sighed, said goodbye, and turned to me, with a distinctly sad expression.

They would come with me for anything, I only have to give them some money—so they can eat, so to speak. And it is a shame. It is really sad that such young girls do this, and there are many of them. Now look at the irony: they despise me, as an Albanian, but I fuck their girls.

The scenario in which regular, young Macedonian women had sex with older Albanian men for small gifts corresponded to some of the worst nightmares for Macedonian workers. As the economic chaos of the 1990s undermined their ability to affirm their manhood in public, male workers had turned to the more intimate space of kinship to regain existential mileage—not as workers but as comrades and patriarchs. Darko, for instance, recalled the informal working conditions of the early transition as bonding experiments when his connections with colleagues, neighbors, and managers allowed him to survive the country's economic devastation. Through fictive, quasi-kin relationships, he managed to get odd jobs as a subcontractor, first in Macedonia and then in Russia and Ukraine, where his masculinity was validated in many sexual encounters with impoverished local women.

Once home, Darko and others lost much of their economic and social charm. In Construx, they found an ethnically homogeneous space that they were able to control thanks to the comradely connections they forged abroad. To expand these spaces of uncontested manhood, construction workers heightened their symbolic control over the relational lives of their wives and daughters—a form of retraditionalized manhood that relied on monopolizing women's emotional and/or sexual attentions to prevent challenges posed by interethnic intimacies.[26] And yet, as Gani's story demonstrates, without status and money, that patriarchal dream proved impossible. Without that illusion of control over their kinship networks, Macedonian men felt increasingly emasculated, forced to face their own frailty.

Managing Masculinities in the Workplace

In practice, the postsocialist reemergence of patriarchal masculinity depended on women's unrecognized labor. To ensure that construction sites or the intimate spaces of the household constituted uncontested spaces of male authority, wives, coworkers, and even daughters added a "third shift of governance work to their usual double shift of professional and domestic labour."[27] At the Nest, Construx's newest and most difficult site, managing workers' masculinity fell to Natalia, the site manager, who had a long history of helping workers navigate their conflicted patriarchal aspirations. And yet, in a climate of illiquidity Natalia found it increasingly hard to reconcile workers' conflicts without infringing upon the company's hierarchy and jeopardizing her own financial stability.

A woman in her mid-fifties, Natalia had over thirty years of experience directing sites. Workers used to call her "auntie," teasing her for her tendency to speak quickly in a single breath. And yet, she was highly respected and listened to carefully, even when what she had to say caused significant disagreement. Unlike male managers, Natalia did not avoid conflict. When problems arose, she called workers into her office one by one and addressed their issues directly. "I try to help them," Natalia told me after one of these events.

> Some of them are hotheads, and you need to take them apart little by little. And once they leave the office, they don't even know their names! But they know I mean well! If they need an extra job, and somebody from the neighborhood comes and sees me about a problem, I hook them up. What can I do? They are *my* workers!

A strong woman who singlehandedly saved her household from bankruptcy after her husband lost his job, Natalia saw her management style as that of a postsocialist mother. When "*her* workers" needed help, she came to the rescue—not by indulging their performances but by finding ways to confront them that leveraged and reinforced their sense of (male) responsibility. Thanks to Natalia's often invisible labor, workers remained focused and disciplined, while her negotiating skills ensured that some materials trickled in so that workers could still maintain a semblance of dignity—an unending task of foreseeing, recombining, and strategizing about workers and buildings that often gave her headaches but that she thought of as her inescapable burden.

> As a woman on the construction site, you are disadvantaged. You need to know twice as much as a man knows in order to be taken seriously. And it is a constant fight! Oh, oh—you can't imagine the labor [*maka*] that it entails. My brain has to go twice as fast, and I need to be one step ahead of them. I need to know beforehand what they will think once I give them directions! Over the years, I have learned how to do it and how to play the game. You know, construction workers play games all the time. Did you notice? With you too! They test you all the time—but I have learned how to play their games, and now I can turn them around on their heads if I want to.

It was true. The workplace was a constant tease where one's masculinity was often called into question based on imaginary metrics. "Hey Fabio," the *Kapetan* (foreman) once asked me while we were all sitting idly after (or before) a break. "So, do you like sex with men? You know, *gnaca gnaca gnaca*" (hitting one hand closed as a fist with the palm of the other open hand, as to signify anal intercourse). Suddenly, all the workers turned to me with slight smiles on their faces. Embarrassed, I laughed. "I don't know. I've never tried! If you want, we can go and find out together. Shall we?" There was a second of suspense while ten pairs of eyes swung back to the Kapetan's surprised face, and I wondered if my spicy rebuttal was, in fact, too direct. Then everyone laughed. Amused, the Kapetan patted me on the shoulder and shook my hand approvingly. "You know I am joking, right?" Others echoed the sentiment: "We're only joking."

Sometimes salacious, these jokes were the markers of workers' social intimacy, a space reserved for those willing to respect workers' aspiration for (male-centric) equality. Western anthropologists, local workers, temporary subcontractors, passing buyers, even Natalia, the site supervisor—everyone who spent enough time in the workplace was tested in the same way: "They always try to get me drunk. They pass me rakija and watch to see if I drink," Natalia told me. "So, I drink. A little sip. But then they pass it to me again—and then I do not drink. I fake it." The ruse, Natalia admitted, did not fool workers, but that was not the point. The point was recognizing their performances of masculinity and letting them have symbolic wins that quietly reinforced the gendered hegemony of the workplace—allowing workers to feel like true men while simultaneously avoiding the trouble they got into by drinking too much unsupervised.

Natalia was convinced that the main reason workers respected her (and, to her surprise, me) was that she had taken on the burdensome and silent task of managing their masculinity—embodying perfectly the retraditionalized gendered roles of the postsocialist workplace. That relationship, however, limited Natalia's ability to express herself on the construction site. As an auntie, Natalia had to curb her femininity and reserve it for private occasions.

When I was younger, I wanted to dress nicely. I wanted to look gorgeous. But I was on construction sites every day! How can you dress pretty here? It is not just because of the dirt, although of course you do not want to ruin your dresses like that. You cannot wear a skirt around here. You see them? How can I be respected with a skirt? Or with a sleeveless blouse? You know what they would say or think? I can't do that—and over time I lost the habit of dressing up. Now I only dress up at weddings.

In her youth, Natalia sometimes came to work with heels and went straight from the construction sites to cafés, where she was often the only woman. During my research, she wore a long gray apron and woolen sweatshirts that her husband had been paid with and that they had not been able to resell to others. Instead of affirming herself as a middle-class professional as she did during her youth, Natalia hid her body—a mixture of calculation and resignation that removed any symbol of untamed independence from the workplace. Her old sweatshirt camouflaged Natalia's alterity from the workplace, allowing *her* workers to imagine the site as an oasis of manhood—where she figured not as a professional manager, nor as an object of male conquest but as their unswerving, nurturing guardian.[28]

Sorosoides, Women, and Other Gay Things

In the mid-2000s, women's rights organizations, supported by international funds including USAID and UNWOMEN, pressured the Macedonian government to take action against gender gaps in Macedonian society. Happy to project itself as a neoliberal champion of meritocracy, the VMRO–DPMNE passed antidiscrimination laws and set forth national strategies that included gender-sensitive measures.[29] This led to a surge of women in politics. Between 1990 and 2006, the number of women elected to Parliament increased from less than 8 percent to over 34 percent in 2014, with some rising to prominent positions in the inner circle of Gruevski's regime.[30] Slowly, more and more women appeared in management roles in private companies—an increased visibility that made women's contribution to public life more evident and, paradoxically, threatening.[31]

These affirmative steps, too small to be significant, nonetheless provided ammunition for the VMRO–DPMNE regime's ideology. In speeches that targeted dispossessed working-class males, the VMRO–DPMNE magnified women's gains as a "wave of emancipation coming from Western countries"— a dangerous attack against Macedonia's customs and families.[32] In Gruevski's 2015 speech, the clash assumed civilizational proportions—an epic struggle between the traditional gender values of "real" Macedonians and the queer, feminine influence of "little Macedonians" and their foreign allies.

The VMRO–DPMNE's gendered paranoia blamed the experience of dispossessed male workers especially on international actors, paradigmatically summarized in the defamatory campaign against George Soros, a Hungarian-American Jewish financier known for his global speculation and philanthropic work—ironically criticized by both left and right for funding "open" market societies and democratic participation. In the regime's propaganda, Soros and "*Sorosoid(es)*" (literally, followers of Soros) became derogatory terms used to describe the dispossession felt by male workers—a way of blaming Macedonian workers' worsening economic and social conditions on a lingering queering of society. As a label for anyone who criticized the government, the term *Sorosoid* leveraged the gendered anxiety of male workers to suppress voices of dissent as threats to the Macedonian nation[33] and its patriarchal order.

On construction sites, fears about queer and feminine influences resonated among blue-collar workers, fueled by experiences of economic marginalization. As the company became increasingly entangled in financial debt, blue-collar workers found it harder and harder to find meaning within their pointless workdays or to justify their labor to managers or even to their families. Paid with continuing delay, workers felt they were drowning in an existential black hole where they failed as breadwinners, husbands, and fathers—losing their reputation daily while the company seemed to shift its interests toward urbanism or architectural design divisions, sectors where most of the employees were women.

It was understandable that Construx workers felt this economic shift as a crisis of masculinity. While construction sites stood still, the offices of Construx's designers were bustling with activity, accompanied by the rhythmic drumming of hurried heels and female voices. In these locales in the center of Skopje, most new deals were inked, additional capital was raised, and new calls for projects were announced. There, Construx's female sales managers convinced young couples or pensioners to invest their hard-earned savings or to wait a few more months before suing the company for their postponements—a massive amount of emotional and relational labor that administrative, legal, and financial assistants provided to the management to keep the company afloat in spite of the bad decisions of its male directors.

Construx's blue-collar workers resented being left out of the action. But they were especially troubled by how the breakdown of the company's male hierarchy destabilized the construction site's position in the imagined masculine order of the construction world. If the company was going under, they reasoned, it was the director's patriarchal responsibility to let them know, man to men, as had happened many times before in their postsocialist adventures.

Since the beginning of the delays in salaries, however, Construx's male directors were hiding—barricading themselves in their offices or hiding behind administrative excuses. In these circumstances, blue-collar workers lamented that even (female) cleaners and administrative assistants who worked at the company's offices knew more about the future than they did—a *pederski* (queer) approach in which financial debt seemed to have subverted the very gendered foundations of their company.

If workers ascribed the company's crisis to queer, feminine influence, Natalia and Veronika, Construx's office manager, offered a different explanation. Indeed, the two women remarked that Construx's administrative and managerial roles were occupied by more women than in the past. But that was not why the company had broken its promise of male reciprocity. Women such as Natalia and Veronika were heavily invested in nurturing workers' manhood and largely subscribed to workers' postsocialist vision of construction as a male-dominated space—so much so that they both had often shielded male workers from the chaotic challenges of economic disruption. So the problem was not that women had more power than in the past; it was that women in power were structurally prevented from helping workers. In Construx's financial predicament, Natalia and Veronika had found their decision-making power increasingly tied up by male managers—put in double binds, where caring for workers' manhood pitted them against the wishes of the directors and jeopardized their own financial future.

Since November 2013, Veronika's responsibilities had expanded. Answering phones, directing guests and clients, tending to Moustache's volatile whims, she was the first to arrive and the last to leave, forced to run between state agencies, clients, and suppliers with whom Moustache did not want to deal. Like most women in managerial positions, Veronika had access to crucial information about the company's financial standing, which, in the past, she would have slipped to workers—directly or by "facilitating" the director's communications. Yet in a climate of increasing illiquidity, her communications were being heavily scrutinized. Subjected to verbal abuse when something was going wrong and fearful for her job, Veronika refrained from supporting workers and had become the scapegoat for the male directors' own silence.

For women such as Veronika and Natalia, financialization meant having to reevaluate the postsocialist "cultural norms and negotiation of social obligations" that had identified them as stewards of the male-centric workplace.[34] Trapped in positions in which caring for their families meant limiting how they cared for workers, women such as Veronika and Natalia were often overwhelmed by guilt. Natalia could see *her* workers struggle, increasingly angry at each other, as their masculine world fell apart around them. And yet, if she told them what she knew or suspected, she could be fired—an outcome that she could not afford.

Like Natalia, most of the Construx female workforce had to take care of unemployed husbands or sick relatives. Unable to either quit or shape the company's policies, they felt a constant remorse for their silence—a silence that was imposed by their male directors precisely because of the women's growing importance for the company's finances. Sometimes they would come back from Moustache's office, where they had just discussed new plans to win external contracts that could provide a lifeline for the company's other investments, with red eyes and their makeup slightly smudged—marks of a handful of tears, of shame or anger, that had fought their way through their stoic smiles.

Speculating on Letters and "Little Men"

By December 2013, workers had started to become very anxious about the concrete possibility of economic, existential, and masculine collapse from continuing delays on the construction site. As the company's financial maneuvers failed to yield any results except more illiquidity, workers started to anxiously scrutinize the workplace and each other for signs—speculating on what could predict the impending crisis or who was to blame for the continuous decline.

"Fueled by a heightened state of anticipation,"[35] most of these speculations revolved around manhood as an existential space and language that allowed workers to express and negotiate their increasing precariousness. As their male-centric world fell apart around them, workers' banter and jokes turned into bitter exercises of masculine denigration. For a moment, calling into question another worker's manhood chased away their sense of existential nothingness—until it evaporated, feeding a desolate climate of suspicion and resentment. The more workers engaged in threatening and abusive exchanges, the more they were forced to spend time defusing and negotiating anger and resentment—an emotional labor that, without Natalia's active participation, consumed their energies and eroded the possibility of collective organization. As Krste put it, his male colleagues seemed to suffer from a schizophrenic condition in which their apparently idle stances hid brewing hostility that teetered on the brink of explosion through their own muted acts of compassion.

Take, for example, stories about sexual prowess. I witnessed countless moments in which male workers shared graphic details of their sexual lives to create horizontal bonds among themselves and seal their common belonging to the male-centric ecosystem of the construction site. By late 2013, however, this sedimented experience of masculinity was filled with suspicions. In the context of illiquidity and meaningless work, sexual anecdotes appeared to single out "lesser men." The result was indeed a schizophrenic atmosphere in which denigrating each other's masculinity was immediately followed by hurried attempts to defuse tensions and cap their mounting rage.

"Have you ever fucked a black woman?" asked Risto, an otherwise reserved worker, his expression somewhere between a smile and lust. Before any of those present could answer, he shrugged his shoulders ("Of course you haven't," he added) and went on to brag about his manly exploits.

> Back then during the transition, that was a good time. I was in Ukraine, working for a construction company there. You know, they were so poor and hungry, with literally nothing to eat. But the women—ufff, they were so beautiful! Slender, tall, blonde . . . and they would come with you just for a piece of bread! We used to go to a restaurant, throw the bouncer a few dollars, and close it up for the night. And then women would come, and we could choose whether to let them in or not.

As exaggerated as this account might have been, it prompted other workers to rant about their past sexual adventures with impoverished Ukrainian or Russian women, accompanying their stories with giggles and gestures toward Kutliac, a worker who had been very silent and seemed visibly uncomfortable. Maliciously, Risto taunted him until a flustered Kutliac felt compelled to assert his own male prowess.

> I too had a lot of women when I worked abroad. I was working for a very important construction company, Ilinden. Did you see the Olympic games? There, we worked in one of those cities. And back then I was responsible for feeding them all, you know, I was the cook there. But, oh man, we would have weekends free, we would sail in a boat across the Black Sea, and you can imagine the girls there! Oh! I fucked there as well!

"Yeah right, you did," commented other workers, not too impressed with Kutliac's story, moving on in scorn. Risto, however, was not done. A "gypsy" like Kutliac had no chance of sleeping with beautiful Russian women, he said in a mocking tone. Clearly distressed, Kutliac started mumbling—he was not a gypsy, what did they know, he was not a gypsy! "Don't believe them, Fabio," he finally managed to articulate amid a long litany of heavy breaths and indistinguishable slurs. Suddenly, workers around us dispersed, amused or worried. Darko, after exchanging reproaching glances with Risto, called Kutliac back to work with a dry and hurried gesture. Relieved as much as insulted, Kutliac continued to mumble as he disappeared into the comforting depth of the Nest's dusty underground, dragging his wounded manhood with him.

By 2014 insinuations of ethnic and gender impurity such as those addressed to Kutliac proliferated. Often these slurs targeted workers who stood out because of phenotypical or behavioral characteristics. Another common target was Gjorgj, the union representative, who also had a darker skin tone. Gjorgj had a technical degree, the same qualification that Natalia held, which helped him land private jobs; unlike other workers, he always had some spare cash. Both Kutliac and Gjorgj tried to downplay these slurs at first. But after several months of being taunted as gypsies who "liked to take it from behind," they were on the verge of exploding. Often only the intervention of a colleague, who jumped in with a joke, a pat on the shoulder, or fictive requests for help, helped them avoid physical altercations.

Arguably, defusing tension constituted a form of care through which workers helped one another avoid the escalation of conflicts. And yet, unlike the efforts of Natalia, this emotional labor did not restore the trust eroded by each insult. In an increasingly tense workplace, repairing relationships highlighted Kutliac's and Gjorgj's dependency on other workers' mediations—a strange form of care that neither erased individual blame nor left individual agency intact. And yet, other workers reasoned, what else could they do? If they were not ready to quit, there were few alternatives for avoiding open confrontations—even if these acts of care ended up undermining, rather than encouraging, collective solidarity.

Increasingly nasty challenges and poisonous forms of care made it harder for workers to build on their shared manhood to make collective decisions and support each other at critical moments. After a trip abroad, I had returned to the worksite on a cold day in January 2014, right after the Orthodox New Year, which, by chance, coincided with a meeting where workers planned to discuss their delayed payments and weigh their options. The atmosphere was not very positive. "How come you are back, and you have nothing for us?" Kapetan barked, with a tense voice. "You should offer a round [*treba da ne chastis*]!" Unprepared, I mumbled that I had no idea and did not know where to go. Several pairs of eyes looked around the room, silently wondering about the "coincidence." Why had I shown up, empty-handed, on *that* day? Was I informed by someone? Had Moustache sent me to spy? As the silence became more awkward, Dino, one of the least proactive workers, offered to come with me and supervise my purchase—a welcome end to increasingly tense speculations.

Laden with four liters of wine, sodas, snacks, and other sweets, we came back just as the Kapetan finished summarizing the company's recent troubles and their impact on workers' precarious lives. Then the union's representative, Gjorgj, took the floor, reading two letters he had written. The first letter officially convened the workers' assembly; the second was a statement, written in legal and union-standardized language, in which workers demanded to be officially informed of the status of the company's finances by the director and, in particular, why they were experiencing delays in payment.

Gjorgj had barely finished reading when an inarticulate hubbub rose from the audience. Darko jumped in: "This is too strong. We cannot make demands; it is *his* company. We cannot impose things!" Natalia, torn between her roles, made the same point: "Exactly, this is absurd. We need to ask him, but not in such a confrontational way!" The Kapetan agreed: "Yes, indeed, we need to beg him [*da go zamolime*] to tell us." Uneasy, Gjorgj looked around and, seeing that most of the workers agreed, walked out to smoke a cigarette. Eventually, Bojan sat down at the table, took the pencil, and said, "How about this. Respected Director, we depend on you." The sound of positive affirmations came from around the room, while workers, now comfortable with having toned their demands down to a language of benevolent patriarchal relations, offered alternative formulations. The atmosphere quickly became cordial and jovial, and workers unanimously (and chaotically) applauded the final text. "Respected Director, we depend on you. We all have families [*familiarni lugje*] and debts. We know that you are temporarily in crisis, but we beg you [*ve zamoluvame*] to tell us when you will pay us." As they slowly walked out, Darko told me: "You see? That is the problem with having a union in a private company. It simply does not work; the patron [*gazda*] is the one who decides, and we simply work for the money."

With the patriarchal spirit of the letter, Darko, Kapetan, and others tried to reconcile their conflicting experiences of what they felt was required from them within an increasingly oppressive political and economic landscape.

Despite their dwindling role, workers felt entitled to being recognized and acknowledged as the creators of the new Skopje—a role some suggested they needed to take back with highly masculine and aggressive stances. In practice, however, that was impossible. There was little that workers could do to take control over their lives—except challenge one another and then spend considerable labor containing their growing frustration.

In this chaotic landscape, Darko and Kapetan appealed to patriarchal solidarity, a form of masculinity that they had utilized in the 1990s to navigate difficult labor relations and forge the hierarchical dependencies that had brought them to Russia, Ukraine, and ultimately, Construx. Darko, Kapetan, and others reasoned that a surfeit of economic and social pressures prevented them from being "real" Macedonian males. Yet they could be men—vicariously, through the director. If workers were increasingly unable to come together on their own, the letter provided a glimmer of hope that Moustache would reinforce their common bonds of dependency. Through these bonds, workers might reinstate an aspect of their manhood—reconstituting a masculine bond through their shared dependence on his patriarchal authority.

This time, however, the plan backfired. Instead of reinforcing vertical and horizontal bonds, the letter revealed workers' vulnerability and disorganization—an open wound in their collective identity that could be exploited to discourage them further. In an exaggerated performance, Moustache called Gjorgj and pretended to be furious about their use of the word "crisis." How did they dare betray him and the company, spreading such vile accusations? Progressively losing sight of the purpose of his performance, an increasingly angry Moustache promised to fire Gjorgj if he did not reveal who wrote the letter. Under pressure and tired of being challenged and questioned, Gjorgj cracked. Natalia, Darko, and the Kapetan were promptly summoned for a meeting. "So Gjorgj, the coward, implicated me, and us, you see, even if we were the ones who tried to calm the waters," Natalia told me. "We went, and the Moustache started shouting, aggressively, before daring us to quit, right there and then, if we had no stomach for work."

The incident left workers even more confused and vulnerable. Whatever patriarchal reciprocity and interdependence they had hoped to reinstate through their letter had broken down in myriad humiliating challenges—confronting them with the unacceptable option of quitting. Back in the workplace, things were even worse. Instead of helping solidify a unique space of interdependent or horizontal manhood, months of increasingly nasty jokes had broken lines of communication and solidarity apart. Some workers, including Gjorgj, snitched on others, and Kapetan and Darko were determined to make them pay—as if that could eliminate the toxicity of their work environment. But was Gjorgj the only villain? Other workers began to doubt their leaders' intentions. After all, Kapetan and Darko had championed the letter—and they advised everyone to think individually, rather than collectively, about what to do next.

Suspicions and rumors spread like wildfire. Some suggested that Gjorgj had not only spied but also stolen money from their common union fund right before leaving to work abroad. Others argued that Darko and the Kapetan had intentionally given bad advice to push other workers out and increase their chances of being paid. Finally, everyone turned on Krste, the new night watchman, whose job was rumored to be a reward for having spied on them. Increasingly casting blame on or being suspicious of one another, workers independently dismantled the few spaces of collective action and solidarity that had begun to emerge. Krste suffered a nervous breakdown. A few others, including Gjorgj, left. Meanwhile, those who remained blamed each other for their failure to act together and advocate for change—a situation that, most workers agreed, left them very few opportunities to be "real" Macedonians.

Impossible Manhood and the Regime

For over a year, I took pictures of workers' lives on the construction site. In retrospect, these snapshots detail the daily changes in the tenor of workers' relationships in their attempt to deal with the challenging environment created by illiquidity. In the early phase of my research, their hardened, sometimes massive bodies met the camera in comradely hugs and playful postures—attempts to enchant an everyday working routine that they felt slipping out of their grasp (see Chapter 4). But as winter descended on Skopje, convivial moments became increasingly interspersed with resigned smiles and bitter reflections, with idle gazes that wandered around empty, bare rooms, meeting only the steam of their own breath.

By early 2014, delays in salaries and the lack of meaningful work had disrupted the idea that Construx's blue-collar workers were, in fact, contributing meaningfully to the company's activities. Unlike other postcrisis contexts such as in Egypt[36] or Ukraine,[37] where workers' inability to express their manhood had prompted them to participate in nationalist movements, Macedonian construction workers seemed stuck—unable or unwilling to contest their precarious economic conditions, especially if that involved anything more than appealing to their managers' benevolence. Such refusals to act collectively, however, were the result of deeply gendered conflicts—a chaotic reshuffling of gendered hegemony that workers tried (and failed) to inherit, inhabit, or improvise.

Since the collapse of socialism, Macedonian workplaces had seen a retraditionalization of gender roles, where men identified a "safe" space of masculinity in the household or the firm. Yet as financial opportunities turned into illiquidity, blue-collar workers found that forms of socialist or postsocialist homosociality were proving inadequate in addressing the declining importance of their work. While workers tried to appeal to their managers' patriarchal duty, which had helped them get lucrative jobs abroad in the 1990s, there was little the directors could do to return dignity to their roles. And yet, despite the failure of their masculine world, workers struggled to see themselves through the revanchist forms of manhood cultivated by the VMRO–DPMNE. While receptive to the regime's denunciation of queering forces, blue-collar workers could neither dismiss their previous socialities nor reconcile ethnomasculine manhood with their precarious conditions.

Stuck in uncharted and dysfunctional labor relations, workers grew frustrated as they experimented with multiple ineffectual modalities of manhood. Unable to embrace their male identity as an asset that propelled them into a future of wealth, prestige, or even normalcy, men's speculation turned inward to torturing ruminations and poisonous suspicions. Confusing, exhausting, sometimes even exhilarating, this form of speculative masculinity meant creating and defusing conflicts in a landscape where no one quite knew what being a man really meant, except that it implied an endless fracturing and mending of relationships—a much harder task than building or tearing apart brick walls.

Just like the forced-credit pyramid scheme described in Chapter 3, in which collaborative relationships of in-kind exchanges turned into forms of dispossession, workers' constant doubts about one another's masculinity transformed their spaces of solidarity into moments of social exclusion that undermined their own capacity to support each other and act collectively. Meanwhile, women and non-heterosexual males found themselves thrown off balance.[38] Often brought into the spotlight, women such as Natalia and Veronika were targeted as the causes of male workers' troubles—feminizing or queering the workplace, not because of what they could do but because of the caring acts they were forced to abandon. No longer stewards of male-centric workplaces but increasingly dependent on the director's whims, Natalia and Veronika now bore another burden in addition to their unrecognized domestic, workplace, and emotional labor: guilt.

As this speculative landscape corroded existing gendered paradigms and relationships, one social institution emerged as solid and invulnerable: the VMRO–DPMNE regime. Paradoxically, men who had been struggling to make ends meet because of the regime's economic and political hierarchies found themselves cherishing the idea of becoming its dependent. It was not that Construx's workers hoped to suddenly solve all their problems through the regime. Certainly, some imagined that they would be paid more regularly and would be spared (some of) their constant emotional turmoil if Construx joined Gruevski's political circle.

Most, however, knew that companies in Gruevski's circle were plagued by other forms of precarity—based on labor rather than on financial exploitation. When workers evoked Gruevski's regime, then, it was to avoid blaming each other or to excuse their own powerlessness. Pointing fingers at Gruevski as the ultimate guilty party in their own miserable circumstances, workers recast themselves as pawns in a pyramid of manhood and agency—one where Gruevski occupied the uncontested summit, an anchor of sorts that granted workers some respite from their already schizophrenic male sociality.

6 Finance and the Pirate State

GENTLE HILLS, covered by ripening grains and vineyards; stalls and stalls heaped with tomatoes, sold by the bagful; long lines of rakija glasses and juicy meats roasting on charcoal. These sensuous pleasures, offered within a splendid landscape that echoes with distant tales of Ottoman intrigue and heartfelt laughter, define the Republic of Macedonia as a remote but hedonistic land— free from the competitive anxieties of Wall Street hedge funds or the dramatic stories that permeate the credit associations of shantytowns often studied by anthropologists of finance. Beneath Macedonia's bucolic landscape, however, simmer deep tensions. Rooted in a long legacy of financial scarcity and debt, these economic contradictions came to a boiling point during the global financial crisis and became a crucial tool for Gruevski's authoritarian regime. Consider the following joke:

> There is a German, an Italian, and a Macedonian worker. The German tells the others that he gets 2,000 euro per month; 1000 he spends on rent and food, and 1000 he doesn't know what to do with. The Italian earns 1500 euro per month; 1000 he spends on rent and food, and he doesn't know where to spend the other 500. Then the Macedonian jumps in. "Hey, my friends. I earn 250 euro per month. Each month I spend 500 on bills and food, and the other 250, I don't know where they come from!"

Just like the workers in the joke, most of my interlocutors had a cynical attitude toward their financial troubles. Many claimed not to know how they scrambled enough money together to survive. Certainly, it was not through official employment. Their declared salaries were either too low or uncertain,

148

as companies seemed increasingly unable to pay each other and their employees. To cover their everyday expenses, many workers contracted debt, which they did not know when or if they would be able to repay—especially if they lacked some degree of patronage from the VMRO–DPMNE government. Their employers, however, were not all doing so poorly. After consolidating Skopje's urban mafia, a handful of oligarchs had been prospering—proof that workers' debts were part of a larger process of dispossession intrinsic to Nikola Gruevski's authoritarian rule.

Who these oligarchs were, where their money came from, and how they made it disappear were questions that lingered in the air—creating a whirlwind of suspicions that, for a decade, empowered the regime rather than its opposition. Few citizens believed that Skopje 2014, with its nationalist statues, neo-baroque façades, and usurped public parks, was in the public interest; even fewer believed the "coincidental" nature of accidents happening to opponents of the regime, whose buildings were sometimes blocked, shut down, or even destroyed by inspectors, or whose participation in protests was disrupted by mobs of "spontaneous" counterprotesters. Escalating a sense that the regime was involved in every domain of social life, these public stunts and the rumors that accompanied them undermined citizens' confidence that they could do anything to stop a government determined to literally bulldoze anyone who stood in its way.

Sustained by an "attempt to divine and manipulate the visible and the invisible"[1] political and financial workings of the regime, this climate of self-defeating speculation reached a paradoxical apex on April 27, 2017. On the night that a new SDSM government was to be installed, after two years of political crisis,[2] the VMRO–DPMNE let a mob of paid thugs and angry citizens storm the *Sobranje* (Assembly), Macedonia's legislative chamber. In dramatic videos, members of Parliament could be seen jumping from balconies, barricading themselves behind doors, or preparing to fight for their lives, while police officers stood idly by and refused to intervene. Outside the building, a surreal climate of fear and anticipation muffled the city's noises while incredulous citizens following the spotty coverage were inundated with rumors of an impending coup.

In the following months, I discussed the incident with several people who had been inside the Assembly. Some of them had hidden in dark hallways or crawled under desks. There they had waited, trapped, counting the minutes before they would be discovered and beaten. Others had tried to put up a fight—what they described as a last heroic stand before a grim ending. Almost in tears, these seasoned men and women could not yet believe that they had made it out alive and, in most cases, unscathed. Why on earth did Gruevski allow the police to come to their rescue after initially refusing their calls for help? And why did the president, a close Gruevski ally, back down from declaring martial law after having completely outplayed them?

Similar feelings of powerlessness were ubiquitous throughout my research. Construction workers and failed businessmen insisted that their economic fortunes were controlled by Gruevski's whims and financial schemes. Indeed, Gruevski had been able to attract international credit lines as well as low-risk/ high-reward investments, finding himself flush with (borrowed) money at a time when most of the country's businessmen were deep in debt. However, Gruevski's regime had revealed surprising limits—atypical for other authoritarian governments in the region. Companies such as Construx that were not aligned with the regime had managed to hang on to their businesses, despite finding themselves marginalized by public investment. Even if, as my interlocutors suggested, Gruevski had utilized the secret police to wiretap companies, organize money-laundering schemes, and demand racket payments, he had been unable to stop those facts from resurfacing in the public sphere—a marked ineptitude in mobilizing the deep state and its violence, which hardly put Gruevski's regime in the same league as the police states of Recep Tayyip Erdogan (Turkey) or Vladimir Putin (Russia).

In this book, I have suggested that in order to understand the characteristics and flavor of Gruevski's authoritarian power, it is necessary to examine its ability to latch on to and manipulate Macedonia's financial expansion. Gruevski was inept at mobilizing state violence in part because his regime was not rooted in the deep structures of the state, including the intelligence community. Instead, the regime radiated an aura of power thanks to its ability to manipulate an ecosystem of unpaid debt, delayed materials, and unsavory deals. This infrastructure of relationships depended on the international conjuncture that had emerged during the global financial crisis, when international investors suddenly turned to "hostile" places such as Macedonia.[3] Gruevski rode this specific financial wave to generate a pervasive but fragile political domination, where dysfunctional credit relationships amplified the regime's grip on the country even when its economic benefits remained elusive. Behind the shiny façade of neo-baroque buildings lingered unstable economic schemes based on recursive exploitation—hardly the kind of rock-solid foundation that could lead to a coup d'état.

Relational Finance

The surprising contradictions of the VMRO–DPMNE regime stemmed from its increasing reliance on financialization to generate unstable social relationships. In that economic landscape, state power and financial processes intermingled with personal connections—a stark departure from the antiseptic, impersonal forms of violence generated by economic abstraction in Western economies.[4] In the Macedonian case, the violence of finance did not emerge from people's livelihood's being regimented by mechanical processes, such as credit scores, but from new dependencies between people with differential access to economic resources—between the regime and oligarchs, between would-be investors and local bureaucrats, and between employers and workers.

Undoubtedly, Macedonia is a small country where the relational dimension of finance is made particularly manifest. Relying on personal connections rather than black-box algorithms to contract consumer/public debt or forced in-kind exchanges, Macedonia hardly constitutes an example of the high-tech environments where increasingly exotic debt products define a baroque relationship between finance and the real world. But does finance behave very differently in more complex environments? As recent studies in science and technology demonstrate, algorithms replicate the social biases of their creators.[5] And aren't machines and calculations deployed to fulfill the needs and interests of managers (or sometimes, engineers) in the most sophisticated contemporary hedge funds? Wall Street speculators do not operate in a social void. Instead, financial brokers often make decisions about hedging debt-based products that are based on geopolitical or even emotional considerations. These products then travel across the globe and are utilized or negotiated by individuals or communities who aim to fulfill different relational needs—from caring for one's family, to affirming one's gendered and personal identity, to influencing a community's political future.[6]

If, then, finance has a strong relational component, it is crucial to understand its variations. Different processes of financial expansion engender different relational landscapes in different cultural, historical, and geopolitical contexts. It is clear, for instance, that Macedonia was perceived by foreign investors as a "frontier" landscape—a context that enticed certain desperate EU businessmen more than successful ones. For distressed entrepreneurs, Macedonia was ripe with a promise of masculine profit, a predatory attitude that was not achievable elsewhere. For workers, however, the inflow of finance appeared as a process of feminization that disrupted their centrality to the production process and restructured the patriarchal responsibilities on construction sites. Couched in predatory attitudes toward women, financial expansion framed encounters between different groups of men in crisis and resulted in fractured collective identities—often one of the spaces of social paralysis that amplified the attraction of Gruevski's regime.

These gendered contradictions involved collusion between international investors and the regime but also conflicts within the local community—a palimpsest of gendered interactions that demonstrates how Macedonia's financial expansion was, from its inception, radically shaped by deep social relations. The ascent of Gruevski's regime was not, then, a process of re-embedding relationships in a landscape whose sociality had been emptied by finance—a Polanyian double movement that authors such as Mikuš[7] have associated with the rise of far-right politics in Croatia. Instead, both the predatory expectations of international actors and domestic workers and the processes of financialization were guided and enmeshed with expectations, hopes, and dreams that were enabled by a particular political conjuncture.

In the wake of the global financial crisis, it is increasingly urgent to account ethnographically for the uncanny political landscapes that generate or follow financial expansion.[8] Anthropologists have a rich canon of political economic approaches to draw from, spanning (post)Marxist to feminist perspectives.[9] If the Macedonian case teaches us anything, it is that we ought to reinterpret these approaches to focus on both the structures that shape our interlocutors' actions and imaginations and the generative forces of financialization—whatever their uncertain routes and forms might be.[10] The dramatic and surreal tensions between investors, political leaders, and workers highlight more than "friction" between global capitalism and local reality. Instead, the moral quandaries and paradoxes of financialization are indicative of the emergence of entirely new political processes, kicked into existence by the encounter between finance and a variety of social actors.[11]

Weaving together different layers of the social fabric, the expansion of finance creates new opportunities for situated interests, actors, and sensibilities to shape a society's politics—both at the existential and the physical level. Financialization interacts with material mechanisms of power—allowing a few individuals who control the flow of credit and money to dictate taxation rules, shape infrastructural development, and manipulate the value and meaning of labor in both economic and social terms. As it allows for a growing centralization of power, financial expansion is fueled by new social imaginaries and expectations—hopes and dreams that reflect a country's geopolitical status and can enchant their dispossession, making citizens active participants or, as in the case of Macedonian workers, confused supporters of increasingly oppressive and authoritarian political structures.

Rentier Aspirations and Enchantment at the Periphery

Since the spectacular collapse of the global financial firm Lehman Brothers in 2008 and the ensuing global credit crunch, the illusory character of financial speculation has come under heavy scrutiny. Many public commentators rushed to expose the absurdity of Wall Street greed and the economic strategies behind social inequality. For these commentators, the absurdity of the crisis centered on the ruthless expansion of the credit supply. Helped by years of stagnant salaries and a weaker social safety net, commercial banks, mortgage companies, and other financial institutions worked hard to offer new financial products to an ever-expanding range of consumers. The more debt they underwrote, the more virtual assets they could sell to the financial market. Repackaged as credit-based products that would yield streams of future profit, financial instruments such as mortgages, derivatives, collateral obligations, and credit default swaps circulated among algorithms and traders in London, Tokyo, Singapore, Frankfurt, and New York—fueled by the self-reinforcing conviction that value would continue to increase as long as markets existed, independent of the creditworthiness of their origins.

Anthropologists, however, noted that one does not need to be particularly greedy to join the dangerous dance of speculative finance. Financial professionals have rather banal motives when entering into complex and predatory financial schemes that range from the willingness to do a good job to the satisfaction with earning large sums of money. Rather than eccentric "wolves of Wall Street," brokers and traders resemble office employees—numb to the risk implied by future credit instruments, normalizing their participation in speculative trading as just another aspect of their daily routine.[12]

But what about common citizens? Why do we seem so willing to buy into speculative credit schemes and believe their promises of otherworldly wealth? Perhaps, anthropologists suggest, the expansion of financial markets is akin to magical thinking, where occult beliefs of future wealth obscure the dispossession suffered at the hand of a continuously evolving "casino capitalism."[13] How else could we explain the proliferation of Ponzi or pyramid schemes in which investors are promised exceptional rewards paid for by the capital put in by new members rather than by actual profits? "Bridg[ing] the gap between present and future"[14] in places that are experiencing social transitions, fast money schemes embody hopes for financial returns that vindicate a society's perceived flaws, including its postcolonial marginality, through the quasi-mystical action of political, and sometime religious, leaders.[15]

Similar social aspirations, rooted in Macedonia's deep-seated history of peripheralization, coalesced around Gruevski's regime and his financial schemes. Plagued by an unproductive economy since World War II, socialist Macedonia's access to subsidized credit fueled and limited the possibilities of progress. When Yugoslavia collapsed and the Macedonian economy imploded, citizens found themselves in a devastated social landscape. Overnight, common Macedonians mutated from employed and proud socialist subjects to jobless embodiments of Europe's exclusionary politics. Stuck in a politically contested country and ignored by the same international financial flows that had nurtured them under socialism, Macedonians came to interiorize their struggle for economic survival as proof of their inherent flaws as a nation.[16]

Things started to change at the time of the global financial crisis. Unlike other European citizens, Macedonians had not had the luxury of accumulating financial debt during the 1990s. This (enforced) clean slate turned into an asset during the global financial crisis, when central banks were making money increasingly cheap but the markets were dominated by instability. Suddenly, the commitment of international organizations to extending precautionary aid to small, peripheral countries such as Macedonia attracted a host of speculators, investors, and businessmen eager to cash in on the comparatively higher returns offered by Macedonian bonds or to extract some profits from European money.

But if European investors were making out like bandits, why should Macedonians abstain from extracting all that they could from European finance? The regime certainly tried to hammer home this perspective and insisted that the influx of European money constituted a turning point in the country's history. Thanks to Gruevski's business acumen, Macedonians did not need to beg for a seat at the European table. They could simply take a seat and perhaps even reverse their fortunes. The regime encouraged local bureaucrats and businessmen to rethink their own sedimented experiences of peripheralization not as evidence of their inferiority but as testimony to a new interdependence with Europe. Receiving EU funds by virtue of their under-development gave power to both Macedonian businessmen and bureaucrats. It was time to use this power to extract money from their European partners rather than simply comply with their procedures and expectations.

The process, however, was not seamless. The sudden inflow of money to Gruevski's coffers was paralleled by an equal disinvestment in the private sector—a painful reminder of decades of financial starvation. Scores of small- and large-scale businessmen hoped to latch on to public investment, such as the Skopje 2014 project, to recover some funds and make up for the collapse of horizontal arrangements that had kept companies afloat financially and existentially during the transition. Nagged by the financial expectations of these domestic businessmen and citizens, the regime could not invest in the country while also maintaining a solvent profile for international investors. Instead, the regime enabled concentric circles of forced credit, which condemned companies that were not politically aligned to financial hardship and pushed citizens to believe in the VMRO–DPMNE credit schemes as their best chance for improving their economic fortunes—a "faith" not rooted in economic optimism but driven by fear, cynicism, and doubt that the regime cultivated over time.

Macedonians' embrace of the regime as a scheme for turning their tormented belonging into a source of exploitative gain provides a different insight from that of typical ethnographic accounts of the routes that finance takes to bleed into the social fabric of a society. The credibility of Gruevski's promises of wealth was not due to the regime's ability to redistribute wealth. What sustained the regime's aura was "its failures to deliver services"[17] and its capacity to propagate material inequalities and conscious (self)exploitation. This paradox calls for a conceptual apparatus able to simultaneously embrace hopes and fears, desires and failures—a theoretical approach in which the gloomy materiality of Macedonian forced-credit practices can be read through the sedimented experiences of financial dispossession. This approach offers a nuanced understanding of the tactical maneuvering of political elites and businessmen but also workers as they operate in the folds of economic transformation.

Defining that material and existential space is likely to remain a subject of debate among anthropologists of finance. In this book, I found it useful to map the paradoxes of financialization through the concept of illiquidity, understood not only as a property of the market but as a political and economic conjuncture that became normative and spread expectations of rent through-out Macedonian society. Classically, rent refers to unearned profits from ownership of land or other resources. But if one conceives of property eth-nographically, rent expresses a predatory attitude—the act of inhabiting rela-tionships of inequality and turning them into profit.[18] At once a social imag-inary and a material relation, rent embraces aspirations for profit and forms of recursive exploitation alike, reverberating along class and geopolitical cleavages.[19]

In the Macedonian case, the rentier aspirations defined a zero-sum land-scape where one's existential or material desires for (normal) wealth and po-litical recognition could often be expressed only through shabby and des-perate scams or extractive actions. When these speculative desires failed to materialize, illiquidity became extremely productive for Gruevski's regime, amplifying citizens' sense of economic inadequacy and galvanizing their sup-port for political leaders who appeared able to domesticate global finance.[20] Dynamic and unsettling, Macedonian illiquidity constituted aspirations, hopes, and dreams that thrived precisely because, under Gruevski, the gaps between the periphery and the center, between oligarchs and citizens, wid-ened exponentially.

This ghastly landscape eroded Macedonian citizens' dreams—leaving be-hind contorted aspirational forms unable to fully account for one's existential change, let alone shape a "leisure class"[21] or a national bourgeoisie.[22] Instead, illiquidity fostered an environment of failed deals in which extractive hopes and nightmares collided without a clear sense of direction, accountability, or responsibility. In a speculative context starved of cash, these rentier aspira-tions and the scams they promoted made authoritarianism plausible. It was the regime's fault, repeated the culpable and innocent alike. If forced-credit night-mares and existential drama were a material "appearance of the state,"[23] citi-zens felt compelled to join in or be irrevocably doomed.

Predatory Authoritarianism

Both as a hope of overcoming geopolitical subordination and as a desire to escape economic exploitation, illiquidity reveals a complex social landscape that connects financialization to global populism. This point is particularly salient today as social scientists are increasingly asked to analyze the crisis of contemporary democracies. Considering the impact of illiquidity and rent can help move beyond "populism," a concept that often naturalizes liberalism as the only viable political model and obfuscates the different class relations expressed by phenomena as diverse as Brexit, Trumpism, and Putinism.[24]

A non-populist theory of the contemporary authoritarian moment doesn't only consist in highlighting the role of high-income individuals and the middle class in the renaissance of authoritarian states. Such a theory dwells on the dialectic between aspiration and reality within different social groups— considering the meaning of hopes for financial profit in places, both far and near, where years of economic stagnation and insecurity have created an uncanny resonance for non-democratic messages.[25] But a non-populist theory also considers how finance mediates a country's history of entanglement in the global economic and political order. Finally, this theoretical approach must consider how financialization may, in fact, not devolve into widespread access to wealth but legitimize a proliferation of constraints to citizens' economic well-being—what Vahabi and Durant conceptualize as a political economy of predation in which finance sabotages spaces of economic independence and forces individuals into technofeudal relationships.[26] In short, a non-populist theory rightly thinks about what happens when financial expansion makes rent a legitimate object of social desire and legitimizes predatory social relations as a way to claim (or maintain) a place in the world.

So, what does the Macedonian case tell us about the pull of illiberal messages among dispossessed citizens? It is interesting to note that, when compared to other moments of mass disillusionment that led to illiberal politics in the past century, Macedonian far-right forces lacked coherent organization and mass. Macedonian workers who supported Gruevski never took part in protests, participated in the local life of their party, or organized into fascist squads. Similarly, the elections of most global "populist" leaders were not preceded by social demonstrations comparable to the massive marches that preceded or legitimized totalitarian regimes in the early twentieth century.[27] Even more noteworthy is the fact that, unlike in early fascist regimes, most contemporary "populisms" do not actually redistribute wealth—except upward. Instead, they propose new, heightened forms of the very same extractive politics that oligarchs and financial elites have successfully implemented since the 1980s in Moscow, Washington, and elsewhere.[28]

Could it be that post–global financial crisis authoritarianism is thriving precisely because it presents itself as a solid alternative to a widespread sense of failure—what Gökarıksel describes as an individual and collective nihilism?[29] Perhaps one of the most provocative insights that can be derived from the Macedonian case is that Gruevski's regime did not have a core of solid corporative practices and ideologies. Instead, it consisted of a tight circle of oligarchs and their associates operating in a power vacuum—a reversed Ponzi scheme of sorts, maintained by the lucid disappointment following everyday failures to navigate forms of predatory finance. Blue-collar, male construction workers I interviewed intuitively understood that their attempts to conjure away illiquidity with horizontal relationships were not really working. They rejected the extreme dimensions of the regime's propaganda that they had in any case no means to embrace. And yet, haunted by a financial landscape in which they did not fit, they could not see any other solid political or existential option.[30]

Hopelessness and feeling trapped in an "unhomely present,"[31] abandoned by classless progressive movements[32]—these feelings are all too common in the global rustbelts described by ethnographers.[33] The financial crisis that started in 2007 forced Western societies to look in the mirror, bringing inequality and power to the fore of political debates. Globally, this generated powerful waves of movements, which failed spectacularly often because of the opposition of liberal-minded elites—a scenario that seems uncannily similar to the 1930s.[34] What was left to global working classes, if not illiberal politics? Perhaps, workers in Illinois, Poland, and Macedonia reasoned, they were doomed. But at least, if they voted for illiberal leaders, they would not be the only ones.

Of course, workers' despair did not just happen. Instead, making political alternatives unrealistic was one of the significant accomplishments of the Macedonian regime—which combined well with its unforeseen ability to harness financial expansion in shaping construction activities. This peculiar economic configuration was the result of years of postsocialist neglect and in a longer trajectory that allowed "local elites [to] deliberately stunt social transformation."[35] Yet it also signified a departure from the lack of investment in social and public projects of the 1990s. Unlike the fragmented, hollow politics typical of the early transition, Gruevski invested in selective urban projects and infrastructure as well as in (some) sectors of the public administration. His government offered citizens the illusion of participating in building a state—albeit a hierarchical one—engaged in defying nothing less than the entire Euro-Atlantic status quo. This promise of irredentist corporativism helped him channel a brewing desire for non-representative politics—a political ferment stoked by crisis throughout the world that, elsewhere in the

Balkans and especially in Bosnia and Herzegovina, had led to massive grass-roots activism.[36] Rather than an expression of what Mujanović calls "elastic authoritarianism," a political expression of longstanding patrimonial inequalities,[37] Gruevski's authoritarian project fed on an ideological rupture with the past and a new access to finance—both enabled by the chaos of the global financial system.

It would be limiting to understand such a political project, in its material and existential dimension, as a hybrid regime—a Frankenstein of neoliberal authoritarian policies, defined by its lack (of institutional strengths, of democracy, of market economy) rather than its features.[38] Yes, Gruevski implemented a series of neoliberal measures. He did simplify bureaucracy, reduce taxation, and make the country a "haven" for foreign investors, whose inflow of capital he utilized to capture domestic businesses. But didn't fascist regimes also implement austerity, creating unstable alliances with the very industrial and financial interests they set out to dismantle?[39] Didn't Margaret Thatcher, former prime minister of the UK, utilize neoliberalism to curtail democratic participation by dismantling trade unions and reducing access to public services?[40] Indeed, scholars of neoliberalism such as Martin Konings suggest that "free markets" are created and regulated by the state. Since the global financial crisis, neoliberal "freedom" has taken on an increasing illiberal flavor[41]—an "Authoritarian Fix," perhaps necessary to resolve the contradictions of financial expansion.[42]

Calling Macedonia's regime "hybrid," then, demonstrates a certain analytical anachronism, which ignores the longer-term entanglements between states and finance at the core of advanced economies, reserving the hybrid label for "non-Western" places such as Macedonia, where those contradictions are more explicit. But doesn't Gruevski's brand of authoritarianism, able to fuel rentier paradoxes while preventing the formation of a rentier class that could endanger the regime, merit its own analytical space?

Perhaps one way to capture Gruevski's paradoxical successes and his inherent contradictions is to reject the hybrid label and to understand his political project as a predatory regime—a pirate state of sorts that attempted "through the threat of violence . . . to insert [it]self within a global sea" of finance.[43] Not unlike the golden era of piracy, Gruevski's regime was empowered by the restructuring of hegemonic roles within the international and European communities and the liminal window of financial opportunities offered by the crisis.[44] Much like mates on buccaneer vessels, Macedonians had been rejected by Europe, condemned to a purgatory of economic stagnation and irrelevance. Didn't it make sense to join the crew of Gruevski "the Voivode," who claimed the heritage of bandits and rebels who had fought the Ottoman occupation in the early twentieth century and set sail to pillage the imperial convoys of global finance or build their own treasure island?[45]

One, a Hundred, or a Thousand Financializations?

Water, land, illnesses (and illness prevention), hog farms, food, embryos, work, cities, debt, and even finance itself—everything seems to be susceptible to financialization. Understandably, scholars who had embraced this concept in its infancy are today experiencing an increasing financialization fatigue. Natascha van der Zwan, for instance, has recently called for limiting the concept to the "financialization of finance"—the introduction of specific modes of calculation that subordinate financing processes to neoliberal markets.[46] But if we adopt that perspective, what should be done with places such as Macedonia—where financial expansion appears in very different forms, often only obliquely related to the rationality of financial markets?[47]

Considering the case of Macedonia alongside other experiences of financial expansion, however, highlights the predatory but social and participatory character of financialization. Instead of being an anomaly, the predatory flavor of Macedonia's illiquidity offers a prism for understanding the political impact of financial dynamics in other, more developed economies. Certainly, Gruevski's piratical domination was largely a consequence of Macedonia's legacy of peripheralization and geopolitical liminality during the global financial crisis—a structural condition that explains why, even after his regime ended, new "democratic" forces have relied on very similar mechanisms of power. Yet, if the VMRO–DPMNE's authoritarian project emerged as the "'best possible political shell' for a still-evolving, and inevitably crisis-prone, predatory, finance-dominated accumulation regime," it was largely thanks to a mixture of utter disillusionment and hidden-away hope.[48]

To readers interested in contemporary politics, this sounds eerily familiar. Isn't the resurgence of cryptofascism seen in European countries also built on a progressive embrace of predatory socialities and repressed anticipation of change, facilitated by payment crises and illiquidity?[49] Aren't rentier expectations and mutual oppressions key relational horizons that materialize the ebbs and flows of global finance in thriving economies such as the US or Australia? These "individual, conscious strategies of social betterment" work also as "processes of co-optation for maintaining power"[50] precisely because of their capacity to normalize authoritarianism even in more developed economies.[51]

Disposing of a unitary concept of financialization would obscure, rather than clarify, the growing political similarities between the periphery and the core of the world system. Instead of delimiting the concept, I suggest that it is more productive to defetishize how we understand and describe finance and its expansion. Moving away from thinking of finance as either an external force that impacts the relational world or an inherent logic to capital allows researchers to listen carefully to the disquieting whispers of interlocutors far and near and let local stories of economic decline and frustrated hopes affect how we conceptualize global political and economic trends. From this viewpoint, financialization becomes a social process, the result of concrete relationships, imaginary fears, repressed aspirations, and desperate struggles.

Following those threads, I have focused on the financial and existential paradoxes that induced a motley crew of social actors to support an authoritarian regime against their best interests. This deeply distressing landscape, made up of scams between international investors and local contractors, failed deals, and sour masculine jokes, suggests that finance empowered a small circle of individuals connected to an emerging authoritarian regime.[52] Yet that political result depended on myriad social interactions situated beyond the secretive world of oligarchs and elites. Instead, if financial expansion proves fertile for authoritarian projects, it is precisely because it intersects, enmeshes, and *becomes* a variety of political relationships, from the redefinition of the value of labor to the re-evaluation of social identities.

Understanding the complex relational dimension of finance means dwelling on the series of historically sedimented and idiosyncratic political conundrums that both lead to and follow from financial expansion. If my study is to serve as a blueprint (or a warning sign), this approach involves a slow unearthing of trends nested within troves of contradictory results—a weedy mess, as Schuster calls it, not just because, as we know, life is complicated but because finance entangles peoples' lives in increasingly complex chains of value and debt.[53] The result is a textured world made of conflict, doubt, and sometimes laughter, framed by political blows and material struggles; a world of imagined powerlessness and real exploitation that led Macedonians into a downward spiral of authoritarian politics, one unsteady step at a time, in what looked like an endless downfall—until it dissolved in the deafening silence of a failed revolution.

Notes

Introduction

1. Aaron Z. Pitluck, Fabio Mattioli, and Daniel Souleles, "Finance Beyond Function: Three Causal Explanations for Financialization," *Economic Anthropology* 5, no. 2 (2018): 157–71.

2. Fabio Mattioli, "Debt, Financialization, and Politics," in *A Research Agenda for Economic Anthropology*, ed. James Carrier (Cheltenham, UK: Edward Elgar, 2019), 56–73.

3. Rudolph Hilferding, *Finance Capital: A Study of the Latest Phase of Capitalist Development* (London: Routledge, 1910; 1981). Regarding the convergence between industrial and financial elites in Italy in the 1930s, see Clara Elisabetta Mattei, "Austerity and Repressive Politics: Italian Economists in the Early Years of the Fascist Government," *European Journal of the History of Economic Thought* 24, no. 5 (2017): 998–1026; and in the US in the 1970s, see Youn Ki, "Industrial Firms and Financialization in Late Twentieth-Century America," presented at the 30th Annual SASE Conference on Global Reordering: Prospects for Equality, Democracy, and Justice, Doshisha University, Kyoto, June 23–25, 2018.

4. Giovanni Arrighi suggests that financialization is caused by a decline of hegemony, when a collapse in profits by dominant states is offset by the relocation of production, war investments, and colonialism, leading to increasing international conflicts (*The Long Twentieth Century: Money, Power, and the Origins of Our Times* [London: Verso, 1994], 27–84). See also Rosa Luxemburg, *The Accumulation of Capital* (New York: Routledge, 2003); David Harvey, *The New Imperialism* (New York: Oxford University Press, 2003); David Harvey, *Limits to Capital* (New York: Verso, 2007); Thomas Piketty, *Capital in the Twenty-First Century* (Cambridge, MA: Harvard University Press, 2014).

5. Paul Langley, *The Everyday Life of Global Finance: Saving and Borrowing in*

Anglo-America (London: Oxford University Press, 2008), 20–41; Randy Martin, *Financialization of Daily Life* (Philadelphia: Temple University Press, 2002), 1–12.

6. Melissa García-Lamarca and Maria Kaika, "'Mortgaged Lives': The Biopolitics of Debt and Housing Financialisation," *Transactions of the Institute of British Geographers* 41, no. 3 (2016): 313.

7. Marieke de Goede, *Virtue, Fortune, and Faith: A Genealogy of Finance* (Minneapolis: University of Minnesota Press, 2005); Karen Ho, *Liquidated: An Ethnography of Wall Street* (Durham, NC: Duke University Press, 2009); Maurizio Lazzarato, *The Making of the Indebted Man: An Essay on the Neoliberal Condition* (Boston: MIT Press, 2012).

8. See for instance Petra Krippner, *Capitalizing on Crisis: The Political Origins of the Rise of Finance* (Cambridge, MA: Harvard University Press, 2011); Costas Lapavitsas, *Profiting Without Producing: How Finance Exploits Us All* (London: Verso, 2013); Ewa Karwowski and Engelbert Stockhammer, "Financialisation in Emerging Economies: A Systematic Overview and Comparison with Anglo-Saxon Economies," *Economic and Political Studies* 5, no. 1 (2017): 60–86.

9. Léna Pellandini-Simányi, Ferenc Hammer, and Zsuzsanna Vargha, "The Financialization of Everyday Life or the Domestication of Finance? How Mortgages Engage with Borrowers' Temporal Horizons, Relationships and Rationality in Hungary," *Cultural Studies* 29, nos. 5–6 (2015): 733–59; Hedwig Amelia Waters, "The Financialization of Help: Moneylenders as Economic Translators in the Debt-Based Economy," *Central Asian Survey* 37, no. 3 (2018): 403–18; Ariel Wilkis, *The Moral Power of Money: Morality and Economy in the Life of the Poor*, Culture and Economic Life (Stanford, CA: Stanford University Press, 2017).

10. Douglas R. Holmes, *Economy of Words: Communicative Imperatives in Central Banks* (Chicago: University of Chicago Press, 2013); Eleni Tsingou, "Club Governance and the Making of Global Financial Rules," *Review of International Political Economy* 22, no. 2 (2015): 225–56; Caitlin Zaloom, *Out of the Pits: Traders and Technology from Chicago to London* (Chicago: University of Chicago Press, 2006).

11. Andrea Lagna, "Derivatives and the Financialisation of the Italian State," *New Political Economy* 21, no. 2 (2016): 167–86.

12. Manolis Kalaitzake, "The Political Power of Finance: The Institute of International Finance in the Greek Debt Crisis," *Politics & Society* 45, no. 3 (2017): 389–413.

13. Brett Williams, *Debt for Sale: A Social History of the Credit Trap* (Philadelphia: University of Pennsylvania Press, 2005); Julia Elyachar, *Markets of Dispossession: NGOs, Economic Development, and the State in Cairo* (Durham, NC: Duke University Press, 2005), 37–65.

14. Sibel Kusimba, "'It Is Easy for Women to Ask!': Gender and Digital Finance in Kenya," *Economic Anthropology* 5, no. 2 (2018): 247–60; Ana Flavia Badue and Florbela Ribeiro, "Gendered Redistribution and Family Debt: The Ambiguities of a Cash

Transfer Program in Brazil," *Economic Anthropology* 5, no. 2 (2018): 261–73; Caroline Schuster, *Social Collateral: Women and Microfinance in Paraguay's Smuggling Economy* (Oakland: University of California Press, 2015), 1–26.

15. Laura Bear et al., "Gens: A Feminist Manifesto for the Study of Capitalism," Theorizing the Contemporary, Cultural Anthropology (website), March 30, 2015; Fabio Mattioli, "Debt, Financialization, and Politics"; Martijn Konings, "Neoliberalism and the American State," *Critical Sociology* 36, no. 5 (2010): 741–65; Hadas Weiss, "Financialization and Its Discontents," *American Anthropologist* 117, no. 3 (2015): 506–18.

16. Noelle Stout, "Petitioning a Giant: Debt, Reciprocity, and Mortgage Modification in the Sacramento Valley," *American Ethnologist* 43, no. 1 (2016): 158–71.

17. Philip Abrams, "Notes on the Difficulty of Studying the State (1977)," *Journal of Historical Sociology* 1, no. 1 (1988): 58–89; Timothy Mitchell, "The Limits of the State: Beyond Statist Approaches and Their Critics," *American Political Science Review* 85, no. 1 (1991): 77.

18. See Natascha van der Zwan, "Finance and Democracy: A Reappraisal," presented at the 30th Annual SASE Conference on Global Reordering: Prospects for Equality, Democracy, and Justice, Doshisha University, Kyoto, June 23, 2018; or Brett Christophers, "The Limits to Financialization," *Dialogues in Human Geography* 5, no. 2 (2015): 183–200.

19. Lagna, "Derivatives and the Financialisation," 168.

20. Bear et al., "Gens: A Feminist Manifesto." See also Susana Narotzky and Niko Besnier, "Crisis, Value, and Hope: Rethinking the Economy: An Introduction to Supplement 9," *Current Anthropology* 55, no. S9 (2014): S4–16.

21. Lagna, "Derivatives and the Financialisation." Lagna shows that while most governments utilize financial tools, they do not do so in isolation from global dynamics. Rather, financialization constitutes a space where global agendas (in the Italian case he examines, European-driven austerity) can favor the emergence of domestic political leaders (i.e., a new coalition of center left and neoliberal reformers) and disrupt earlier power networks (i.e., traditional business owners accustomed to thriving through public debt-fueled spending) because of restriction or expansion in the flow of liquidity and credit.

22. Sidney Mintz, *Sweetness and Power: The Place of Sugar in Modern History* (London: Penguin Books, 1985); Fernando Ortiz, *Cuban Counterpoint: Tobacco and Sugar* (Durham, NC: Duke University Press, 1995); Fernando Coronil, *The Magical State: Nature, Money, and Modernity in Venezuela* (Chicago: University of Chicago Press, 1997).

23. Susana Narotzky, "Rethinking the Concept of Labour," *Journal of the Royal Anthropological Institute* 24, no. S1 (2018): 32. There is merit in the exploration of the perspective of specific communities, studying either the sociality of elites (see Hirokazu Miyazaki, *Arbitraging Japan* [Berkeley: University of California Press, 2013];

Zaloom, *Out of the Pits: Traders and Technology*; or, regarding the morality of debt-related practices among marginalized communities, Michael Herzfeld, *Evicted from Eternity: The Restructuring of Modern Rome* [Chicago: University of Chicago Press, 2009]). The approach I offer here, however, takes the idea that finance defines a relational space as a methodological prompt to focus on contradictions and entanglements between, rather than within, communities of people related to finance.

24. See Daniel Souleles, *Songs of Profit, Songs of Loss: Private Equity, Wealth, and Inequality*, Anthropology of Contemporary North America (Lincoln: University of Nebraska Press, 2019); Horacio Ortiz, "A Political Anthropology of Finance: Profits, States and Cultures in Cross-Border Investment in Shanghai," *HAU: Journal of Ethnographic Theory* 7, no. 3 (2017): 325–45; Lotta Björklund Larsen, *A Fair Share of Tax: A Fiscal Anthropology of Contemporary Sweden* (London: Palgrave Macmillan, 2018); and Douglas R. Holmes, *Economy of Words: Communicative Imperatives in Central Banks* (Chicago: University of Chicago Press, 2013), for a clear picture of how a small circle of individuals operating in different financial spheres can shape particular global political conjunctures.

25. Anna Tsing, "Inside the Economy of Appearances," *Public Culture* 12, no. 1 (2000): 217. While anthropologists have been particularly attentive in portraying how financial failures are mobilized to stress the quasi-magical potency of individual entrepreneurs (see Laura Bear, "Capitalist Divination: Popularist Speculators and Technologies of Imagination on the Hooghly River," *Comparative Studies of South Asia, Africa and the Middle East* 35, no. 3 [2015]: 409), the Macedonian case shows the role of illiquidity in shaping the emergence of an entire coordinated, structured, and organized political regime.

26. After shadowing workers or managers for as long as twelve hours on the construction site, I decided against colonizing the (little) time they had left to spend with their families. The book relies mainly on secondhand information regarding household financial practices and consumption. When we shared convivial moments, it was as colleagues or friends, outside of a research framework.

27. Melissa Fisher, *Wall Street Women* (Durham, NC: Duke University Press, 2012), 95–119.

28. See Antonio Gramsci, *Prison Notebooks, Volume 1*, ed. Joseph A. Buttigieg and Antonio Callari (New York: Columbia University Press, 1992). See also Pitluck, Mattioli, and Souleles, "Finance Beyond Function"; Kate Crehan, *Gramsci's Common Sense* (Durham, NC: Duke University Press, 2016).

29. In this book, thinking about praxis does not mean understanding social action through cultural, rather than economic, structures, as David Graeber appears to frame it (*Debt: The First 5,000 Years* [Brooklyn, NY: Melville House, 2011]). Instead, my approach takes seriously the Marxist claim that capital, and especially financial capital, is, at its core, a social relation (Michael Blim, *Made in Italy: Small-Scale*

Industrialization and Its Consequences [New York: Praeger, 1990]; Mintz, *Sweetness and Power*; Anwar Shaikh, *Capitalism: Competition, Conflict, Crises* [Oxford: Oxford University Press, 2016]).

30. See Hannah Appel, "Occupy Wall Street and the Economic Imagination," *Cultural Anthropology* 29, no. 4 (2014): 602–25; Larisa Kurtović and Azra Hromadžić, "Cannibal States, Empty Bellies: Protest, History and Political Imagination in Post-Dayton Bosnia," *Critique of Anthropology* 37, no. 3 (2017): 262–96.

31. See for instance the revival of in-kind dealings and favors of the postsocialist period (Douglas Rogers, "Moonshine, Money, and the Politics of Liquidity in Rural Russia," *American Ethnologist* 32, no. 1 [2005]: 63–81).

32. Katherine Verdery, *What Was Socialism, and What Comes Next?* (Princeton, NJ: Princeton University Press, 1996); Caroline Humphrey, *The Unmaking of Soviet Life: Everyday Economies After Socialism* (Ithaca, NY: Cornell University Press, 2002).

33. Olga Shevchenko, *Crisis and the Everyday in Postsocialist Moscow* (Bloomington: Indiana University Press, 2008), 15–34.

34. See Čarna Brković, *Managing Ambiguity: How Clientelism, Citizenship and Power Shape Personhood in Bosnia and Herzegovina* (New York: Berghahn Books, 2017), 37–56.

35. See Miladina Monova, "'We Don't Have Work. We Just Grow a Little Tobacco': Household Economy and Ritual Effervescence in a Macedonian Town," in *Economy and Ritual in Postsocialist Times*, ed. Stephen Gudeman and Chris Hann (New York: Berghahn Books, 2015), 160–190.

36. To this day, Greece claims that the name Macedonia denotes its northern region. To resolve the impasse, Macedonia changed its name to North Macedonia in 2019. Because the book refers to facts happening before the name change, I use the name Macedonia, which, at the time, was the constitutional name of the country.

37. Stef Jansen, "After the Red Passport: Towards an Anthropology of the Everyday Geopolitics of Entrapment in the EU's 'Immediate Outside,'" *Journal of the Royal Anthropological Institute* 15, no. 4 (2009): 815–32.

38. Ognen Vangelov, "Stalled European Integration, the Primordialization of Nationalism, and Autocratization in Macedonia Between 2008 and 2015," *Intersections: East European Journal of Society and Politics* 3, no. 4 (2017): 17–40.

39. Nikica Mojsoska-Blazevski, "Supporting Strategies to Recover from the Crisis in South Eastern Europe, Country Assessment Report: The Former Yugoslav Republic of Macedonia," Budapest: International Labour Organization, 2011, p. 17.

40. Paul Langley, "The Performance of Liquidity in the Subprime Mortgage Crisis," *New Political Economy* 15, no. 1 (2010): 77.

41. Anastasia Nesvetailova, *Financial Alchemy in Crisis: The Great Liquidity Illusion* (Chicago: University of Chicago Press, 2010), 75.

42. Bruce G. Carruthers and Arthur L. Stinchcombe ("The Social Structure of

Liquidity: Flexibility, Markets, and States," *Theory and Society* 28, no. 3 [1999]) suggest that illiquidity is an "issue in the sociology of knowledge" (p. 353) because it enables "artifices of indifferences" (Duncan Wigan, "Financialisation and Derivatives: Constructing an Artifice of Indifference," *Competition & Change* 13, no. 2 [June 2009]: 157–72) upon which traders can exchange disparate objects as equal (see also Aaron Z. Pitluck, "Watching Foreigners: How Counterparties Enable Herds, Crowds, and Generate Liquidity in Financial Markets," *Socio-Economic Review* 12, no. 1 [2014]: 5–31; Nesvetailova, *Financial Alchemy*). The Macedonian case, however, suggests that illiquidity too can be construed not as an object of knowledge but as a power relation where local actors exploit global contradictions for multiple goals.

43. Ian Hardie, *Financialization and Government Borrowing Capacity in Emerging Markets* (London: Palgrave Macmillan, 2012), 1–34.

Chapter 1

1. Till Mayer, "Macedonian Capital Skopje Gets Kitsch Makeover via Skopje 2014 Project," *Spiegel Online*, November 12, 2013.

2. Prva Arhi Brigada, First Architectural Uprising, March 28, 2009 [прво архитетонско востание 28.03.2009].

3. Deana Kjuka, "Urban Renewal or Nationalist Kitsch? Skopje 2014 Stirs Controversy," *Radio Free Europe*, December 2, 2013.

4. Meta.mk, "Karpoš 4 Are Gathering Signatures to Save Their Parks, the Mayor 'Gives' His Support," September 23, 2015.

5. Karen Dawisha, *Putin's Kleptocracy: Who Owns Russia?* (New York: Simon & Schuster, 2014), 13–35.

6. Tamta Khalvashi, "Peripheral Affects: Shame, Publics, and Performance on the Margins of the Republic of Georgia," PhD diss., Department of Anthropology, University of Copenhagen, 2015; Mateusz Laszczkowski, "Building the Future: Construction, Temporality, and Politics in Astana," *Focaal* 60 (2011): 77–92; Mateusz Laszczkowski, "'Demo Version of a City': Buildings, Affects, and the State in Astana," *Journal of the Royal Anthropological Institute* 22, no. 1 (2016): 148–65.

7. Bruce Grant, "Edifice Complex: Architecture and the Political Life of Surplus in the New Baku," *Public Culture* 26, no. 3 (2014): 405.

8. Max Holleran, "'Mafia Baroque': Post-Socialist Architecture and Urban Planning in Bulgaria," *British Journal of Sociology* 65, no. 1 (2014): 21–42.

9. Laura L. Adams and Assel Rustemova, "Mass Spectacle and Styles of Governmentality in Kazakhstan and Uzbekistan," *Europe-Asia Studies* 61, no. 7 (2009): 1249–76; Laura Adams, *The Spectacular State: Culture and National Identity in Uzbekistan* (Durham, NC: Duke University Press, 2010), 21–68.

10. See Mateusz Laszczkowski and Madeleine Reeves, "Introduction," *Social Analysis* 59, no. 4 (2015): 1–14; Christina Schwenkel, "Post/Socialist Affect: Ruination

and Reconstruction of the Nation in Urban Vietnam," *Cultural Anthropology* 28, no. 2 (2013): 252–77.

11. The intuition that urban space, rather than affect, enables the spectral and visceral qualities of authoritarian rule to become so concrete that they are able to invade citizens' intimate reflections, follows the intuition of Marxist thinkers such as Henry Lefebvre and David Harvey. Unlike gentrification or the urban spectacles observed in Western cities, Skopje's façades expand the domain of the political, allowing the VMRO–DPMNE's authoritarian regime to encroach on Macedonians' lives. (Ida Susser, *Norman Street: Poverty and Politics in an Urban Neighborhood* [Oxford: Oxford University Press, 1982]; Jacqueline Kennelly and Paul Watt, "Sanitizing Public Space in Olympic Host Cities: The Spatial Experiences of Marginalized Youth in 2010 Vancouver and 2012 London," *Sociology* 45, no. 5 [2011]: 765–81). The hyper-political urban interactions and identities forged by Skopje 2014 pushed citizens out of their comfort zones and into the constricting embrace of the VMRO–DPMNE regime.

12. Asher Ghertner, *Rule by Aesthetics: World-Class City Making in Delhi* (New York: Oxford University Press, 2015), 1–22.

13. Oleg Golubchikov, "World-City-Entrepreneurialism: Globalist Imaginaries, Neoliberal Geographies, and the Production of New St Petersburg," *Environment and Planning A: Economy and Space* 42, no. 3 (2010): 626.

14. David Harvey, *The Condition of Postmodernity: An Enquiry into the Origins of Cultural Change* (Oxford: Blackwell, 1989), 327.

15. Seventy percent of the total value of contracts for Skopje 2014, worth 452 million euro, were awarded to five companies—Beton, Granit, Strabag AG, Beton Stip, and Bauer BG (*Prizma*, "Skopje 2014 Uncovered," 2019)—most of which were connected to important oligarchs who were, or were to become, close to the VMRO–DPMNE.

16. See Jean Despeyroux, "Le Séisme de Skopje: Ses Enseignements en Matière de Protection Antisismique—Aperçu des Problèmes de la Construction Antisismique en Yougoslavie et de la Reconstruction de Skopje," in *The Earthquake in Skopje: Its Teachings Regarding Antiseismic Protection: Summary of the Problems of the Antiseismic Construction in Yugoslavia and in Skopje*, edited by UNESCO Assistance Mission (Amsterdam: UNESCO Press, 1963), 145–77. Estimates from Ottoman, Yugoslav, and Macedonian sources calculate the city's population at 33,000 citizens in 1902–3; 43,847 in 1913; 102,604 in 1958; 197,341 in 1961; 408,143 in 1981; and 506,926 in 2004 (Ivan Ivanovski, "Decoding Postsocialist Transition on the Case of Skopje: Housing in the Arena of Private Interest and the Emergence of New Urban Prototypes," master's thesis, Department of Architecture, Dessau Institute of Architecture, 2008; Petar Todorov, "Skopje, od Pochetok na XIX Vek do Krajot na Osmanlinskoto Vladeenje, Скопје Од Почетокот На XIX Век До Крајот На Османлиското Владеење," (PhD diss., Institute of History, University of Ss. Cyril and Methodius, Skopje, 2013). Current estimates suggest that Skopje has around 550,000 inhabitants, although in the

absence of an accurate census, urban planners generally assume the population to be closer to 800,000.

17. Savezni Zavod za Statistiku, (*Statistical Yearbook of Yugoslavia*), (Belgrade: Savezni Zavod za Statistiku, 1987), p. 634.

18. Ljubica Spaskovska, "Building a Better World? Construction, Labour Mobility and the Pursuit of Collective Self-Reliance in the 'Global South,' 1950–1990," *Labor History* 59, no. 3 (2018): 331–51.

19. See Beton, "History of Beton," 2016. Granit built the Homs-Salet highway in Syria in 1969 and took part in the construction of the Zwentendorf nuclear power plant in Austria in 1972. In 1974, Granit won a contract worth 160 million USD for a military base in Kuwait, and in 1978 it built streets and highways in Benghazi, Libya. In the following years, the company won contracts for other military airfields in Iraq, Libya, and Algeria worth more than 350 million USD (Granit, "About Us," 2019).

20. Johanna Bockman, "From Socialist Finance to Peripheral Financialization: The Yugoslav Experience" (presentation with Fabio Mattioli, Center for Place, Culture and Politics, CUNY Graduate Center, November 15, 2017).

21. Spaskovska, "Building a Better World?," 331.

22. Makstat Database 2019a, "Completed Construction Works Abroad," State Statistical Office.

23. Makstat Database 2019b, "Employed by Type of Ownership of the Business Entities and Sectors of Activities, by Year," State Statistical Office.

24. Holly Watts and Saska Cvetkovska, "Tory Chairman Refuses to Name Macedonian Business Partners," *The Guardian*, May 25, 2015; Claire Duffin and Ruth Sutherland, "SamCam's Fashion Line's Links with a Macedonian Tycoon," *Daily Mail*, February 17, 2017.

25. Meta.mk, "Karpoš 4 Are Gathering"; *Scoop*, "Key Players in the Media Business: Who Owns the Media in Macedonia?," April 21, 2016.

26. Sinisa Marusic, "Macedonia's SJO Says Secret Police Ran Illegal Wiretapping," BalkanInsight, November 18, 2016.

27. Meta.mk, "'Transparency Macedonia': Tenders for Security Tailored Especially for SGS," February 10, 2016.

28. Martin Dimitrov, "From Spies to Oligarchs: The Party, the State, the Secret Police, and Property Transformations in Postcommunist Europe" (presented at the *1989: Twenty Years After* conference, University of California, Irvine, 2009).

29. Meri Jordanovska, "Todor Mircevski: Liceto Sto go Povrzuva 'Eksiko' so Kamcev (Тодор Мирчевски – лицето што го поврзува „Ексико" со Камчев), Призма (*Prisma*), March 31, 2015. See also Vlatko Stojanovksi, "Сашо Мијалков станал газда на „Софија Градба", „Жито Полог", „Пелагонија" и на „Здравје Радово"!"*Fokus*, November 16, 2017.

30. Meri Jordanovska and Vlado Apostolov, "Od Tesorot na MVR 'Ispumpani'

860.000 evra, Од трезорот на МВР „испумпани" 860.000 евра," Призма (*Prisma*), September 28, 2016; Meri Jordanovska, "Direktorot na Makedonski Telekom bil sopstvenik na misteriosnata 'Eksiko' Директорот на Македонски Телеком бил сопственик на мистериозната „Ексико"," Призма (*Prisma*), May 27, 2016.

31. Vlado Apostolov, "'Adora' na Cifliganec partner so famoznata 'Eksiko'," („Адора" на Чифлиганец партнер со фамозната „Ексико",) Призма (*Prisma*), June 25, 2015.

32. Harold Lydall, *Yugoslavia in Crisis* (New York: Clarendon Press, 1989), 24.

33. Industrial output also increased over 5 percent annually (David Dyker, *Yugoslavia: Socialism, Development, and Debt* [London: Routledge, 1990], 91; Barbara Einhorn, *Citizenship in an Enlarging Europe: From Dream to Awakening* [New York: Palgrave, 2006]).

34. James Gapinski, *The Economic Structure and Failure of Yugoslavia* (New York: Praeger, 1993), 7.

35. Dyker, *Yugoslavia: Socialism*, 49; Einhorn, *Citizenship in an Enlarging Europe*.

36. Susan Woodward, *Socialist Unemployment: The Political Economy of Yugoslavia, 1945–1990* (Princeton, NJ: Princeton University Press, 1995), 168, 187.

37. Woodward, *Socialist Unemployment*, 223–25.

38. Dyker, *Yugoslavia: Socialism*, 119. Despite a fall in exports, which grew only 2.9 percent each year between 1973 and 1979, compared to 7 percent during the period between 1966 and 72, international loans continued to fuel Yugoslav consumer standards thanks to an artificial and high exchange rate (Mihail Petkovski, "Deviznite Kursevi i Nacionalnata Ekonomska Politika," ("Девизните Курсеви И Националната Економска Политика"), PhD diss., Department of Economy, University of Ss. Cyril and Methodius, Skopje, 1989), 287; see also Woodward, *Socialist Unemployment*, 253.

39. Gligorov, 1952, in Woodward, *Socialist Unemployment*, 168.

40. Sekretarijat za Stoki i Promet, August 12, 1956. Macedonian National Archives, Skopje, Republic of Macedonia.

41. Woodward, *Socialist Unemployment*, 291; Lydall, *Yugoslavia in Crisis*, 83.

42. Lydall, *Yugoslavia in Crisis*, 190.

43. Woodward, *Socialist Unemployment*, 225.

44. Lydall, *Yugoslavia in Crisis*, 178.

45. In the 1960s, Yugoslavia tried to reschedule its debt with Western powers. In the case of the UK, several departments were inclined to decline the Yugoslav request to postpone repayments for over 40 million USD. To avoid a diplomatic embarrassment and potential friction with other allies, the UK Embassy in Belgrade and the Foreign Office offered to extend the terms of an expired loan for the rebuilding of Skopje, repackaged together with commercial credits for raw and industrial materials. See Telegram 102 from Belgrade to Foreign Office, March 15, 1966, FO371/189036, National Archives, London, United Kingdom.

46. Izvestaj za Rabota na Sojuzniot Devizen Inspektorat, Oddelenje vo Skopje, za 1975 Godina, February 1975, F-295, Box 3, Folder 1, Savezni Devizni Inspektorat 1975 Opšta Arhiva, Macedonian National Archives, Skopje, Republic of Macedonia, p. 20.

47. Izvestaj za Rabota, Savezni Devizni Inspektorat, Macedonian National Archives, p. 21.

48. The accumulation and distribution of foreign currency became a crucial political issue in Yugoslavia. Until 1971, companies that accumulated foreign currency were forced to surrender a large quota to the National Bank. This system disadvantaged republics like Croatia, whose tourist industries generated approximately half of the SFRY inflows of foreign currency (Davorka Matić, "Is Nationalism Really That Bad? The Case of Croatia," in *Democratic Transition in Croatia: Value Transformation, Education, and Media*, edited by Sabrina P. Ramet and Davorka Matić [College Station: Texas A&M University Press, 2007], 343) and was abandoned after significant popular protest (Jana Bacević, *From Class to Identity: The Politics of Education Reforms in Former Yugoslavia* [Budapest: CEU Press, 2014], 63; Alvin Rubinstein, "The Yugoslav Succession Crisis in Perspective," *World Affairs* 135, no. 2 [1972]: 109).

49. Izvestaj za Rabota, Savezni Devizni Inspektorat, Macedonian National Archives, p. 22.

50. Izvestaj za Rabota, Savezni Devizni Inspektorat, Macedonian National Archives, p. 42.

51. Izvestaj za Rabota, Savezni Devizni Inspektorat, Macedonian National Archives, p. 46.

52. Informacija, December 1974, F-297, Box 3, Folder 5, Savezni Devizni Inspektorat 1975 Opšta Arhiva, Macedonian National Archives, Skopje, Republic of Macedonia.

53. Lydall, *Yugoslavia in Crisis*, 173.

54. Izvestaj za Rabota, Savezni Devizni Inspektorat, Macedonian National Archives, p. 26.

55. Woodward, *Socialist Unemployment*, 228.

56. Petkovski, "Deviznite Kursevi," 283.

57. Dyker, *Yugoslavia: Socialism*, 125.

58. Aktivnost u Prekršajnom Postupku, 1981, F-527, Box 9, Folder 11, Savezni Devizni Inspektorat 1981 Opšta Arhiva, Macedonian National Archives, Skopje, Republic of Macedonia.

59. Podsetnik za Kontrola Deviznog Poslovanje, 29 December 1981, F-524, Box 9, Folder 7, Savezni Devizni Inspektorat 1980 Opšta Arhiva, Macedonian National Archives, Skopje, Republic of Macedonia.

60. Potvrdjenje za Telefonski Razgovor, 23 August 1982, F-582, Box 10, Folder 81, Savezni Devizni Inspektorat 1982 Opšta Arhiva, Macedonian National Archives, Skopje, Republic of Macedonia.

61. Gapinski, *Economic Structure*, 5.

62. A similar process was documented also in Slovenia, where "directors of export-oriented companies had to adopt one of the various forms of cooperation with the secret police and the military intelligence service as well as form links with the Yugoslav Foreign trade bank (*Jugobanka*) and federal (i.e., Serbian) export companies. Without their support, they could not have penetrated the large Soviet market." (Jurij Fifkfak et al., *Biti Direktor v Casu Socializma: Med Idejami in Praksami*, edited by Jurij Fikfak and Joze Princic (Ljubljana, Slovenia: Zalozba ZRC, 2008), 272.

63. Martin Dimitrov, "From Spies to Oligarchs: The Party, the State, the Secret Police, and Property Transformations in Postcommunist Europe," (presented at the *1989: Twenty Years After* conference, University of California, Irvine, 2009), 15.

64. Christian Nielsen, "The Symbiosis of War Crime and Organized Crime in the Former Yugoslavia" (presented at the *Money and the Shifting Locations of Eastern Peripheries* conference, Zagreb, 2009); Rado Pezdir, *Slovenska Tranzicija od Kardelja do Tajkunov* (Ljubljana: Časnik Finance, 2008).

65. Ljubica Spaskovska, "Building a Better World? Construction, Labour Mobility and the Pursuit of Collective Self-Reliance in the 'Global South', 1950–1990," *Labor History* 59, no. 3 (2018): 331–51.

66. Yugoslavia: Internal Security Capabilities, October 29, 1985, CIA-RDP86S00588R000300320007-5, General CIA Records, CREST Online Collection, p. 5.

67. Katherine Verdery, *My Life as a Spy: Investigations in a Secret Police File* (Durham, NC: Duke University Press, 2018), 74.

68. *Plus*, October 29, 1992; *Plus*, November 5, 1992; *Plus*, November 12, 1992; *Plus*, November 25, 1992; *Plus*, December 3, 1992; *Plus*, December 10, 1992; *Fokus*, p. 8, December 6, 1996; *Fokus*, pp. 10–11, August 11, 1996; *Fokus*, p. 10, November 14, 1996; *Fokus*, pp. 4–7, November 28, 1996.

69. AIM, "Armiski Spiunski Skandal," December 12, 1996.

70. Yugoslavia, General CIA Records, CREST Online, p. 2.

71. *Plus*, p. 10, November 5, 1992.

72. Trajko Slaveski, "Privatization in the Republic of Macedonia: Five Years After," *Eastern European Economics* 35, no. 1 (1997): 41.

73. Francesco Strazzari, "The Decade Horribilis: Organized Violence and Organized Crime Along the Balkan Peripheries, 1991–2001," *Mediterranean Politics* 12, no. 2 (2007): 185–209.

74. Risto Karajkov, "The End of a Bad Privatization," Osservatorio Balcani e Caucaso, October 5, 2007.

75. After placing Sašo Mijalkov inside the military intelligence service, Gruevski enlisted the help of a former director of the UBK, Slobodan Bogoevski. A seasoned intelligence operative, Bogoevski was at the center of the KOS smear campaign and managed to remain vital to Macedonian politics by sharing his contacts with Greek

oligarchs, Gruevski, and the SDSM (Adela Gjorgjioska, "The Case of the Macedonian Telekom: An Entangled Web of International Political and Business Corruption," Lefteast, December 28, 2015).

76. Vesna Bozinovska, "Kade Isceznaa 50 milioni Evra?!" ("Каде исчезнаа 50 милиони евра?!"), Вечер (Vecer), 2006.

77. Dimitrov, "From Spies to Oligarchs."

78. CBRF 2016; Nova TV 2014. Controversial Serbian businessman Jovica Stevanovic, also known as Gazda Nini, owned Rado Banka and subsequently purchased the already troubled Makedonska Banka, the third largest in the country, from members of the VMRO–DPMNE (allegations have recently been made that Gruevski took bribes to facilitate this transaction; see Sinisa Marusic, "Macedonia PM Accused of Bribery over Bank Sale," BalkanInsight, April 17, 2014.

79. Mijat Lakicević, "Makedonski Scenario 3," Peščanik, May 25, 2017. Leaked Macedonian counterintelligence documents suggest that during Gruevski's regime the Serbian Security Information Agency was very active in Macedonia. According to the dossier, Zivaljević had regular contact with Ivan Stoijlković, the leader of the Serb Party in Macedonia, and was deeply involved in promoting pro-Gruevski and pro-Russian propaganda. His activities included publishing inflammatory editorials in Serbian media close to the Serbian ruling party, as well as facilitating Stojilkovic's meetings with Russian officials on the creation of a neutral (i.e., non-NATO) military zone in the Balkans (Stevan Dojcinović et al., "Investigation: Serbia's Involvement in the Macedonian Crisis," *Balkanist*, May 30, 2017). Since 2008, Macedonia "has been undergoing strong subversive propaganda and intelligence activity implemented through the Embassy of the Russian Federation" (Aubrey Belford et al., "Leaked Documents Show Russian, Serbian Attempts to Meddle in Macedonia," OCCRP, June 4, 2017.) According to leaked intelligence documents, three agents of the Russian's Foreign Intelligence Service, supervised by four agents of the military Main Intelligence Directorate, based in Sofia, tried to recruit "a critical mass of military trained persons . . . to be used for accomplishing Russian interests" (Belford et al., "Leaked Documents"). In his ten years in government, Gruevski had often been helped by Russian oligarch Sergei Samsonenko, who took part in some of the murky schemes that allowed Kamcev (and Mijalkov) to acquire domestic companies (Goran Lefkov, "Samsonenko: Successful in Macedonia—Under Scrutiny in Russia," Scoop English, December 5, 2016; "Key Players in the Media Business: Who Owns the Media in Macedonia?", Scoop, April 21, 2016; Sonja Risteska, "Macedonia: A New Russian Frontier," in *The Russian Economic Grip on Central and Eastern Europe*, edited by Ognian Shentov [Abingdon, UK: Routledge, 2018]). In exchange, the VMRO–DPMNE facilitated Samsonenko's investments in real estate. During Gruevski's government, Samsonenko built a new sports hall, a hotel, and a church in the VMRO–DPMNE-controlled municipality of Aerodrom and was made honorary consul to Macedonia. This emerging Russian influence was

echoed at the political level by the Macedonian president, Gjorge Ivanov, who showed a deep fascination with the political systems built by autocrats, such as Putin and Erdogan (Sinisa Marusic, "Macedonians Divided Over President's Support for Erdogan," BalkanInsight, July 8, 2013). Putin returned the courtesy extended to him in 2016 when he publicly denounced the collapse of Gruevski's regime as the result of an intervention by external powers (Aleksandar Vasovic, "Russia Accuses NATO, EU and Albania of Meddling in Macedonia," Reuters, March 2, 2017).

80. Andrew Graan, "Counterfeiting the Nation? Skopje 2014 and the Politics of Nation Branding in Macedonia," *Cultural Anthropology* 28, no. 1 (2013): 161–79; Melissa Aronczyk, *Branding the Nation: The Global Business of National Identity* (Oxford: Oxford University Press, 2013), 63–81; Manuel Aalbers, "The Financialization of Home and the Mortgage Market Crisis," *Competition & Change* 12, no. 2 (2008): 148–66.

81. Srdjan Jovanovic-Weiss (paper presented at Forum Skopje 2009: *The Aftershock of the Postmodernism*, Mala Stanica, Skopje, Macedonia, June 8–14, 2009).

82. Dorina Pojani, "Cities as Story: Redevelopment Projects in Authoritarian and Hybrid Regimes," *Journal of Urban Affairs* 40, no. 5 (2018): 716–17.

83. Forestalling escape routes or forcing citizens to inhabit uncomfortable positions are classic examples of the political and disciplining value of space. Haussmannian urbanism, for instance, obliterated the complex and tortuous street grid of old Paris, substituting boulevards to facilitate access for troops needed to impose order on revolt-prone, working-class French subjects (David Harvey, *Paris, Capital of Modernity* (New York: Routledge, 2005). Large boulevards were also installed during the rebuilding of Skopje after the 1963 earthquake. The idea was to redefine the pre-modern, Ottoman character of Skopje and make it a modernist city, ready for massive car use and open to circulation (Ines Tolic, *Dopo il Terremoto: La Politica della Ricostruzione negli Anni della Guerra Fredda a Skopje* [Reggio Emilia, Italy: Diabasis, 2011]). Within this urban social engineering, post-Ottoman (i.e., Turkish and Albanian) subjects were relegated to a monumental space on the right bank of the Vardar River, which came to be known as Carsija (Fabio Mattioli, "Unchanging Boundaries: The Reconstruction of Skopje and the Politics of Heritage," *International Journal of Heritage Studies* 20, no. 6 [2014]: 599–615.

84. Rory Archer, "The Moral Economy of Home Construction in Late Socialist Yugoslavia," *History and Anthropology* 29, no. 2 (2018): 141–62; Brigitte Le Normand, *Designing Tito's Capital: Urban Planning, Modernism, and Socialism in Belgrade* (Pittsburgh: University of Pittsburgh Press, 2014), 147–88.

85. Rozita Dimova, *Ethno-Baroque: Materiality, Aesthetics and Conflict in Modern-Day Macedonia* (New York: Berghahn Books, 2013), 115–43.

86. Aihwa Ong, "Hyperbuilding: Spectacle, Speculation, and the Hyperspace of Sovereignty," in *Worlding Cities: Asian Experiments and the Art of Being Global*, edited by Ananya Roy and Aihwa Ong (London: Wiley-Blackwell, 2011), 209.

87. After household coal and wood heating and industrial production, the construction industry was the third leading cause of the exceptional levels of pollution found in Macedonia (MEPP, Air Quality Assessment Report for the Period 2005–2015 [Skopje: Macedonian Environment Information Center, 2017]). According to developers and architects, the construction expansion promoted alongside the Skopje 2014 project produced significant dust and debris that could not be easily dispersed, given the reduced air circulation in the city caused by bigger buildings and smaller green areas. A recent study called "Skopje Grows" shows that in the neighborhoods of Debar Maalo and Bunjakovec alone, the green area has been reduced from 21 percent of the total surface in 1991 to 13.8 percent in 2012 and is projected to be only 4.5 percent in 2020 (Reactor–Research in Action, and Arhitektri, "Skopje Raste: Policy Study on the Effects of Urban Planning Methodology and Practice: Case Studies of Debar Maalo and Bunjakovec," Skopje, 2013, accessed October 26, 2018, http://reactor.org.mk/CMS /Files/Publications/Documents/SkopjeRaste.pdf).

88. Among other things, citizens lamented that Skopje 2014 had eroded precarious neighborhood arrangements that allowed Skopje to survive the ethnic conflicts in the early 2000s (Vasiliki Neofotistos, *The Risk of War: Everyday Sociality in the Republic of Macedonia* [Philadelphia: University of Pennsylvania Press, 2012], 84–100; Goran Janev, "Ethnocratic Remaking of Public Space– Skopje 2014," *EFLA Journal* 1 [2011]: 33–36).

89. David Atkinson and Denis Cosgrove, "Urban Rhetoric and Embodied Identities: City, Nation, and Empire at the Vittorio Emanuele II Monument in Rome, 1870–1945," *Annals of the Association of American Geographers* 88, no. 1 (1998): 28–49; Federico Caprotti, *Mussolini's Cities: Internal Colonialism in Italy, 1930–1939* (Youngstown, OH: Cambria Press, 2007); Lamartine Da Costa and Plinio Labriola, "Bodies from Brazil: Fascist Aesthetics in a South American Setting," *International Journal of the History of Sport* 16, no. 4 (1999): 163–80; Marla Stone, "Staging Fascism: The Exhibition of the Fascist Revolution," *Journal of Contemporary History* 28, no. 2 (1993): 215–43.

90. Janev, "Ethnocratic Remaking."

91. Ophélie Veron, "Contesting the Divided City: Arts of Resistance in Skopje," *Antipode* 48, no. 5 (2016): 1441–61; Mattioli, "Unchanging Boundaries."

92. Balint Magyar, *Post-Communist Mafia State: The Case of Hungary* (Budapest: CEU Press, 2016).

93. The relationships between associates of the regime continue. The most important prosecutor for crimes of corruption and organized crimes, Jovo Ilievski, is also a relative of Sašo Mijalkov. Zoran Stavrevski, former minister of finance, was Gruevski's *kum* (Meta.mk, "'Transparency Macedonia'"). Dejan Pandelevski, the director of the construction company ISKRA, partly owned by Orka Holding and Eksiko, was *kum* to Mile Janakievski, the former minister of transport and communications.

94. Aaron Z. Pitluck, Fabio Mattioli, and Daniel Souleles, "Finance Beyond Function: Three Causal Explanations for Financialization," *Economic Anthropology* 5, no. 2 (2018): 157–71.

95. See also Ana Flavia Badue and Florbela Ribeiro, "Gendered Redistribution and Family Debt: The Ambiguities of a Cash Transfer Program in Brazil," *Economic Anthropology* 5, no. 2 (2018): 261–73; Smitha Radhakrishnan, "Of Loans and Livelihoods: Gendered 'Social Work' in Urban India," *Economic Anthropology* 5, no. 2 (2018): 235–46.

96. Dimova, *Ethno-Baroque*; Andrew Graan, "Counterfeiting the Nation? Skopje 2014 and the Politics of Nation Branding in Macedonia," *Cultural Anthropology* 28, no. 1 (2013): 161–79.

97. Ivan Rajković, "From Familial to Familiar: Corruption, Political Intimacy and the Reshaping of Relatedness in Serbia," in *Reconnecting State and Kinship*, edited by T. Thelen and E. Alber (Philadelphia: University of Pennsylvania Press, 2018), 133.

98. Fernando Coronil, *The Magical State: Nature, Money, and Modernity in Venezuela* (Chicago: University of Chicago Press, 1997), 317.

99. Dave Wilson, "Shaping the Past and Creating the Future: Music, Nationalism, and the Negotiation of Cultural Memory at Macedonia's Celebration of Twenty Years of Independence," *Music and Politics* 13, no. 2 (2019): 2.

Chapter 2

1. National Bank of the Republic of Macedonia, *Financial Stability Report for the Republic of Macedonia 2014*, October 2015.

2. The public debt of the Western Balkan region increased, on average, from 33 percent of GDP in 2008 to 49.9 percent in 2013. In the same period, Central and Eastern Europe saw its public debt grow from 32.5 percent of GDP to 52.8 percent (Raiffeisen RESEARCH, "CEE Banking Sector Report: New Normal and 10% Thresholds," June 9, 2016).

3. See Neil Smith, "Gentrification and the Rent Gap," *Annals of the Association of American Geographers* 77, no. 3 (1987): 462–65; and Judy Whitehead, "Rent Gaps, Revanchism and Regimes of Accumulation in Mumbai," *Anthropologica* 50, no. 2 (2008): 269–82, regarding rent gaps. Llerena Guiu Searle (*Landscapes of Accumulation: Real Estate and the Neoliberal Imagination in Contemporary India*, South Asia Across the Disciplines [Chicago: University of Chicago Press, 2016], 146) suggests that India tried to present the country as an abstract land for speculation but faced significant struggles to make its construction and real estate practices readable to foreign investors.

4. See Michela Sacchioli, "Il Lavoro negli Anni della Crisi: L'Italia Paga il Conto, la Disoccupazione è Cresciuta del 108%," *La Repubblica*, April 29, 2015.

5. Blim, *Made in Italy*, 11.

6. Raffaele Ricciardi, "Industrial Production, Italy Lost 22% from the Beginning of the Crisis" ("Produzione Industriale, l'Italia Ha Perso il 22% dallo Scoppio della Crisi"), *La Repubblica*, September 23, 2016.

7. Ilaria Vesentini, "In Italy 2 Companies Close Down Every Hour: In 5 Years 60,000 Firms Were Lost" ("In Italia Chiudono Due Imprese Ogni Ora: In Cinque Anni Perse 60mila Aziende"), *Il Sole 24 Ore*, January 23, 2014.

8. See Kimberley Coles, *Democratic Designs: International Intervention and Electoral Practices in Postwar Bosnia-Herzegovina* (Ann Arbor: University of Michigan Press, 2007), 63; Peter Redfield, "The Unbearable Lightness of Ex-Pats: Double Binds of Humanitarian Mobility," *Cultural Anthropology* 27, no. 2 (2012): 358–82; Emil Røyrvik, *The Allure of Capitalism: An Ethnography of Management and the Global Economy in Crisis* (New York: Berghahn Books, 2011); Paul Green, "Mobility, Subjectivity and Interpersonal Relationships: Older, Western Migrants and Retirees in Malaysia and Indonesia," *Asian Anthropology* 14, no. 2 (2015): 150–65; Filippo M. Zerilli and Julie Trappe, "Expertise and Adventure: In/Formalization Processes Within EU Rule of Law Capacity Building Programs," *Anuac* 6, no. 2 (2017): 103–8.

9. Ho, *Liquidated*, 1.

10. Holmes, *Economy of Words*, 21; Tsing, "Inside," 118.

11. Martha Poon, "Scorecards as Devices for Consumer Credit: The Case of Fair, Isaac & Company Incorporated," *Sociological Review* 55 (2007): 284–306.

12. Caroline Schuster, "Weedy Finance: The Political Life of Resilience in the Paraguayan Countryside" (paper delivered at the Seminar of Anthropology, May 1, 2019, University of Melbourne); Noelle Stout, "Petitioning a Giant: Debt, Reciprocity, and Mortgage Modification in the Sacramento Valley," *American Ethnologist* 43, no. 1 (2016): 158–71.

13. Alfonso Garcia Mora, Andrey Milyutin, and Simon Walley, *Europe and Central Asia Housing Finance Crisis Prevention and Resolution: A Review of Policy Options* (Washington, DC: World Bank, 2013), 10.

14. Aleksandar Janev, "Fanfari za 3.8 Milijardi, Fabriki za Polovina Milijarda Evra," ("Фанфари за 3,8 милијарди, фабрики за половина милијарда евра"), Призма (*Prisma*), January 23, 2017.

15. Graan, "Counterfeiting the Nation? Skopje 2014," 167.

16. Marjana Janchevska, "The Importance of FDI in the Macedonian Economy," master's thesis, Department of Economics, University of Ljubljana, 2014.

17. As Llerena Searle (*Landscapes of Accumulation: Real Estate and the Neoliberal Imagination in Contemporary India*, South Asia Across the Disciplines [Chicago: University of Chicago Press, 2016]) demonstrates, the lack of common metrics to evaluate a country's business climate can significantly affect investment decisions. In this context, FDI, or Macedonia's position in global business climate ranking, assumed an increased relevance.

18. Janev, "Fanfari za 3.8 milijardi."

19. Dorothee Bohle, "European Integration, Capitalist Diversity and Crises Trajectories on Europe's Eastern Periphery," *New Political Economy* 23, no. 2 (2018): 239–53.

20. Branimir Jovanovic, "The Real Price of the Cheap Labour Force," 2016.

21. Ian Bruff, "The Rise of Authoritarian Neoliberalism," *Rethinking Marxism* 26, no. 1 (2014): 124. Politically, deficit and public debt have been vilified as major social problems by leaders in the UK, France, Italy, and Germany, even when the consequences of balancing the budget have been socially disastrous—the Greek crisis being a case in point (Robert Skidelski, "Cameron Is Right to Warn of Another Recession, but Wrong to Blame the World," *The Guardian*, November 18, 2014). Leaders who implemented different economic policies have been pressured to resign, as in the case of Berlusconi in Italy, or boycotted, as in the cases of Portugal and Greece (Rachel Donadio and Elisabetta Povoledo, "Berlusconi Resigns After Italy's Parliament Approves Austerity Measures," *New York Times*, November 13, 2011; Patricia Kowsmann, "Portugal President Reappoints Prime Minister, Despite Lack of Majority," *Wall Street Journal*, October 22, 2015). See also Bernard Connolly, *The Rotten Heart of Europe: The Dirty War for Europe's Money* (London: Faber and Faber, 1995); John Agnew, "How Many Europes? The European Union, Eastward Enlargement and Uneven Development," *European Urban and Regional Studies* 8, no. 1 (2001): 29–38.

22. Rodrigo Fernandez and Angela Wigger, "Lehman Brothers in the Dutch Offshore Financial Centre: The Role of Shadow Banking in Increasing Leverage and Facilitating Debt," *Economy and Society* 45, nos. 3–4 (2016): 407–30; Angela Wigger, "The Political Interface of Financialisation and the Regulation of Mergers and Acquisitions in the EU," *Journal of European Integration* 34, no. 6 (2012): 623–41.

23. Francesca Gambarotto and Stefano Solari, "The Peripheralization of Southern European Capitalism Within the EMU," *Review of International Political Economy* 22, no. 4 (2015): 788–812; Pasquale Tridico, "The Impact of the Economic Crisis on EU Labour Markets: A Comparative Perspective," *International Labour Review* 152, no. 2 (2013): 175–90.

24. Fernandez and Wigger, "Lehman Brothers."

25. Servaas Storm and C. W. M. Naastepad, "Europe's Hunger Games: Income Distribution, Cost Competitiveness and Crisis," *Cambridge Journal of Economics* 39, no. 3 (2015): 959–86.

26. Stefano Solari and Giandemetrio Marangoni, "The Making of the New European Periphery: The Evolving Capitalisms Within the Monetary Union" (presented at the Euromemorandum Conference, Vienna, 2012); Luigi Orsi and Stefano Solari, "Financialisation in Southern European Economies," *Économie Appliquée* 63 (2010): 5–34; Engelbert Stockhammer, "Peripheral Europe's Debt and German Wages: The Role of Wage Policy in the Euro Area," *International Journal of Public Policy* 7, no. 1 (2011): 83–96.

27. Manolis Kalaitkaze, "The Political Power of Finance: The Institute of International Finance in the Greek Debt Crisis," *Politics & Society* 45, no. 3 (2017): 710.

28. Fernandez and Wigger, "Lehman Brothers," 420.

29. Stephen Bell and Andrew Hindmoor, "Structural Power and the Politics of Bank Capital Regulation in the United Kingdom," *Political Studies* 65, no. 1 (2017): 103–21.

30. Tsingou, "Club Governance."

31. See Kees van der Pijl, Otto Holman, and Or Raviv, "The Resurgence of German Capital in Europe: EU Integration and the Restructuring of Atlantic Networks of Interlocking Directorates After 1991," *Review of International Political Economy* 18, no. 3 (2011): 384–408. These events pushed authors such as Gambarotto and Solari ("Peripheralization of Southern European") but also Arjan Vliegenthart ("Bringing Dependency Back In: The Economic Crisis in Post-Socialist Europe and the Continued Relevance of Dependent Development," *Historical Social Research / Historische Sozialforschung* 35, no. 2 [2010]: 242–65) to recognize that Southern European countries had lost their centrality within the EU and had converged toward the subordinate, peripheral position occupied by Eastern Europe. However, it would be a mistake to downplay the economic and political edge that PIIGS maintain over their Eastern European neighbors (Bela Belojevikj and Fabio Mattioli, "Etnografia Di Una Crisi Normale: Crisiscape, Vrski e Riflessione Antropologica a Skopje, Macedonia," in *Oltre Adriatico e Ritorno: Percorsi Antropologici Tra Italia e Sudest Europa*, edited by Antonio Pusceddu and Tiziana Lofranco [Milano: Meltemi, 2017], 57–86). It is useful to understand how different paths toward financialization intersect, clash, and influence one another.

32. Despite its economic, and recently, political choices, Europeanness is often heralded as an example of multiculturalism that, in practice, erases traces of past peripheralization. While some countries such as France or the UK have had public and intellectual discussions about their colonial past, mostly thanks to intellectuals from the Global South such as Fanon, Trouillot, Asad, and Césaire, the EU as a whole has not. Italian colonialism is denied in public or otherwise portrayed as a benevolent, necessary process, devoid of atrocities (Rosario Forlenza, "Sacrificial Memory and Political Legitimacy in Postwar Italy: Reliving and Remembering World War II," *History & Memory* 24, no. 2 [2012]: 73–116; Angelo Del Boca, *Italiani Brava Gente?* [Milan: Neri Pozza, 2005]; Nicola Labanca, *Oltremare: Storia dell'Espansione Coloniale Italiana* [Bologna: Il Mulino, 2007]; Alberto Burgio, *Nel Nome della Razza: Il Razzismo nella Storia d'Italia 1870–1945* [Bologna: Il Mulino, 1999]). Similarly, the EU presents itself as a land of quality, excellence, and technology, obliterating centuries of famine, poverty, and resettlement. As Kristín Loftsdóttir, Andrea L. Smith, and Brigitte Hipfl ("Introduction," in *Messy Europe: Crisis, Race, and Nation-State in a Postcolonial World* [New York: Berghahn Books, 2018]) suggest, however, these kinds of racializing currents have continued to underpin the European project—and have increasingly resurfaced after the global financial crisis.

33. Larry Wolff, *Inventing Eastern Europe: The Map of Civilization on the Mind of the Enlightenment* (Stanford, CA: Stanford University Press, 1994); Maria Todorova, *Imagining the Balkans* (New York: Oxford University Press, 1997); Robert Aman, "The EU and the Recycling of Colonialism: Formation of Europeans Through Intercultural Dialogue," *Educational Philosophy and Theory* 44, no. 9 (2012): 1010–23.

34. BBC, "Romania and Bulgaria EU Migration Restrictions Lifted," January 1, 2014.

35. József Böröcz, "Introduction: Empire and Coloniality in the 'Eastern Enlargement' of the European Union," in *Empire's New Clothes: Unveiling European Enlargement*, edited by József Böröcz and Melinda Kovacs (Holly Cottage, UK: Central European Review, 2001); Agnes Gagyi, "'Coloniality of Power' in East Central Europe: External Penetration as Internal Force in Post-Socialist Hungarian Politics," *Journal of World-Systems Research* 22, no. 2 (2016): 349–72; Tanja Petrović, "European New Colonialism," *Belgrade Journal of Media and Communications* 2, no. 4 (2013): 111–28.

36. Bohle, "European Integration," 243; Gagyi, "'Coloniality of Power,'" 354; Angela Wigger, "The Political Interface of Financialisation and the Regulation of Mergers and Acquisitions in the EU," *Journal of European Integration* 34, no. 6 (2012): 623–41. Within the Visegrád Four (Czech Republic, Hungary, Poland, and Slovakia), the economic interconnection with Germany allowed Poland, and to a limited extent Slovakia and the Czech Republic, to mitigate the damages due to the crisis. Hungary, however, began to rely on EU transfers and aid when the massive inflow of privatization-linked FDI started to dwindle.

37. The extensive penetration of finance within the economy also bears some resemblance to the Anglo-Dutch financialization path. In contrast to the Baltic states, however, the Anglo-Dutch financialization path provides a low-tax environment through which financial capital can circulate or temporarily be harbored (Bohle, "European Integration").

38. Peter Mooslechner, "Management of Debt Challenges in Europe," Österreichische Nationalbank, 2012, p. 7.

39. National Bank of the Republic of Macedonia, *Financial Stability Report*, p. 83.

40. Raiffeisen Research, *CEE Banking Sector Report*, p. 5.

41. Stephen Gudeman, *Anthropology and Economy* (Cambridge: Cambridge University Press, 2016), 5.

42. Douglas Andrew Yates (*The Rentier State in Africa: Oil Rent Dependency and Neocolonialism in the Republic of Gabon* [Trenton, NJ: Africa World Press, 1996], 29), for instance, sees rent as a process where profit is generated by political elites dedicated to unproductive activities—what Thorstein Veblen defined as a "leisure class" (*The Theory of the Leisure Class: An Economic Study of Institutions* [New York: Modern Library, 1934 (1899)], 1). See also Michael Schatzberg, *The Dialectics of Oppression*

in Zaire (Bloomington: Indiana University Press, 1988); Gordon Tullock, *The Economics of Special Privilege and Rent Seeking*, Studies in Public Choice (Amsterdam: Springer, 1989); Anne Krueger, "The Political Economy of the Rent-Seeking Society," *American Economic Review* 64, no. 3 (1974): 291–303.

43. Central Financing and Contracting Department (CFCD), "Contracted Projects," 2017.

44. As Jasmin Mujanovic (*Hunger and Fury: The Crisis of Democracy in the Balkans* [Oxford: Hurst, 2018], 95–130) suggests, European actors might have tolerated authoritarian politics in the Balkans in exchange for political stability. Yet the Italian case suggests a more direct participation in predatory endeavors.

45. Here I have purposefully altered the details of the project. At the time of writing, there existed neither a Maritime Ministry nor a Sustainable Fishing Project.

46. This was common among expats. See Chris Shore, *Building Europe: The Cultural Politics of European Integration* (New York: Routledge, 2000), 147.

47. Squeezed by the VMRO–DPMNE, rent did not offer many spaces of independence—as in the hawker culture of Naples or the ambiguous "friendships that strangle" observed in Rome (Herzfeld, *Evicted from Eternity*, 143), or the competing brutality found among networks of gang-like politicians in Montenegro (Strazzari, "The Decade Horribilis") or Bulgaria (Venelin Ganev, *Preying on the State: The Transformation of Bulgaria After 1989* [Ithaca, NY: Cornell University Press, 2007]).

48. Elizabeth Dunn and Michael Bobick, "The Empire Strikes Back: War Without War and Occupation Without Occupation in the Russian Sphere of Influence," *American Ethnologist* 41, no. 3 (2014): 405–13.

Chapter 3

1. Jaime Palomera, "How Did Finance Capital Infiltrate the World of the Urban Poor? Homeownership and Social Fragmentation in a Spanish Neighborhood," *International Journal of Urban and Regional Research* 38, no. 1 (2014): 218–35; Aalbers, "Financialization of Home."

2. Nesvetailova, *Financial Alchemy*, 4.

3. For a survey, see Gustav Peebles, "The Anthropology of Credit and Debt," *Annual Review of Anthropology* 39, no. 1 (2010): 225–40; Bill Maurer, "The Anthropology of Money," *Annual Review of Anthropology* 35, no. 1 (2006): 15–36; Jonathan Parry and Maurice Bloch, eds., *Money and the Morality of Exchange* (Cambridge: Cambridge University Press, 1989), 1.

4. Bronislaw Malinowski, *Argonauts of the Western Pacific: An Account of Native Enterprise and Adventure in the Archipelagoes of Melanesian New Guinea* (New York: Routledge, 1978), 176; Paul Bohannan and Laura Bohannan, *Tiv Economy* (Chicago: Northwestern University Press, 1968).

5. Verdery, *What Was Socialism*; Elizabeth Dunn, "Postsocialist Spores: Disease,

Bodies, and the State in the Republic of Georgia," *American Ethnologist* 35, no. 2 (2008): 243–58; Alena Ledeneva, *Russia's Economy of Favours: Blat, Networking and Informal Exchange* (Cambridge: Cambridge University Press, 1998), 34; Davide Torsello, *The New Environmentalism? Civil Society and Corruption in the Enlarged EU* (London: Ashgate, 2012); Brković, *Managing Ambiguity*, 57; David Woodruff, *Money Unmade: Barter and the Fate of Russian Capitalism* (Ithaca, NY: Cornell University Press, 1999), 1.

6. Caroline Humphrey, "Barter and Economic Disintegration," *Man*, New Series, 20, no. 1 (1985): 48–72; Humphrey, *Unmaking of Soviet Life*, 5.

7. Morten Pedersen, "From 'Public' to 'Private' Markets in Postsocialist Mongolia," *Anthropology of East Europe Review* 25, no. 1 (2007): 64–71; Nikolai Ssorin-Chaikov, *The Social Life of the State in Subarctic Siberia* (Stanford, CA: Stanford University Press, 2003); Barbara A. Cellarius, "'You Can Buy Almost Anything with Potatoes': An Examination of Barter During Economic Crisis in Bulgaria," *Ethnology* 39, no. 1 (2000): 73–92; Björklund Larsen, *Fair Share of Tax*, 82.

8. David Sneath, "The 'Age of the Market' and the Regime of Debt: The Role of Credit in the Transformation of Pastoral Mongolia," *Social Anthropology* 20, no. 4 (2012): 491.

9. Stephen Gudeman, *Economy's Tension: The Dialectics of Community and Market* (New York: Berghahn Books, 2012), 1.

10. Graeber, *Debt*, 89.

11. Elizabeth Ferry, "Geologies of Power: Value Transformations of Mineral Specimens from Guanajuato, Mexico," *American Ethnologist* 32, no. 3 (2005): 420–36; Rogers, "Moonshine, Money," 63–81.

12. Bill Maurer, "Payment: Forms and Functions of Value Transfer in Contemporary Society," *Cambridge Anthropology* 30, no. 2 (2012): 15–35.

13. Noelle Stout, "Petitioning a Giant: Debt, Reciprocity, and Mortgage Modification in the Sacramento Valley," *American Ethnologist* 43, no. 1 (2016): 158–71.

14. Palomera, "Finance Capital," 228.

15. Sohini Kar, *Financializing Poverty: Labor and Risk in Indian Microfinance* (Stanford, CA: Stanford University Press, 2018), 14. See also Badue and Ribeiro, "Gendered Redistribution"; Smitha Radhakrishnan, "Of Loans and Livelihoods: Gendered 'Social Work' in Urban India," *Economic Anthropology* 5, no. 2 (2018): 234–45.

16. Larisa Jasarević, *Health and Wealth on the Bosnian Market: Intimate Debt* (Bloomington: Indiana University Press, 2017), 26.

17. Adam Sargent and Gregory Duff Morton, "What Happened to the Wage?," *Anthropological Quarterly* 92, no. 3: 637.

18. The CIA noted that, by 1971, approximately one-third of East-West trade happened in kind. See CREST, "East European Countertrade: The Trend Toward Bilateralism in Trade with the West, An Intelligence Assessment," April 1, 1985, CIA-RDP86S00588R000100130005-0, General CIA Records, p. 7.

19. CREST, "Intelligence Memorandum: The Growing Barter Element in East-West Trade," June 1, 1970, CIA-RDP85T00875R001600030077-4, General CIA Records, p. 2.

20. CREST, "East European Countertrade," p. 1.

21. In the 1980s, countertrade accounted for 30 percent of the exchanges between the West and Poland, Romania, and Yugoslavia. In the assessment of the CIA Office of European Analysis, compensation agreements resulted "in less economic burden than administrative controls on import and domestic austerity measures. The hard currency outlays saved by countertrade transactions may have equaled as much as a third of the region's debt service costs," in CREST, "East European Countertrade," p. iii.

22. CREST, "East European Countertrade," p. 3.

23. Kompenzacija was particularly attractive because it circumvented problems of conversion between the East and the West without utilizing fictive currencies, such as *klirinški dolari*. In 1982, the CIA estimated that kompenzacija was worth between 20 percent and 30 percent of its trade with the West. Yugoslav firms that conducted kompenzacija could hold on to a higher percentage of hard currency instead of surrendering most of it to the central bank—a fact that might have helped companies survive but de facto reduced the country's ability to pay its public debt. See CREST, "East European Countertrade," pp. 7–8.

24. Verdery, *What Was Socialism*, 20; Humphrey, *Unmaking of Soviet Life*, 5; Janos Kornai, *The Socialist System: The Political Economy of Communism* (Oxford: Oxford University Press, 1992), 262.

25. Sobranje Na SRM (1945–1990), Zapiznik of 26th sednica na Republickiot Sobor na Sobranieto na SR Makedonija, 27 Maj 1971, 1–17, Box 212, Folder 1, p. 7.

26. Sobranje Na SRM (1945–1990), Informacija za postignatite rezultati od rabotenjeto na stopanskite organizacii od SR Makedonija, April 1971, 121–197, Box 212, Folder 5, p. 11.

27. Sobranje Na SRM (1945–1990), Likvidnosta na delovnite banki I stopanskite organizacii vo SR Makedonija I nejsinata reperkusija vrs redovnata isplata na licnite dohodi vo rabotnite organisacii, April 1971, Box 212, p. 27. The SFRJ paid only 159.6 million dinars out of the 1.113 billion it had committed to the Republic of Macedonia. At the global level, the 1970s was marked by a process of stagflation. Macedonia was particularly exposed to international stagflation in the first instance, in addition to the Volcker shock and the oil crisis of 1973.

28. Sobranje Na SRM, Likvidnosta, p. 7.

29. Some large Macedonian banks drew the attention of economists, as they needed to use their reserves to execute daily transactions. In the first four months of 1971, these banks ran out of money for about five days. Sobranje Na SRM, Likvidnosta, p. 17.

30. Sobranje Na SRM, Informacija, p. 42.

31. Sobranje Na SRM, Likvidnosta, p. 10. See also Eirik Furubotn and Svetozar Pejovich, "Property Rights, Economic Decentralization, and the Evolution of the

Yugoslav Firm, 1965–1972," *Journal of Law and Economics* 16, no. 2 (1973): 275–302; Chiara Bonfiglioli, "Gender, Labour and Precarity in the South East European Periphery: The Case of Textile Workers in Štip," *Contemporary Southeastern Europe* 1, no. 2 (2014): 7–23.

32. In 1971, Macedonian exports were worth 300 million MKD, while its imports were worth 746 million MKD. Sobranje Na SRM (1945–1990), Zaklucioci vo vrska so stvaranjite dvizenja i nekoj karakteristiki na razvojot na stopanstvoto vo januari-mart 1971 godina, 11 Maj 1971, Box 212, Folder 2, p. 33.

33. Sobranje Na SRM, Informacija, p. 30.

34. Sobranje Na SRM, Informacija, p. 27.

35. Sobranje Na SRM, Likvidnosta, p. 15.

36. The time needed for payment increased from seventy-two days in 1969 to ninety days in 1970. Sobranje Na SRM, Informacija, pp. 43, 51.

37. Sobranje Na SRM, Informacija, p. 49.

38. Sobranje Na SRM, Likvidnosta, pp. 25–26.

39. Katarina Ott, *The Yugoslav Banking System* (Zagreb: Institut za Iavni Financii, 1988).

40. Susan Woodward, *Balkan Tragedy: Chaos and Dissolution After the Cold War* (Washington, DC: Brookings Institution Press, 1995).

41. See Michael Palairet, "Metallurgical Kombinat Smederevo 1960–1990: A Case Study in the Economic Decline of Yugoslavia," *Europe-Asia Studies* 49, no. 6 (1997): 1071–1101.

42. Rob Bryer, "Socialism, Accounting, and the Creation of 'Consensus Capitalism' in America, Circa 1935–1955," *Critical Perspectives on Accounting* 34 (January 2016): 1–35; Robert Horvat and Bojana Korosec, "The Role of Accounting in a Society: Only a Techn(Olog)Ical Solution for the Problem of Economic Measurement or Also a Tool of Social Ideology?," *Naše Gospodarstvo / Our Economy* 61, no. 4 (2015): 32–40.

43. National Bank of the Republic of Macedonia, *Annual Report 2000*, 2001, p. 13; National Bank of the Republic of Macedonia, *Annual Report 1999*, 2000, p. 14.

44. Caroline Humphrey and Stephen Hugh-Jones, *Barter, Exchange and Value: An Anthropological Approach* (Cambridge: Cambridge University Press, 1992), 1.

45. According to the data from Eurostat, Ireland's construction index in 2007 was at 486 and today is at 115; Spain was at 180 in 2006 and today is at 93. Eurostat, *Production in Construction—Annual Data*, 2018.

46. In fact, data from the statistical office suggest that the profitability of the sector radically decreased from a net profit margin of 12.3 percent in 2013 to 5.4 percent in 2014. The sector's debt ratio has increased from 50 percent to 54 percent.

47. Risto Karajkov, "Macedonia: The Building Industry from Boom to Crisis" ("Macedonia: Il Mattone dal Boom alla Crisi"), Osservatorio Balcani e Caucaso, August 12, 2013.

48. Some years later, the government issued bonds to compensate account holders.

49. Khaled Sherif, Michael Borish, and Alexandra Gross, "State-Owned Banks in the Transition: Origins, Evolution, and Policy Responses" (Washington, DC: World Bank, 2003).

50. Edda Zoli, "Cost and Effectiveness of Banking Sector Restructuring in Transition Economies," IMF Working Papers WP/01/157, October 1, 2001.

51. National Bank, *Annual Report 2000*, p. 31. See also Sherif, Borish, and Gross, "State-Owned Banks."

52. IMF, "Country Report No. 15/242: The Former Yugoslav Republic of Macedonia, Staff Report for the 2014 Article IV Consultation" (Washington, DC: International Monetary Fund, 2015).

53. IMF, "Country Report No. 15/242," p. 18.

54. IMF, "Country Report No. 15/242," p. 26.

55. IMF, "Country Report No. 16/356: The Former Yugoslav Republic of Macedonia, Staff Report for the 2016 Article IV Consultation," p. 44 (Washington, DC: International Monetary Fund, 2016).

56. Eric Cloutier, "NPL Monitor for the CESEE," 1H 2016, Vienna Initiative, p. 3.

57. The Gruevski regime promised prosperity and economic benefits to citizens and oligarchs. Young couples received subsidized mortgages through the *kupi kuka kupi stan* program, in which the government would subsidize loans for cheap new buildings—which tended to be built by oligarchs who had received special concessions in the purchase of land.

58. Douglas R. Holmes, *Economy of Words: Communicative Imperatives in Central Banks* (Chicago: University of Chicago Press, 2013), 208.

59. IMF, "Minutes of Executive Board Meeting 09/123-3: Former Yugoslav Republic of Macedonia, 2009 Article IV Consultation," p. 24 (Washington, DC: International Monetary Fund); Biljana Jovanovikj and Danica Unevska Andonova, "The Optimal Level of Foreign Reserves in Macedonia," Working Paper, National Bank of the Republic of Macedonia, p. 5.

60. IEG, "Former Yugoslav Republic of Macedonia," Project Performance Assessment Report 106177, World Bank, June 30, 2016.

61. IMF, "Country Report No. 16/356."

62. National Bank, "Financial Stability Report."

63. IMF, "Country Report No. 15/242."

64. IMF, "Country Report No. 13/178: The Former Yugoslav Republic of Macedonia. Staff Report for the 2013 Article IV Consultation," p. 4 (Washington, DC: International Monetary Fund, 2013); IMF, "Country Report No. 16/356," p. 14.

65. Between 2011 and 2014, Macedonian household NPLs declined from about 8 percent to about 6 percent. During the same period, however, corporate NPLs increased from 10 percent to about 17 percent (World Bank, "FYR Macedonia Partnership Country Program Snapshot April 2015," p. 5 [Washington, DC: World Bank]).

66. Aleksandar Pisarev, "Cross and Crescent Divide Up Macedonia," Balkan-Insight, October 1, 2014.

67. Justin Otten, "Wine Mafia and the Thieving State: Tension and Power at the Crossroads of Neoliberalism and Authoritarianism in 21st Century Macedonia," *Anthropology of East Europe Review* 2 (2013): 2–18.

68. Dimitra Kofti, "Moral Economy of Flexible Production: Fabricating Precarity Between the Conveyor Belt and the Household," *Anthropological Theory* 16, no. 4 (2016): 433–53.

69. Marek Mikuš, *Frontiers of Civil Society: Government and Hegemony in Serbia* (New York: Berghahn Books, 2018), 141.

70. Brković, *Managing Ambiguity*, 83.

71. Sale times for apartments increased from 193 days in 2013 to 234 days in 2014.

72. National Bank, *Financial Stability Report*; Branimir Jovanovic, "When Is There a Kuznets Curve?," 201550, Department of Economics and Statistics, Cognetti de Martiis, Working Papers (Turin, Italy: University of Turin, 2015).

73. Note the difference from postsocialist barter in which companies who had good finances used barter to hide revenues from the state, as in the 1998 Russian financial crisis (Sergei Guriev, Igor Makarov, and Mathilde Maurel, "Debt Overhang and Barter in Russia," *Journal of Comparative Economics* 30, no. 4 [2002]: 635–56). In the Macedonian case, however, kompenzacija could be regulated through official contracts, even if some companies did it through informal channels.

74. Deborah James, *Money from Nothing: Indebtedness and Aspiration in South Africa* (Stanford, CA: Stanford University Press, 2014).

75. Verdery, *What Was Socialism*, 168–203; John Cox, *Fast Money Schemes: Hope and Deception in Papua New Guinea* (Bloomington: Indiana University Press, 2018), 47; Smoki Musaraj, "Tales from Albarado: The Materiality of Pyramid Schemes in Postsocialist Albania," *Cultural Anthropology* 26, no. 1 (2011): 84–110.

76. Verdery, *What Was Socialism*, 91; Woodruff, *Money Unmade*; Humphrey, *Unmaking of Soviet Life*, 24; Douglas Rogers, "Energopolitical Russia: Corporation, State, and the Rise of Social and Cultural Projects," *Anthropological Quarterly* 87, no. 2 (2014): 431–51; Dunn, *Postsocialist Spores*, 249.

Chapter 4

1. Elizabeth Dunn, *No Path Home: Humanitarian Camps and the Grief of Displacement* (Ithaca, NY: Cornell University Press, 2017), 94.

2. Narotzky, "Rethinking the Concept of Labour," 39. See also Sharryn Kasmir and August Carbonella, "Dispossession and the Anthropology of Labor," *Critique of Anthropology* 28, no. 1 (2008): 5–25; Penny Harvey and Christian Krohn-Hansen, "Introduction: Dislocating Labour: Anthropological Reconfigurations," *Journal of the Royal Anthropological Institute* 24, no. S1 (2018): 10–28.

3. Shevchenko, *Crisis and the Everyday*, 15.

188 Notes to Chapter 4

4. Kathleen Millar, "The Tempo of Wageless Work: E. P. Thompson's Time-Sense at the Edges of Rio de Janeiro," *Focaal*, no. 73 (2015): 35; Kathleen Millar, *Reclaiming the Discarded: Life and Labor on Rio's Garbage Dump* (Durham, NC: Duke University Press, 2018). See also Bryonny Goodwin-Hawkins, "Weaving Time in the Textile Valley: Postindustrial Temporality in Rural Northern England," PhD thesis, School of Social and Political Sciences, Faculty of Arts, University of Melbourne, 2013.

5. Tamara Kohn, "Waiting on Death Row," in *Waiting*, edited by Ghassan Hage (Carlton, Australia: Melbourne University Press, 2009), 220.

6. Fordist modes of work were never in the majority in advanced economies, especially in the southeastern periphery of Europe (see Ivan Rajković, "For an Anthropology of the Demoralized: State Pay, Mock-Labour, and Unfreedom in a Serbian Firm," *Journal of the Royal Anthropological Institute* 24, no. 1 [2018]: 47–70; Blim, *Made in Italy*). Yet Fordist workplaces had provided a temporal blueprint for post–World War II workplaces (see E. P. Thompson, *The Making of the English Working Class* [New York: Random House, 1963]). As other ethnographies suggest, it was precisely the disappearance of that ideological framework of progress and discipline that rendered the precariousness of the working classes under financialization particularly problematic (Williams, *Debt for Sale*; Randy Martin, *Financialization of Daily Life* [Philadelphia: Temple University Press, 2002]; Clara Han, *Life in Debt: Times of Care and Violence in Neoliberal Chile* [Berkeley: University of California Press, 2012]; Anne Allison, *Precarious Japan* [Durham, NC: Duke University Press, 2013]).

7. See Engin Isin, "The Neurotic Citizen," *Citizenship Studies* 8, no. 3 (2004): 217–35.

8. Similarly, the capacity to mobilize spatial uncertainty, modulating time and space, has been crucial for protest movements such as the red shirt taxi drivers in Thailand. Without the ability to make mobility in the city uncertain, the movement would have not survived brutal political repression (Claudio Sopranzetti, *Owners of the Map: Motorcycle Taxi Drivers, Mobility, and Politics in Bangkok* [Berkeley: University of California Press, 2017]; Dimitra Kofti, "Moral Economy of Flexible Production: Fabricating Precarity Between the Conveyor Belt and the Household." *Anthropological Theory* 16, no. 4 (2016): 433–53.

9. For traders and other financial brokers who speed up the "decline of the near future" (Jane Guyer, "Prophecy and the Near Future: Thoughts on Macroeconomic, Evangelical, and Punctuated Time," *American Ethnologist* 34, no. 3 [2007]: 411), the cacophony of information and the instantaneous shifts of financial markets present unique opportunities for profit. For these groups, the unpredictability of the global economy constitutes a basis for hedging bets and generating returns and is valued as a positive moral horizon—the literal culture of risk embraced by Wall Street, irrespective of its negative consequences (Ho, *Liquidated*).

10. Typically, workdays began at 7:00 a.m. and ended at 5:00 p.m.

11. Catherine Dolan and Dinah Rajak, "Speculative Futures at the Bottom of the Pyramid," *Journal of the Royal Anthropological Institute* 24, no. 2 (2018): 234.

12. Macedonian banks are owned by foreign investors, with the notable exception of Komercijalna Banka. Stopanska Banka, founded in 1944 and active during socialism, was bought in 2000 by the National Bank of Greece. Alpha Bank is a subsidiary of a Greek bank.

13. Despite making concessions to local municipal mayors—including sponsorships for a local basketball team and the building of a church—Construx had refused to align itself with the ruling party.

14. Guyer, "Prophecy and the Near," 407.

15. Zaira Tiziana Lofranco ("Refurnishing the Home in Post-War Neoliberalism: Consumption Strategies in the Sarajevan Household Economy," *Human Affairs* 25, no. 1 [2015]) argues that home improvement and consumption loans became crucial tools through which former Yugoslav citizens reappropriateed symbolically the economic downturn of postsocialism.

16. The Macedonian Health Fund gives workers vouchers for medical services every month only if the employer has paid his dues (which are linked to salaries).

17. Ghassan Hage, "Waiting Out the Crisis: On Stuckedness and Governmentality," in *Waiting*, edited by Ghassan Hage (Carlton, Australia: Melbourne University Press), 97.

18. Months of work, even without pay, counted toward the total they needed to qualify for the benefits from state pensions.

19. Dolan and Rajak, "Speculative Futures," 234.

20. Rajković, "For an Anthropology," 49.

21. Ernesto de Martino, *Magic: A Theory from the South* (Chicago: HAU Books, 2015).

22. Upon releasing the building permit, each investor has to pay the local administration a fixed municipal tax (around 10–12 percent of the overall value of the building) for such infrastructural work.

23. That, too, was a temporal strategy to defer and defuse emergencies, which had the unpleasant downside of crowding the administrative offices with inquirers in search of answers.

24. If one takes Michael Burawoy's (*The Radiant Past: Ideology and Reality in Hungary's Road to Capitalism* [Chicago: University of Chicago Press, 1992]) ethnographic study of a Hungarian steel factory as paradigmatic of working rhythms under market socialism, it seems clear that workers were largely able to avoid bursts of activity. Burawoy explicitly compares this experience with his work in a similar factory in the US, where the very oppressive work regimes and tight scheduling created constant scrap materials, "hot" periods of work, and impressively long hours around the holiday season. Burawoy did not have to rush to finish his quotas in the Hungarian firm,

not because the work was easier but because of the horizontal forms of solidarity and flexibility that allowed workers to cooperate by having more autonomy in dividing piece rates and activities.

25. Zygmunt Bauman, *Liquid Modernity* (Cambridge: Polity, 2000), 54.

26. Dave Wilson (*Music Making Space: Musicians, Scenes, and Belonging in the Republic of Macedonia*, PhD diss., Department of Ethnomusicology, UCLA, 2015, iii) utilizes the term "sociovirtuosity" to identify how Macedonians "employ and shape various notions of race, ethnicity, musicality, the future, and the past in the service of making spaces for alternative belonging."

27. Daniel M. Knight and Charles Stewart, "Ethnographies of Austerity: Temporality, Crisis and Affect in Southern Europe," *History and Anthropology* 27, no. 1 (2016): 1–18; Noelle Mole, *Labor Disorders in Neoliberal Italy: Mobbing, Well-Being, and the Workplace* (Bloomington: Indiana University Press, 2011), 38.

28. Galina Oustinova-Stjepanovic ("A Catalogue of Vice: A Sense of Failure and Incapacity to Act Among Roma Muslims in Macedonia," *Journal of the Royal Anthropological Institute* 23, no. 2 [2017]: 338–55) describes a very similar process for Roma Sufi communities who tried and failed to introduce new, more stringent religious practices. While for many Roma this process evoked an image of past defeats and marginalization, for construction workers it mobilized a clear path of downfall—from their centrality during socialist times to their current obsolescence, at least in politically disconnected companies.

29. Jon Schubert, "'A Culture of Immediatism': Co-Optation and Complicity in Post-War Angola," *Ethnos* 83, no. 1 (2018): 9. Sally Babidge ("Sustaining Ignorance: The Uncertainties of Groundwater and Its Extraction in the Salar de Atacama, Northern Chile," *Journal of the Royal Anthropological Institute* 25, no. 1 [2019]: 83–102) describes a similar phenomenon, whereby companies banked on their ability to spread uncertainty about the effects of mining, thus perpetuating processes of (potentially) harmful extraction.

30. Craig Jeffrey, "Timepass: Youth, Class, and Time Among Unemployed Young Men in India," *American Ethnologist* 37, no. 3 (2010): 465.

Chapter 5

1. For workers, "queer" constituted a gendered and ethnic category for all the processes that could affect and reduce their own ethnomasculinity. To reproduce this perspective, I use feminine(-ze) and queering rather interchangeably.

2. Carla Freeman, "Is Local: Global as Feminine: Masculine? Rethinking the Gender of Globalization," *Signs: Journal of Women in Culture and Society* 26, no. 4 (2001): 1007–37.

3. Juanita Elias and Christine Beasley, "Hegemonic Masculinity and Globalization: 'Transnational Business Masculinities' and Beyond," *Globalizations* 6, no. 2 (2009): 281–96.

4. See Blim, *Made in Italy*, 10; Andrea Muehlebach, "On Affective Labor in Post-Fordist Italy," *Cultural Anthropology* 26, no. 1 (2011): 68.

5. Linda McDowell, "Life Without Father and Ford: The New Gender Order of Post-Fordism," *Transactions of the Institute of British Geographers* 16, no. 4 (1991): 404.

6. Doreen Massey, *Spatial Divisions of Labour: Social Structures and the Geography of Production* (London: Palgrave, 1984), 222.

7. See Aihwa Ong, *Spirits of Resistance and Capitalist Discipline: Factory Women in Malaysia* (Albany: State University of New York Press, 1987).

8. Freeman, "Is Local: Global," 24. Adrienne Roberts ("Financing Social Reproduction: The Gendered Relations of Debt and Mortgage Finance in Twenty-First-Century America," *New Political Economy* 18, no. 1 [2013]: 21–42; "Finance, Financialization, and the Production of Gender," in *Scandalous Economics: Gender and the Politics of Financial Crises*, edited by Aida Hozic and Jacqui True, 57–78 [New York: Oxford University Press, 2016]) also describes how financialization did not bring about substantial emancipation for women.

9. This was the case especially in the development context (see Lamia Karim, *Microfinance and Its Discontents: Women in Debt in Bangladesh* [Minneapolis: University of Minnesota Press, 2011]; Schuster, *Social Collateral*, 66.

10. See Fisher, *Wall Street*, 95; Sohini Kar and Caroline Schuster, "Comparative Projects and the Limits of Choice: Ethnography and Microfinance in India and Paraguay," *Journal of Cultural Economy* 9, no. 4 (2016): 347–63.

11. Hage, "Waiting Out," 98.

12. Angela McRobbie, "Reflections on Feminism, Immaterial Labour and the Post-Fordist Regime," *New Formations* 70, no. 17 (2011): 68.

13. See Pippa Norris and Roland Inglehart, *Cultural Backlash: Trump, Brexit, and Authoritarian Populism* (New York: Cambridge University Press, 2019).

14. Like many scholars interested in populism, Irena Stefoska and Darko Stojanov ("A Tale in Stone and Bronze: Old/New Strategies for Political Mobilization in the Republic of Macedonia," *Nationalities Papers* 45, no. 3 [2017]: 358) suggest that if Skopje 2014 and its masculine statues mobilized Macedonians, it was because they offered empty signifiers that could be embraced by anyone who shared "a frustration with the status quo." Here, I agree with their analysis. Skopje 2014 and Gruevski's gender ideology generated chaos and paradoxes rather than cohesive new models of identity. Yet I suggest that the act of eroding gender hierarchies and proliferating existential anxieties was, in and of itself, crucial for pushing citizens to subject themselves to the regime.

15. See Robert Connell and James Messerschmidt, "Hegemonic Masculinity Rethinking the Concept," *Gender & Society* 19, no. 6 (2005): 829–59; Gerald Creed, *Masquerade and Postsocialism: Ritual and Cultural Dispossession in Bulgaria* (Bloomington: Indiana University Press, 2011), 70; Matthew Gutmann, *The Meanings of Macho: Being a Man in Mexico City* (Oakland: University of California Press, 1996).

16. Stefoska and Stojanov ("Tale in Stone," 361) argue that this is also a claim against the "diminutive" role that Macedonia was assigned in the SFRJ.

17. Zsófia Lóránd, "Socialist-Era New Yugoslav Feminism Between 'Mainstreaming' and 'Disengagement': The Possibilities for Resistance, Critical Opposition and Dissent," *Hungarian Historical Review* 5, no. 4 (2016): 861.

18. See Chiara Bonfiglioli, "Gender, Labour and Precarity in the South East European Periphery: The Case of Textile Workers in Štip," *Contemporary Southeastern Europe* 1, no. 2 (2014): 7–23; "Feminist Translations in a Socialist Context: The Case of Yugoslavia," *Gender & History* 30, no. 1 (2018): 240–54. Older women I spoke with explicitly confirmed that they had been able to enjoy socialist equality only in the very short period of their lives after being employed but before being married. Obtaining a job emancipated women temporarily from paternal control at home. Once they were married, young brides were faced with new forms of practical and ethical subordination. As many older men and women made clear, women rarely rose to prominent positions in the political or economic life of socialist countries. Libora Oates-Indruchová ("The Void of Acceptable Masculinity During Czech State Socialism: The Case of Radek John's Memento," *Men and Masculinities* 8, no. 4 [2006]: 428–50) signals that in the Czech case, official discourses that referred to work often expunged women from the narrative. Similarly, Éva Fodor ("Smiling Women and Fighting Men: The Gender of the Communist Subject in State Socialist Hungary," *Gender & Society* 16, no. 2 [2002]: 240–63) shows that Hungarian women were treated as if their commitment to the household, itself dictated by socialist policies, prevented them from giving total loyalty to the party (see also Rory Archer and Goran Musić, "Approaching the Socialist Factory and Its Workforce: Considerations from Fieldwork in (Former) Yugoslavia," *Labor History* 58, no. 1 [2017]: 44–66; Garth Massey, Karen Hahn, and Duško Sekulić, "Women, Men, and the 'Second Shift' in Socialist Yugoslavia," *Gender & Society* 9, no. 3 [1995]: 359–79; Kristen Ghodsee, *The Red Riviera: Gender, Tourism, and Postsocialism on the Black Sea* [Durham, NC: Duke University Press, 2005], 41).

19. Elizabeth Brainerd, "Women in Transition: Changes in Gender Wage Differentials in Eastern Europe and the Former Soviet Union," *Industrial & Labor Relations Review* 54, no. 1 (2000): 138–62.

20. See Ivan Simić, "Gender Policies and Amateur Sports in Early Yugoslav Socialism," *International Journal of the History of Sport* 34, no. 9 (2017): 848–61; John Haynes, *New Soviet Man: Gender and Masculinity in Stalinist Soviet Cinema* (Manchester, UK: Manchester University Press, 2003); Barbara Einhorn, *Citizenship in an Enlarging Europe: From Dream to Awakening* (New York: Palgrave, 2006). As Eliot Borenstein (*Overkill: Sex and Violence in Contemporary Russian Popular Culture* [Ithaca, NY: Cornell University Press, 2008]) shows, while pornography had existed in Russia since the Czarist era, it had very little to do with eroticism. Configured as an intellectual exercise that utilized foul language and forbidden imagery, it was soon

pushed underground by the moralizing censorship of the Soviet regime. Because the socialist state conceived of the social and aesthetic dominance of males as being in tension with the egalitarian charge of the industrial worker, the Soviet representations of men and women were moralized rather than inscribed in a sexual context.

21. Ulf Brunnbauer, ed., *(Re)Writing History: Historiography in Southeast Europe After Socialism (Studies on South East Europe)* (Münster, Germany: LIT, 2004), 262–96; Stefan Troebst, "Historical Politics and Historical 'Masterpieces' in Macedonia Before and After 1991," *New Balkan Politics*, no. 6 (2003).

22. In the USSR, especially in Ukraine, ethnicity constituted a political tool for the communist leadership. Ukrainians were first forced to assimilate Russian culture. Subsequently, the USSR co-opted national(ist) hierarchies within the party structure (Rogers Brubaker, *Nationalist Politics and Everyday Ethnicity in a Transylvanian Town* [Princeton, NJ: Princeton University Press, 2006]; Francine Hirsch, *Empire of Nations: Ethnographic Knowledge and the Making of the Soviet Union* [Ithaca, NY: Cornell University Press, 2005]; Emily Channell-Justice, "Left of Maidan: Self-Organization and the Ukrainian State on the Edge of Europe" [PhD diss., Department of Anthropology, CUNY Graduate Center, 2016]).

23. See Gary Bertsch, "Ethnicity and Politics in Socialist Yugoslavia," *Annals of the American Academy of Political and Social Science* 433, no. 1 (1977): 88–99. At the same time, Yugoslav socialism, especially the central organs such as the League of Communists of Yugoslavia, embedded modernist aspirations to erase ethnic specificities (Fabio Mattioli, "Unchanging Boundaries: The Reconstruction of Skopje and the Politics of Heritage," *International Journal of Heritage Studies* 20, no. 6 [2014]: 599–615). Albanian males who lived in Yugoslavia perceived the socialist state as a force that imposed a ceiling on their careers, pushing them into fringe, private professions—a situation perhaps similar to that of ethnic Germans in Romania, who were often excluded from major political roles and suspected of being allies of Western powers (Katherine Verdery, *National Ideology Under Socialism* [Berkeley: University of California Press, 1991]).

24. See Dubravka Zarkov, "Feminism and the Disintegration of Yugoslavia: On the Politics of Gender and Ethnicity," *Social Development Issues* 24, no. 3 (2003): 59–68; Spyros Sofos, "Inter-Ethnic Violence and Gendered Constructions of Ethnicity in Former Yugoslavia," *Social Identities* 2, no. 1 (1996): 73–92; Sasho Lambevski, "Suck My Nation: Masculinity, Ethnicity and the Politics of (Homo)Sex," *Sexualities* 2, no. 4 (1999): 397–419; Julie Mostov, "Sexing the Nation / Desexing the Body: Politics of National Identity in the Former Yugoslavia," in *Gender Ironies of Nationalism: Sexing the Nation*, edited by Tamar Mayer (London: Routledge, 2000), 89–112; Elissa Helms, *Innocence and Victimhood: Gender, Nation, and Women's Activism in Postwar Bosnia-Herzegovina* (Madison: University of Wisconsin Press, 2013), 158; Marko Zivkovic, "Ex-Yugoslav Masculinities Under Female Gaze, or Why Men Skin

Cats, Beat Up Gays and Go to War," *Nationalities Papers* 34, no. 3 (2006): 257–63. In places such as Bosnia, Kosovo, or to a lesser extent, Macedonia, however, vulnerable men from different ethnic backgrounds found new spaces for collective identity in reaffirming their joint superiority over women's bodies (Stef Jansen, "Of Wolves and Men: Postwar Reconciliation and the Gender of Inter-National Encounters," *Focaal*, no. 57 [2010]: 33–49)—a process of aggressively hegemonic gender solidarity that can be observed at play even among working-class citizens who have become far-right supporters. See also Wendy Bracewell, "Rape in Kosovo: Masculinity and Serbian Nationalism," *Nations and Nationalism* 6, no. 4 (2000): 563–90; Nitzan Shoshan, *The Management of Hate: Nation, Affect, and the Governance of Right-Wing Extremism in Germany* (Princeton, NJ: Princeton University Press, 2016), 15; Douglas R. Holmes, *Integral Europe: Fast Capitalism, Multiculturalism, Neofascism* (Princeton, NJ: Princeton University Press, 2000), 109; Don Kalb and Gábor Halmai, *Headlines of Nations, Subtexts of Class: Working Class Populism and the Return of the Repressed in Neoliberal Europe* (New York: Berghahn Books, 2011), 17.

25. Dimova, *Ethno-Baroque: Materiality*; Ilká Thiessen, *Waiting on Macedonia: Identity in a Changing World* (Toronto: Broadview, 2007), 105; Vasiliki Neofotistos, "The Balkans' Other Within: Imaginings of the West in the Republic of Macedonia," *History and Anthropology* 19, no. 1 (2008): 17–36; "Cultural Intimacy and Subversive Disorder: The Politics of Romance in the Republic of Macedonia," *Anthropological Quarterly* 83, no. 2 (2010): 279–315; *The Risk of War: Everyday Sociality in the Republic of Macedonia* (Philadelphia: University of Pennsylvania Press, 2012), 65.

26. See Verdery, *What Was Socialism*; Susan Gal and Gail Kligman, *The Politics of Gender After Socialism: A Comparative-Historical Essay* [Princeton, NJ: Princeton University Press, 2000], 63; Tetyana Bureychak, "Masculinity in Soviet and Post-Soviet Ukraine: Models and Their Implications," in *Gender, Politics, and Society in Ukraine*, edited by Olena Hankivksy and Anastasiya Salnykova (Toronto: Toronto University Press, 2011), 325–61; Zarana Papic, "From State Socialism to State Nationalism: The Case of Serbia in Gender Perspective," *Refuge: Canada's Journal on Refugees* 14, no. 3 (1994): 10–14; Elza Ibroscheva, "Caught Between East and West? Portrayals of Gender in Bulgarian Television Advertisements," *Sex Roles* 57, no. 5 (2007): 409–18; Ericka Johnson, *Dreaming of a Mail-Order Husband: Russian-American Internet Romance* (Durham, NC: Duke University Press, 2007), 88. Postsocialist economies did not always imply increased control (or politicization) of women's bodies. At the same time, however, these new sexual markets set the stage for sex-work migratory patterns that irreversibly affected the lives of women in countries such as Romania, Russia, and Bosnia (Victor Malarek, *The Natashas: The New Global Sex Trade* [Toronto: Penguin Books, 2004, 158]).

27. Jane Pollard, "Gendering Capital: Financial Crisis, Financialization and (an Agenda for) Economic Geography," *Progress in Human Geography* 37, no. 3 (2013):

405. As the transition morphed into a recession, the rise of a survival economy forced many women to invest most of their energy within the household (Rogers, "Moonshine, Money," 70). In some cases, this was a welcome change. Edward Snajdr ("Ethnicizing the Subject: Domestic Violence and the Politics of Primordialism in Kazakhstan," *Journal of the Royal Anthropological Institute* 13, no. 3 [2007]: 603–20) describes the retraditionalization of Kazakh society as a result of women's preference for non-modern identities that privileged strong, patriarchal families. In other cases, women's retrenchment into the private sphere followed the erasure of socialist institutions (Peggy Watson, "Eastern Europe's Silent Revolution: Gender," *Sociology* 27, no. 3 [1993]: 471). Of course there were exceptions: those segments of the female workforce that had been highly educated during socialism, or at the margins of socialist markets, were relatively easily integrated into a capitalist market economy, at least in its early stages when state structures still mattered (Rebecca Jean Emigh and Iván Szelényi, *Poverty, Ethnicity, and Gender in Eastern Europe During the Market Transition* [Westport, CT: Greenwood, 2001], 6; Peter F. Orazem and Milan Vodopivec, "Winners and Losers in Transition: Returns to Education, Experience, and Gender in Slovenia," *World Bank Economic Review* 9, no. 2 [1995]: 201–30; Suzanne LaFont, "One Step Forward, Two Steps Back: Women in the Post-Communist States," *Communist and Post-Communist Studies* 34, no. 2 [2001]: 203–20; Frances Pine, "Dealing with Fragmentation: Consequences of Privatization for Rural Women in Central and Southern Poland," in *Surviving Post-Socialism: Local Strategies and Regional Responses in Eastern Europe and the Former Soviet Union*, edited by Susan Bridger and Frances Pine [London: Routledge, 1998], 106–23).

28. Perhaps nurtured by the socialist attitude that Natalia infused in their everyday interactions, workers preferred to embody an ethos of modest paternalism—in stark contrast to descriptions of European construction sites where women were often the target of predatory behaviors (see Jacqueline Watts, "Leaders of Men: Women 'Managing' in Construction," *Work, Employment & Society* 23, no. 3 [2009]: 512–30; Andrew Agapiou, "Perceptions of Gender Roles and Attitudes Toward Work Among Male and Female Operatives in the Scottish Construction Industry," *Construction Management and Economics* 20, no. 8 [2002]: 697–705). Workers stressed the "dignity" rather than the deprecative dimension of their homosociality even in their visual presentation. When I asked them to strike a pose for a portrait, most of them purposely covered with jackets or other clothing the lone playboy-style calendar that someone had hung in one of the break rooms. They chose to highlight tools or aspects of their working routines in the background and assumed composed, intense stares—closer to the iconography of socialist pamphlets rather than the aggressive postures of Gruevski's macho statues.

29. UNWOMEN, "Writing Women into the Budget: FYR Macedonia Welcomes Its First Strategy on Gender-Responsive Budgeting," August 2012.

30. UNDP, "Strengthening Women's Political Participation," Istanbul, 2016, p. 16; Marcia Greenberg and Kara MacDonald, "Women's Political Participation in the Republic of Macedonia: Opportunities to Support Women in Upcoming Elections—and Beyond," August 2000, Development Alternatives, Inc.; Katerina Ristova-Aasterud, "The Gender Dimension of the EU Enlargement: Case Study of Macedonia as a Candidate Count" (presented at the ECPG Conference, University of Lausanne, June 8, 2017), p. 14.

31. During the decade of Gruevski's rule, the gender gap remained essentially the same, with Macedonia at the 69th position globally (for context, Russia is 75th and Turkey 130th. See World Economic Forum, *The Global Gender Gap Report 2015*, Geneva, 2015, p. 16.) According to the State Statistical Office, *Employees and Net Wages, Statistical Review: Population and Social Statistics* (2007 and 2015), Skopje, in 2006, 11,727 women were employed in the central public administration (CPA) versus 27,616 men; in 2014, the CPA employed 15,557 women and 32,806 men. This means a slight increase in the number of women employed in the CPA (from 29.8 percent to 32.2 percent), which had an overall increase of 9,000 employees, or 18 percent or the workforce. Women also increased their presence in other public sectors that were, however, already predominantly female. These include education (from 56.1 percent to 60.6 percent), social work, and healthcare (from 60 percent to 70.3 percent). In the private sector, the ratio between women and men employed in the manufacturing sector did not change between 2006 and 2014, while women increased their participation in the wholesale and retail sector (from 38.3 percent to 43.2 percent).

32. In the words of the head of the Macedonian antidiscrimination agency, nominated by the VMRO–DPMNE, Western influence had caused a recent rise in the divorce rate (Sinisa Marusic, "Macedonian Divorce Rate Blamed on Women's Rights," BalkanInsight, August 16, 2013). Interestingly, he failed to note that the divorce rate fell in line with the country's economic performance and the spread of illiquidity. In fact, divorces had decreased from 11 percent in 2004 to 8 percent in 2009, only to drastically rise in 2010 to 12 percent and gradually climb to 16 percent in 2015, according to data from the State Statistical Office.

33. Vasiliki Neofotistos, "The Rhetoric of War and the Reshaping of Civil Society in North Macedonia," *Slavic Review* 78, no. 2 (2019): 357.

34. Ainur Begim, "How to Retire like a Soviet Person: Informality, Household Finances, and Kinship in Financialized Kazakhstan," *Journal of the Royal Anthropological Institute* 24, no. 4 (2018): 781.

35. Laura Bear, Ritu Birla, and Stine Simonsen Puri, "Speculation: Futures and Capitalism in India," *Comparative Studies of South Asia, Africa and the Middle East* 35, no. 3 (2015): 388.

36. Sherine Hafez, "No Longer a Bargain: Women, Masculinity, and the Egyptian Uprising," *American Ethnologist* 39, no. 1 (2012): 37–42.

37. Channell-Justice, "Left of Maidan"; Emily Channell-Justice, "'We're Not Just Sandwiches': Europe, Nation, and Feminist (Im)Possibilities on Ukraine's Maidan," *Signs: Journal of Women in Culture and Society* 42, no. 3 (2017): 717–41.

38. See Jane Pollard, "Gendering Capital: Financial Crisis, Financialization and (an Agenda for) Economic Geography," *Progress in Human Geography* 37, no. 3 (2013): 403–23.

Chapter 6

1. Laura Bear, "Capitalist Divination: Popularist Speculators and Technologies of Imagination on the Hooghly River," *Comparative Studies of South Asia, Africa and the Middle East* 35, no 3 (2015): 408.

2. In early 2015, the opposition broadcast tape recordings that exposed the regime's corrupt practices. Suddenly, Macedonians had proof not only of Gruevski's violence and paranoia but also of the regime's inability to control the state machinery. Emboldened, a wide coalition of students, activists, and members of the opposition party mobilized thousands of Macedonians, leading to the occupation of universities and daily marches in the country's capital. To stop these massive protests, Gruevski tried to provoke ethnic conflicts in the northern town of Kumanovo with a two-day battle between special forces and "terrorists," most likely ethnic Albanian criminals, that destroyed an entire neighborhood. When that failed, he reshuffled the government, created an independent prosecutor's office to investigate his government's operations, and planned to hold early elections—while doing everything in his power to circumvent lawful voting procedures (VMRO–DPMNE affiliates had registered up to sixty, sometimes deceased voters in apartments of fifty square meters and given passports to migrants from cities in Albania) or push local courts and journalists into obstructing or discrediting formal inquiries into his past abuses. Gruevski's stalling tactics proved successful. In the 2016 elections, the VMRO–DPMNE won fifty-one seats but proved unable to secure the support of ten more members of Parliament and form a government. After several months of negotiations and boycott from the VMRO–DPMNE, the leader of the opposition, Zoran Zaev, secured a governing coalition.

3. For what "hostile" means in relation to capitalism, see Giovanni Arrighi and Fortunata Piselli, "Capitalist Development in Hostile Environments: Feuds, Class Struggles, and Migrations in a Peripheral Region of Southern Italy," *Review* (Fernand Braudel Center) 10, no. 4 (1987): 649.

4. The question of economic abstraction can be traced back to early debates between formalists and substantivists. See Stephen Gudeman, *The Anthropology of Economy: Community, Market, and Culture* (London: Wiley, 2001), 20; Graeber, *Debt*, 103.

5. Joy Buolamwini, and Timnit Gebru, "Gender Shades: Intersectional Accuracy Disparities in Commercial Gender Classification," Conference on Fairness, Accountability, and Transparency, in *Proceedings of Machine Learning Research* 81 (2018): 1–15.

6. Pitluck, Mattioli, and Souleles, "Finance Beyond Function," 5.

7. Marek Mikuš, "Contesting Household Debt in Croatia: The Double Movement of Financialization and the Fetishism of Money in Eastern European Peripheries," *Dialectical Anthropology* (May 2019): 1–21.

8. Christine Trampusch ("The Financialization of the State: Government Debt Management Reforms in New Zealand and Ireland," *Competition & Change* 23, no. 1 [2019]: 3–22) suggests that the outcomes of financialization are different depending on which agents within the state structure initiate it.

9. Anthropological approaches that centered on political economy were a major driving force in the discipline in the 1970s and 1980s, particularly in the work of Eric Wolf (*Europe and the People Without History* [Berkeley: University of California Press, 1982]), Sidney Mintz (*Sweetness and Power*), Katherine Verdery (*The Vanishing Hectare: Property and Value in Postsocialist Transylvania* [Ithaca, NY: Cornell University Press, 2003]), Ida Susser (*Norman Street*), and Michael Blim (*Made in Italy*). This is not to say that other dominant anthropological approaches to finance completely overlooked the political significance of their case studies. On the contrary, anthropologists interested in Wall Street finance have produced very poignant studies of the cultural assumptions that forged "markets." Peeking behind the doors of traders' pits and into investment funds' hallways, seminal works, such as those by Karen Ho (*Liquidated*), highlighted the political implications of such human (and sometimes technological) performances (Martha Poon, "Scorecards as Devices for Consumer Credit: The Case of Fair, Isaac & Company Incorporated," *Sociological Review* 55 [2007]: 284–306). Almost at the same time, studies that focused on vulnerable populations (see Sohini Kar, *Financializing Poverty: Labor and Risk in Indian Microfinance* [Stanford, CA: Stanford University Press, 2018]; Schuster, *Social Collateral*) articulated political relationships beyond the cultural and performative realm and within that of wealth inequality. Credit for poor women, new forms of digital and mobile money, and mortgages for immigrant populations created new imbalances between the poor and the rich before and after the crisis that often reduced local communities to cogwheels of global financial markets (García-Lamarca and Kaika, "'Mortgaged Lives'"). What often struck me as important as I assessed this literature in light of the Macedonian case was that the two levels of analysis are implicitly connected. Indeed, specific political assumptions and relations between elites make it easier (or harder) for vulnerable populations to be embedded within the global financial mechanism. These everyday financial debts, meanwhile, generate new forms of sociality that contest or corroborate formal political processes—the very forms of government that feed (or regulate) the work of financial traders and wealth managers (Ortiz, "Political Anthropology," 325). Indeed, as the dysfunctional dynamics between workers, managers, and investors demonstrate, their concrete shapes *matter* a great deal—but can be understood only through an organic analysis of a context's political and economic relations (see

also Patrick Neveling and Luisa Steur, "Introduction: Marxian Anthropology Resurgent," *Focaal* 82 [2018]: 1–15).

10. Bear et al., "Gens."

11. As Rebekah Plueckhahn and Terbish Bayartsetseg ("Negotiation, Social Indebtedness, and the Making of Urban Economies in Ulaanbaatar," *Central Asian Survey* 37, no. 3 [2018]: 438–56) suggest, clashes between different logics and practices determine the political configuration of different financial landscapes.

12. Ho, *Liquidated*, 2013; Hirokazu Miyazaki, "Between Arbitrage and Speculation: An Economy of Belief and Doubt," *Economy and Society* 36, no. 3 (2007): 404.

13. Jean Comaroff and John Comaroff, *Millennial Capitalism and the Culture of Neoliberalism* (Durham, NC: Duke University Press, 2001).

14. Leonie Schiffauer, "Dangerous Speculation: The Appeal of Pyramid Schemes in Rural Siberia," *Focaal* 81 (2018): 69.

15. John Cox, "Fast Money Schemes Are Risky Business: Gamblers and Investors in a Papua New Guinean Ponzi Scheme," *Oceania* 84, no. 3 (2014): 289–305, and *Fast Money Schemes: Hope and Deception in Papua New Guinea* (Bloomington: Indiana University Press, 2018); Smoki Musaraj, "Tales from Albarado: The Materiality of Pyramid Schemes in Postsocialist Albania," *Cultural Anthropology* 26, no. 1 (2011): 84–110; Verdery, *What Was Socialism*, 169.

16. Oustinova-Stjepanovic, "Catalogue of Vice," 338.

17. Schubert, *Working the System*, 13.

18. Since the work of Max Gluckman ("Analysis of a Social Situation in Modern Zululand," *Bantu Studies* 14, no. 1 [1940]: 1–30), anthropologists have discussed property as a relationship between people mediated by things. See also Verdery, *Vanishing Hectare*.

19. In financialized economies, rent has increasingly been analyzed as an ability to monopolize the means and infrastructure of value realization (i.e., financial means of payment) rather than those of production (Tullock, *Economics of Special*; Krueger, *Political Economy*). Nevertheless, even where rents are described as a cultural process, motivating, for instance, the predisposition toward risk among financial professionals, they are often within reach in Western countries. Instead of indicating a simple "return independent from labour" (Gudeman, *Anthropology and Economy*, 5) or the ownership of strategic assets such as property or payment networks, the rents I encountered in Macedonia were largely made of future dreams, past sources of bitterness, and contemporary exploitations.

20. There is no doubt that some individuals close to the VMRO–DPMNE were able to extract handsome rewards from Macedonia's financial expansion and to beef up their offshore accounts. But there were only a handful of people in such positions. For most Macedonians, rent had a different political value that went beyond fostering the support of oligarchs dedicated to unproductive activities (see Yates, *Rentier State*;

Schatzberg, *Dialectics of Oppression*). Dysfunctional financial relationships generated a frontier context in which hopes of financial profit became convoluted, exploitative relationships, lacking a clear sense of why they had come into being.

21. Veblen, *Theory*, 106.

22. Nicos Poulantzas, *Classes in Contemporary Capitalism* (New York: Verso, 1975).

23. John Cox, "The Magic of Money and the Magic of the State: Fast Money Schemes in Papua New Guinea," *Oceania* 83, no. 3 (2013): 175.

24. As Lilith Mahmud ("We Have Never Been Liberal: Occidentalist Myths and the Impending Fascist Apocalypse," Hot Spots, Cultural Anthropology [website], 2016) argues, liberalism should be understood as a historical category closely associated with Western enlightenment rather than the only normative horizon of politics.

25. Don Kalb, "Conversations with a Polish Populist: Tracing Hidden Histories of Globalization, Class, and Dispossession in Postsocialism (and Beyond)," *American Ethnologist* 36, no. 2 (2009): 207–23; David Ost, "Workers and the Radical Right in Poland," *International Labor and Working-Class History* 93 (2018): 113–24; Theodora Vetta, "Nationalism Is Back! Radikali and Privatization in Serbia," in *Headlines of Nations, Subtexts of Class: Working Class Populism and the Return of the Repressed in Neoliberal Europe*, edited by Don Kalb and Gábor Halmai, 37–54 (New York: Berghahn Books, 2011); Gilda Zazzara, "'Italians First': Workers on the Right Amidst Old and New Populisms," *International Labor and Working-Class History* 93 (2018): 101–12.

26. See Mehrdat Vahabi, *The Political Economy of Predation* (Cambridge: Cambridge University Press, 2015); Cédric Durant, "De la Prédation à la Rente, Émergence et Stabilisation d'une Oligarchie Capitaliste dans la Métallurgie Russe (1991–2002)," *Géographie Économie et Société* 6, no. 1 (2004): 23–42.

27. Of course, the degree of social support and organization of authoritarian regimes is variable. Certainly, some far-right movements have made white supremacist ideas more widely acceptable in the US and Europe. Robert Horvath (*Putin's Preventive Counter-Revolution: Post-Soviet Authoritarianism and the Spectre of Velvet Revolution* [London: Routledge, 2012], 6) suggests that while Putin did not come to power thanks to a mass movement, his regime is now using various far-right groups to conduct its dirty business, appropriating the very tactics of its grassroots opponents. Paradoxically, even when the regime directly organizes youth groups, the scale of Russian politics allows participants to maintain a degree of personal and collective independence (Julie Hemment, *Youth Politics in Putin's Russia: Producing Patriots and Entrepreneurs* [Bloomington: Indiana University Press, 2015]). That feeling of social possibilities was much more constrained in Gruevski's Macedonia, where quotidian spaces were saturated by a sense of political oppression, especially when they involved economic transactions, even if the regime demonstrated a lesser capacity to mobilize mobs and frame youth groups.

28. Magyar, *Post-Communist*; Bruce Kapferer, "New Formations of Power, the Oligarchic-Corporate State, and Anthropological Ideological Discourse," *Anthropological Theory* 5, no. 3 (2005): 285–99.

29. Saygun Gökarıksel, "The Ends of Revolution: Capitalist De-Democratization and Nationalist Populism in the East of Europe," *Dialectical Anthropology* 41, no. 3 (2017): 207–24.

30. Maura Finkelstein ("Landscapes of Invisibility: Anachronistic Subjects and Allochronous Spaces in Mill Land Mumbai," *City & Society* 27, no. 3 [2015]: 250–71) describes the process of deindustrialization in Mumbai's textile mills as one in which workers who operated these mills in crisis tried to maintain a sense of self-worth despite the declining meaning of their labor. Just like Macedonian construction workers, Mumbai textile workers could neither become "risk-taking" entrepreneurs nor continue with their previous lifestyle. The haunting dimension of their surroundings stemmed from their interstitial position in a disappearing lifestyle—a sort of modern-day bachelor's ball (Pierre Bourdieu, *The Bachelors' Ball: The Crisis of Peasant Society in Béarn*, trans. Richard Nice [Chicago: University of Chicago Press, 2002]).

31. Jeremy Morris, "Hauntology and the Trauma of Social Change: Deindustrializing Communities in Mumbai and Provincial Russia," *City & Society* 30, no. 1 (2018): 149.

32. Ost, *Workers*, 118.

33. See Ariel Russel Hochschild, *Strangers in Their Own Land: Anger and Mourning on the American Right* (New York: New Press, 2016); Christine Walley, *Exit Zero: Family and Class in Postindustrial Chicago* (Chicago: University of Chicago Press, 2013); Ost, *Workers*; Massimiliano Mollona, *Made in Sheffield: An Ethnography of Industrial Work and Politics* (Oxford: Berghahn Books, 2009).

34. Karl Polanyi (*The Great Transformation: The Political and Economic Origins of Our Time* [Boston: Beacon Press, 1944], 236) argued that the political failure to rein in financial logics opened the road for fascist politics in interwar Europe. From his perspective, fascism stemmed from the need to overcome the impasse of liberalism and its inability to fix the globalized market system.

35. Jasmin Mujanović, *Hunger and Fury: The Crisis of Democracy in the Balkans* (New York: Oxford University Press, 2018), 8.

36. See Larisa Kurtović, "Conjuring 'the People,'" *Focaal* 80 (2018): 43–62.

37. Mujanović, *Hunger and Fury*, 45.

38. For a critical review on "competitive authoritarianism" and "hybrid regimes," see Florian Bieber, "Patterns of Competitive Authoritarianism in the Western Balkans," *East European Politics* 34, no. 3 (2018): 337–54.

39. Mattei, "Austerity and Repressive," 1001.

40. Stuart Hall, "The Great Moving Right Show," *Marxism Today*, 1979; Nicos Poulantzas, *State, Power, Socialism* (New York: Verso, 1978).

41. Konings, "Neoliberalism," 743.

42. Ian Bruff, "The Rise of Authoritarian Neoliberalism," *Rethinking Marxism* 26, no. 1 (2014): 125.

43. Jatin Dua, *Captured at Sea: Piracy and Protection in the Indian Ocean* (Berkeley: University of California Press, 2019), 4.

44. Ost ("Workers," 120) refers to this non-corporative dimension of Poland's illiberal regime as that of a "final arbiter." Dunn and Bobick ("Empire Strikes Back," 405) describe a similar process when they emphasize Putin's ability to become the arbiter of a fragile geopolitical conjuncture he had helped to destabilize.

45. Under Gruevski, the VMRO–DPMNE increased its reference to the VMRO movement, which had led guerrilla warfare against the Ottoman Empire, fulfilling "one traditional role of the social bandit" (Keith Brown, *Loyal unto Death: Trust and Terror in Revolutionary Macedonia* [Bloomington: Indiana University Press, 2013], 125).

46. van der Zwan, "Finance and Democracy."

47. Bailey et al. ("Financialising Acute Kidney Injury: From the Practices of Care to the Numbers of Improvement," *Sociology of Health & Illness* 41, no. 5 [2019]: 882–99) suggest that financialization doesn't need acutely abstract financial markets to become a socially relevant force but can produce political effects by virtue of the social relationships it expresses (see also Daniel Tischer, Bill Maurer, and Adam Leaver, "Finance as 'Bizarre Bazaar': Using Documents as a Source of Ethnographic Knowledge," *Organization* 26, no. 4 [2018]: 1–25).

48. Bob Jessop, "Authoritarian Neoliberalism: Periodization and Critique," *South Atlantic Quarterly* 118, no. 2 (2019): 359.

49. Nitzan Shoshan, *The Management of Hate: Nation, Affect, and the Governance of Right-Wing Extremism in Germany*, (Princeton, NJ: Princeton University Press, 2016), 29.

50. Schubert, "'Culture of Immediatism,'" 9.

51. Nur Amali Ibrahim, "Everyday Authoritarianism: A Political Anthropology of Singapore," *Critical Asian Studies* 50, no. 2 (2018): 219–31; Jon Schubert, *Working the System: A Political Ethnography of the New Angola* (Ithaca, NY: Cornell University Press, 2017).

52. For Hugh Gusterson ("Introduction: Robohumans," in *Life by Algorithms: How Roboprocesses Are Remaking Our World*, edited by Caterine Besteman and Hugh Gusterson [Chicago: University of Chicago Press, 2019], 6), "illegible financial maneuvers" that "generate huge profits in short periods of time for small elites" are a defining feature of the contemporary economic system.

53. Caroline Schuster, "Weedy Finance: The Political Life of Resilience in the Paraguayan Countryside" (paper delivered at the Seminar of Anthropology, May 1, 2019, University of Melbourne).

Bibliography

Aalbers, Manuel. 2008. "The Financialization of Home and the Mortgage Market Crisis." *Competition & Change* 12, no. 2: 148–66.

Abrams, Philip. 1988. "Notes on the Difficulty of Studying the State (1977)." *Journal of Historical Sociology* 1, no. 1: 58–89.

Adams, Laura. 2010. *The Spectacular State: Culture and National Identity in Uzbekistan*. Durham, NC: Duke University Press.

Adams, Laura L., and Assel Rustemova. 2009. "Mass Spectacle and Styles of Governmentality in Kazakhstan and Uzbekistan." *Europe-Asia Studies* 61, no. 7: 1249–76.

Agapiou, Andrew. 2002. "Perceptions of Gender Roles and Attitudes Toward Work Among Male and Female Operatives in the Scottish Construction Industry." *Construction Management and Economics* 20, no. 8: 697–705.

Agnew, John. 2001. "How Many Europes? The European Union, Eastward Enlargement and Uneven Development." *European Urban and Regional Studies* 8, no. 1: 29–38.

AIM. 1996. "Armiski Spiunski Skandal," December 12. Accessed October 26, 2018. http://www.aimpress.ch/dyn/pubs/archive/data/199612/61212-002-pubs-sko.htm.

Allison, Anne. 2013. *Precarious Japan*. Durham, NC: Duke University Press.

Aman, Robert. 2012. "The EU and the Recycling of Colonialism: Formation of Europeans Through Intercultural Dialogue." *Educational Philosophy and Theory* 44, no. 9: 1010–23.

Appel, Hannah. 2014. "Occupy Wall Street and the Economic Imagination." *Cultural Anthropology* 29, no. 4: 602–25.

Apostolov, Vlado. 2015. "'Adora' na Cifliganec Partner so Famoznata 'Eksiko' / „Адора" на Чифлиганец партнер со фамозната „Ексико"" ("Adora of Cifliganec Partner with the Famous Eksiko"). Призма (*Prisma*), June 25. Accessed October 26, 2018. http://prizma.mk/adora-na-chifliganets-partner-famoznata-eksiko/.

Archer, Rory. 2018. "The Moral Economy of Home Construction in Late Socialist Yugoslavia." *History and Anthropology* 29, no. 2: 141–62.

Archer, Rory, and Goran Musić. 2017. "Approaching the Socialist Factory and Its Workforce: Considerations from Fieldwork in (Former) Yugoslavia." *Labor History* 58, no. 1: 44–66.

Aronczyk, Melissa. 2013. *Branding the Nation: The Global Business of National Identity*. Oxford: Oxford University Press.

Arrighi, Giovanni. 1994. *The Long Twentieth Century: Money, Power, and the Origins of Our Times*. London: Verso.

Arrighi, Giovanni, and Fortunata Piselli. 1987. "Capitalist Development in Hostile Environments: Feuds, Class Struggles, and Migrations in a Peripheral Region of Southern Italy." *Review* (Fernand Braudel Center) 10, no. 4: 649.

Atkinson, David, and Denis Cosgrove. 1998. "Urban Rhetoric and Embodied Identities: City, Nation, and Empire at the Vittorio Emanuele II Monument in Rome, 1870–1945." *Annals of the Association of American Geographers* 88, no. 1: 28–49.

Babidge, Sally. 2019. "Sustaining Ignorance: The Uncertainties of Groundwater and Its Extraction in the Salar de Atacama, Northern Chile." *Journal of the Royal Anthropological Institute* 25, no. 1: 83–102.

Bacevic, Jana. 2014. *From Class to Identity: The Politics of Education Reforms in Former Yugoslavia*. Budapest: CEU Press.

Badue, Ana Flavia, and Florbela Ribeiro. 2018. "Gendered Redistribution and Family Debt: The Ambiguities of a Cash Transfer Program in Brazil." *Economic Anthropology* 5, no. 2: 261–73.

Bailey, Simon, Dean Pierides, Adam Brisley, Clara Weisshaar, and Thomas Blakeman. 2019. "Financialising Acute Kidney Injury: From the Practices of Care to the Numbers of Improvement." *Sociology of Health & Illness* 41, no. 5: 882–99.

Bauman, Zygmunt. 2000. *Liquid Modernity*. Cambridge: Polity.

BBC. 2014. "Romania and Bulgaria EU Migration Restrictions Lifted," January 1. Accessed June 19, 2019. https://www.bbc.com/news/world-europe-25565302.

Bear, Laura. 2015. "Capitalist Divination: Popularist Speculators and Technologies of Imagination on the Hooghly River." *Comparative Studies of South Asia, Africa and the Middle East* 35, no 3: 408–23.

Bear, Laura, Ritu Birla, and Stine Simonsen Puri. 2015. "Speculation: Futures and Capitalism in India." *Comparative Studies of South Asia, Africa and the Middle East* 35, no. 3: 387–391.

Bear, Laura, Karen Ho, Anna Tsing, and Sylvia Yanagisako. 2015. "Gens: A Feminist Manifesto for the Study of Capitalism." Theorizing the Contemporary, Cultural Anthropology (website). March 30, 2015. Accessed October 26, 2018. https://culanth.org/fieldsights/652-gens-a-feminist-manifesto-for-the-study-of-capitalism.

Begim, Ainur. 2018. "How to Retire like a Soviet Person: Informality, Household

Finances, and Kinship in Financialized Kazakhstan." *Journal of the Royal Anthropological Institute* 24, no. 4: 767–85.

Belford, Aubrey, Saska Cvetkovska, Biljiana Sekulovska, and Stevan Dojcinovic. 2017. "Leaked Documents Show Russian, Serbian Attempts to Meddle in Macedonia." OCCRP, June 4. Accessed October 26, 2018. https://www.occrp.org/en/spooksand spin/leaked-documents-show-russian-serbian-attempts-to-meddle-in-macedonia/.

Bell, Stephen, and Andrew Hindmoor. 2017. "Structural Power and the Politics of Bank Capital Regulation in the United Kingdom." *Political Studies* 65, no. 1: 103–21.

Belojevikj, Bela, and Fabio Mattioli. 2017. "Etnografia di una Crisi Normale: Crisiscape, Vrski e Riflessione Antropologica a Skopje, Macedonia" (Ethnography of a Normal Crisis: Crisiscape, Vrski, and Anthropological Reflection). In *Oltre Adriatico e Ritorno: Percorsi Antropologici tra Italia e Sudest Europa* (Beyond the Adriatic and Back: Anthropological Pathways Between Italy and Southeast Europe), edited by Antonio Pusceddu and Tiziana Lofranco, 57–86. Milan: Meltemi.

Bertsch, Gary. 1977. "Ethnicity and Politics in Socialist Yugoslavia." *Annals of the American Academy of Political and Social Science* 433, no. 1: 88–99.

Beton. 2016. "History of Beton." Accessed October 26, 2018. http://www.beton.com .mk/en/docs/history.pdf.

Bieber, Florian. 2018. "Patterns of Competitive Authoritarianism in the Western Balkans." *East European Politics* 34, no. 3: 337–54.

Björklund Larsen, Lotta. 2018. *A Fair Share of Tax: A Fiscal Anthropology of Contemporary Sweden*. London: Palgrave Macmillan.

Blim, Michael. 1990. *Made in Italy: Small-Scale Industrialization and Its Consequences*. New York: Praeger.

Bockman, Johanna. 2017. "From Socialist Finance to Peripheral Financialization: The Yugoslav Experience." Presentation with Fabio Mattioli, Center for Place, Culture and Politics, CUNY Graduate Center, November 15.

Bohannan, Paul, and Laura Bohannan. 1968. *Tiv Economy*. Evanston, IL: Northwestern University Press.

Bohle, Dorothee. 2018. "European Integration, Capitalist Diversity and Crisis Trajectories on Europe's Eastern Periphery." *New Political Economy* 23, no. 2: 239–53.

Bonfiglioli, Chiara. 2014. "Gender, Labour and Precarity in the South East European Periphery: The Case of Textile Workers in Štip." *Contemporary Southeastern Europe* 1, no. 2: 7–23.

———. 2018. "Feminist Translations in a Socialist Context: The Case of Yugoslavia." *Gender & History* 30, no. 1: 240–54.

Borenstein, Eliot. 2008. *Overkill: Sex and Violence in Contemporary Russian Popular Culture*. Ithaca, NY: Cornell University Press.

Böröcz, József. 2001. "Introduction: Empire and Coloniality in the 'Eastern Enlargement' of the European Union." In *Empire's New Clothes: Unveiling European*

Enlargement, edited by József Böröcz and Melinda Kovacs, 1–50. Holly Cottage, UK: Central European Review.

Böröcz, József, and Mahua Sarkar. 2005. "What Is the EU?" *International Sociology* 20, no. 2: 153–73.

Bourdieu, Pierre. 2002. *The Bachelors' Ball: The Crisis of Peasant Society in Béarn.* Translated by Richard Nice. Chicago: University of Chicago Press.

Bozinovska, Vesna. 2006. "Kade Isceznaa 50 milioni Evra?! Каде исчезнаа 50 милиони евра?!" (Where Did 50 Million Euro Go?). Вечер (Vecer). Accessed October 26, 2018. https://vecer.mk/makedonija/kade-ischeznaa-50-milioni-evra.

Bracewell, Wendy. 2000. "Rape in Kosovo: Masculinity and Serbian Nationalism." *Nations and Nationalism* 6, no. 4: 563–90.

Brainerd, Elizabeth. 2000. "Women in Transition: Changes in Gender Wage Differentials in Eastern Europe and the Former Soviet Union." *Industrial & Labor Relations Review* 54, no. 1: 138–62.

Brković, Čarna. 2017. *Managing Ambiguity: How Clientelism, Citizenship and Power Shape Personhood in Bosnia and Herzegovina.* New York: Berghahn Books.

Brown, Keith. 2013. *Loyal unto Death: Trust and Terror in Revolutionary Macedonia.* Bloomington: Indiana University Press.

Brubaker, Rogers. 2006. *Nationalist Politics and Everyday Ethnicity in a Transylvanian Town.* Princeton, NJ: Princeton University Press.

Bruff, Ian. 2014. "The Rise of Authoritarian Neoliberalism." *Rethinking Marxism* 26, no. 1: 113–29.

Brunnbauer, Ulf, ed. 2004. *(Re)Writing History. Historiography in Southeast Europe After Socialism (Studies on South East Europe).* Münster, Germany: LIT.

Bryer, Rob. 2016. "Socialism, Accounting, and the Creation of 'Consensus Capitalism' in America, circa 1935–1955." *Critical Perspectives on Accounting* 34 (January): 1–35.

Buolamwini, Joy, and Timnit Gebru. 2018. "Gender Shades: Intersectional Accuracy Disparities in Commercial Gender Classification." Conference on Fairness, Accountability, and Transparency. In *Proceedings of Machine Learning Research* 81:1–15.

Burawoy, Michael. 1992. *The Radiant Past: Ideology and Reality in Hungary's Road to Capitalism.* Chicago: University of Chicago Press.

Bureychak, Tetyana. 2011. "Masculinity in Soviet and Post-Soviet Ukraine: Models and Their Implications." In *Gender, Politics, and Society in Ukraine*, edited by Olena Hankivksy and Anastasiya Salnykova, 325–61. Toronto: Toronto University Press.

Burgio, Alberto. 1999. *Nel Nome della Razza: Il Razzismo nella Storia d'Italia 1870–1945* (In the Name of Race: Racism in Italian History 1870–1945). Bologna: Il Mulino.

Caprotti, Federico. 2007. *Mussolini's Cities: Internal Colonialism in Italy, 1930–1939*. Youngstown, OH: Cambria Press.

Carruthers, Bruce G., and Arthur L. Stinchcombe. 1999. "The Social Structure of Liquidity: Flexibility, Markets, and States." *Theory and Society* 28, no. 3: 353–82.

CBRF. 2016. "On Revocation of Banking Licence of the Credit Institution JSCB Euro-Axis Bank and Appointment of Provisional Administration." Accessed October 26, 2018. http://www.cbr.ru/eng/press/PR/?file=27052016_101841eng2016-05-27T10_16_56.htm.

Cellarius, Barbara A. 2000. "'You Can Buy Almost Anything with Potatoes': An Examination of Barter During Economic Crisis in Bulgaria." *Ethnology* 39, no. 1: 73–92.

CFCD. 2017. "Contracted Projects." Accessed October 26, 2018. http://cfcd.finance.gov.mk/?page_id=852.

Channell-Justice, Emily. 2016. "Left of Maidan: Self-Organization and the Ukrainian State on the Edge of Europe." PhD diss., Department of Anthropology, CUNY Graduate Center.

———. 2017. "'We're Not Just Sandwiches': Europe, Nation, and Feminist (Im)Possibilities on Ukraine's Maidan." *Signs: Journal of Women in Culture and Society* 42, no. 3: 717–41.

Christophers, Brett. 2015. "The Limits to Financialization." *Dialogues in Human Geography* 5, no. 2: 183–200.

Cloutier, Eric. 2016. "NPL Monitor for the CESEE." 1H. Vienna Initiative. Accessed October 26, 2018. http://npl.vienna-initiative.com/wp-content/uploads/sites/2/2016/03/NPL-Monitor-1H-2016.pdf.

Coles, Kimberley. 2007. *Democratic Designs: International Intervention and Electoral Practices in Postwar Bosnia-Herzegovina*. Ann Arbor: University of Michigan Press.

Comaroff, Jean, and John Comaroff. 2001. *Millennial Capitalism and the Culture of Neoliberalism*. Durham, NC: Duke University Press.

Connell, Robert, and James Messerschmidt. 2005. "Hegemonic Masculinity Rethinking the Concept." *Gender & Society* 19, no. 6: 829–59.

Connolly, Bernard. 1995. *The Rotten Heart of Europe: The Dirty War for Europe's Money*. London: Faber and Faber.

Coronil, Fernando. 1997. *The Magical State: Nature, Money, and Modernity in Venezuela*. Chicago: University of Chicago Press.

Cox, John. 2013. "The Magic of Money and the Magic of the State: Fast Money Schemes in Papua New Guinea." *Oceania* 83, no. 3: 175–91.

———. 2014. "Fast Money Schemes Are Risky Business: Gamblers and Investors in a Papua New Guinean Ponzi Scheme." *Oceania* 84, no. 3: 289–305.

———. 2018. *Fast Money Schemes: Hope and Deception in Papua New Guinea*. Bloomington: Indiana University Press.

Creed, Gerald. 2011. *Masquerade and Postsocialism: Ritual and Cultural Dispossession in Bulgaria*. Bloomington: Indiana University Press.

Crehan, Kate. 2016. *Gramsci's Common Sense*. Durham, NC: Duke University Press.

CREST Online Collection, General CIA Records, partially available under FOIA Act at https://www.cia.gov/library/readingroom/collection/general-cia-records.

Da Costa, Lamartine, and Plinio Labriola. 1999. "Bodies from Brazil: Fascist Aesthetics in a South American Setting." *International Journal of the History of Sport* 16, no. 4: 163–80.

Dawisha, Karen. 2014. *Putin's Kleptocracy: Who Owns Russia?* New York: Simon & Schuster.

De Goede, Marieke. 2005. *Virtue, Fortune, and Faith: A Genealogy of Finance*. Minneapolis: University of Minnesota Press.

Del Boca, Angelo. 2005. *Italiani Brava Gente?* (Italians Are Good People?) Milan: Neri Pozza.

De Martino, Ernesto. 2012. "Crisis of Presence and Religious Reintegration." Prefaced and translated by Tobia Farnetti and Charles Stewart. *HAU: Journal of Ethnographic Theory* 2, no. 2: 431–50.

———. 2015. *Magic: A Theory from the South*. Chicago: HAU Books.

Despeyroux, Jean. 1968. "Le Séisme de Skopje: Ses Enseignements en Matière de Protection Antisismique. Aperçu des Problèmes de la Construction Antisismique en Yougoslavie et de la Reconstruction de Skopje" (The Skopje Earthquake: Its Teachings on the Subject of Antiseismic Protection. A Look at Problems of Antiseismic Construction in Yugoslavia and at the Reconstruction of Skopje). In *The Earthquake in Skopje: Its Teachings Regarding Antiseismic Protection: Summary of the Problems of the Antiseismic Construction in Yugoslavia and in Skopje*, edited by UNESCO Assistance Mission, 145–77. Amsterdam: UNESCO Press.

Dimitrov, Martin. 2009. "From Spies to Oligarchs: The Party, the State, the Secret Police, and Property Transformations in Postcommunist Europe." Presented at the *1989: Twenty Years After* conference, University of California, Irvine.

Dimova, Rozita. 2013. *Ethno-Baroque: Materiality, Aesthetics and Conflict in Modern-Day Macedonia*. New York: Berghahn Books.

Dojcinovic, Stevan, Saska Cetkovska, Biljiana Sekulovska, Bojana Jovanovic, Bojana Pavlovic, and Aubrey Belford. 2017. "Investigation: Serbia's Involvement in the Macedonian Crisis." *Balkanist*, May 30. Accessed October 26, 2018. https://balkanist.net/investigation-serbias-involvement-in-the-macedonian-crisis/.

Dolan, Catherine, and Dinah Rajak. 2018. "Speculative Futures at the Bottom of the Pyramid." *Journal of the Royal Anthropological Institute* 24, no. 2: 233–55.

Donadio, Rachel, and Elisabetta Povoledo. 2011. "Berlusconi Resigns After Italy's Parliament Approves Austerity Measures." *New York Times*, November 13. Accessed October 26, 2018. https://www.nytimes.com/2011/11/13/world/europe/silvio-berlusconi-resign-italy-austerity-measures.html.

Dua, Jatin. 2019. *Captured at Sea: Piracy and Protection in the Indian Ocean*. Berkeley: University of California Press.

Duffin, Claire, and Ruth Sutherland. 2017. "SamCam's Fashion Line's Links with a Macedonian Tycoon." *Daily Mail*, February 17. Accessed October 26, 2018. http://www.dailymail.co.uk/~/article-4236122/index.html.

Dunn, Elizabeth. 2008. "Postsocialist Spores: Disease, Bodies, and the State in the Republic of Georgia." *American Ethnologist* 35, no. 2: 243–58.

———. 2017. *No Path Home: Humanitarian Camps and the Grief of Displacement*. Ithaca, NY: Cornell University Press.

Dunn, Elizabeth, and Michael Bobick. 2014. "The Empire Strikes Back: War Without War and Occupation Without Occupation in the Russian Sphere of Influence." *American Ethnologist* 41, no. 3: 405–13.

Durant, Cédric. 2004. "De la Prédation à la Rente, Émergence et Stabilisation d'une Oligarchie Capitaliste dans la Métallurgie Russe (1991–2002)" (From Predation to Rent, Emergence, and Stabilization of a Capitalist Oligarchy in the Russian Metallurgic Sector [1991–2002]). *Géographie Économie et Société* 6, no. 1: 23–42.

Dyker, David. 1990. *Yugoslavia: Socialism, Development, and Debt*. London: Routledge.

Einhorn, Barbara. 2006. *Citizenship in an Enlarging Europe: From Dream to Awakening*. New York: Palgrave.

Elias, Juanita, and Christine Beasley. 2009. "Hegemonic Masculinity and Globalization: 'Transnational Business Masculinities' and Beyond." *Globalizations* 6, no. 2: 281–96.

Elyachar, Julia. 2005. *Markets of Dispossession: NGOs, Economic Development, and the State in Cairo*. Durham, NC: Duke University Press.

Emigh, Rebecca Jean, and Iván Szelényi. 2001. *Poverty, Ethnicity, and Gender in Eastern Europe During the Market Transition*. Westport, CT: Greenwood.

Eurostat. 2018. *Production in Construction: Annual Data*. Accessed on October 26, 2018. https://ec.europa.eu/eurostat/.

Fernandez, Rodrigo, and Angela Wigger. 2016. "Lehman Brothers in the Dutch Offshore Financial Centre: The Role of Shadow Banking in Increasing Leverage and Facilitating Debt." *Economy and Society* 45, no. 3: 407–30.

Ferry, Elizabeth. 2005. "Geologies of Power: Value Transformations of Mineral Specimens from Guanajuato, Mexico." *American Ethnologist* 32, no. 3: 420–36.

Fifkfak, Jurij, Joze Princic, Jeffrey Turk, and Tatiana Sencar. 2008. "To Be a Director in Time of Socialism: Between Ideas and Practice." In *Biti Direktor v Casu Socializma: Med Idejami in Praksami*, edited by Jurij Fikfak and Joze Princic, 267–78. Ljubljana, Slovenia: Zalozba ZRC.

Finkelstein, Maura. 2015. "Landscapes of Invisibility: Anachronistic Subjects and Allochronous Spaces in Mill Land Mumbai." *City & Society* 27, no. 3: 250–71.

Fisher, Melissa. 2012. *Wall Street Women*. Durham, NC: Duke University Press.

Fodor, Éva. 2002. "Smiling Women and Fighting Men: The Gender of the Communist Subject in State Socialist Hungary." *Gender & Society* 16, no. 2: 240–63.

Forlenza, Rosario. 2012. "Sacrificial Memory and Political Legitimacy in Postwar Italy: Reliving and Remembering World War II." *History & Memory* 24, no. 2: 73–116.

Freeman, Carla. 2001. "Is Local: Global as Feminine: Masculine? Rethinking the Gender of Globalization." *Signs: Journal of Women in Culture and Society* 26, no. 4: 1007–37.

Furubotn, Eirik, and Svetozar Pejovich. 1973. "Property Rights, Economic Decentralization, and the Evolution of the Yugoslav Firm, 1965–1972." *Journal of Law and Economics* 16, no. 2: 275–302.

Gagyi, Agnes. 2016. "'Coloniality of Power' in East Central Europe: External Penetration as Internal Force in Post-Socialist Hungarian Politics." *Journal of World-Systems Research* 22, no. 2: 349–72.

Gal, Susan, and Gail Kligman. 2000. *The Politics of Gender After Socialism: A Comparative-Historical Essay*. Princeton, NJ: Princeton University Press.

Gambarotto, Francesca, and Stefano Solari. 2015. "The Peripheralization of Southern European Capitalism Within the EMU." *Review of International Political Economy* 22, no. 4: 788–812.

Ganev, Venelin. 2007. *Preying on the State: The Transformation of Bulgaria After 1989*. Ithaca, NY: Cornell University Press.

Gapinski, James. 1993. *The Economic Structure and Failure of Yugoslavia*. New York: Praeger.

García-Lamarca, Melissa, and Maria Kaika. 2016. "'Mortgaged Lives': The Biopolitics of Debt and Housing Financialisation." *Transactions of the Institute of British Geographers* 41, no. 3: 313–27.

Garcia Mora, Alfonso, Andrey Milyutin, and Simon Walley. 2013. *Europe and Central Asia Housing Finance Crisis Prevention and Resolution: A Review of Policy Options*. Washington, DC: World Bank.

Ghertner, Asher. 2015. *Rule by Aesthetics: World-Class City Making in Delhi*. New York: Oxford University Press.

Ghodsee, Kristen. 2005. *The Red Riviera: Gender, Tourism, and Postsocialism on the Black Sea*. Durham, NC: Duke University Press.

Gjorgjioska, Adela. 2015. "The Case of the Macedonian Telekom: An Entangled Web of International Political and Business Corruption." Lefteast, December 28. Accessed October 22, 2018. http://www.criticatac.ro/lefteast/the-case-of-the-macedonian-telekom-an-entangled-web-of-international-political-and-business-corruption/.

Gluckman, Max. 1940. "Analysis of a Social Situation in Modern Zululand." *Bantu Studies* 14, no. 1: 1–30.

Gökarıksel, Saygun. 2017. "The Ends of Revolution: Capitalist De-Democratization and Nationalist Populism in the East of Europe." *Dialectical Anthropology* 41, no. 3: 207–24.

Golubchikov, Oleg. 2010. "World-City-Entrepreneurialism: Globalist Imaginaries, Neoliberal Geographies, and the Production of New St Petersburg." *Environment and Planning A: Economy and Space* 42, no. 3: 626–43.

Goodwin-Hawkins, Bryonny. 2013. "Weaving Time in the Textile Valley: Postindustrial Temporality in Rural Northern England." PhD thesis, School of Social and Political Sciences, Faculty of Arts, University of Melbourne.

Graan, Andrew. 2013. "Counterfeiting the Nation? Skopje 2014 and the Politics of Nation Branding in Macedonia." *Cultural Anthropology* 28, no. 1: 161–79.

Graeber, David. 2011. *Debt: The First 5,000 Years*. Brooklyn, NY: Melville House.

Gramsci, Antonio. 1992. *Prison Notebooks, Volume 1*. Edited by Joseph A. Buttigieg and Antonio Callari. New York: Columbia University Press.

Granit. 2019. "About Us." Accessed October 22, 2018. https://www.granit.com.mk /about-us/.

Grant, Bruce. 2014. "Edifice Complex: Architecture and the Political Life of Surplus in the New Baku." *Public Culture* 26, no. 3: 501–28.

Green, Paul. 2015. "Mobility, Subjectivity and Interpersonal Relationships: Older, Western Migrants and Retirees in Malaysia and Indonesia." *Asian Anthropology* 14, no. 2: 150–65.

Greenberg, Marcia, and Kara MacDonald. 2000. "Women's Political Participation in the Republic of Macedonia: Opportunities to Support Women in Upcoming Elections—and Beyond." Development Alternatives, Inc. August 2000. Accessed October 26, 2018. https://pdf.usaid.gov/pdf_docs/PNACM344.pdf.

Gudeman, Stephen. 2001. *The Anthropology of Economy: Community, Market, and Culture*. London: Wiley.

———. 2012. *Economy's Tension: The Dialectics of Community and Market*. New York: Berghahn Books.

———. 2016. *Anthropology and Economy*. Cambridge: Cambridge University Press.

Guriev, Sergei, Igor Makarov, and Mathilde Maurel. 2002. "Debt Overhang and Barter in Russia." *Journal of Comparative Economics* 30, no. 4: 635–56.

Gusterson, Hugh. 2019. "Introduction: Robohumans." In *Life by Algorithms: How Roboprocesses Are Remaking Our World*, edited by Catherine Besteman and Hugh Gusterson, 1–30. Chicago: University of Chicago Press.

Gutmann, Matthew. 1996. *The Meanings of Macho: Being a Man in Mexico City*. Oakland: University of California Press.

Guyer, Jane. 2007. "Prophecy and the Near Future: Thoughts on Macroeconomic, Evangelical, and Punctuated Time." *American Ethnologist* 34, no. 3: 409–21.

Hafez, Sherine. 2012. "No Longer a Bargain: Women, Masculinity, and the Egyptian Uprising." *American Ethnologist* 39, no. 1: 37–42.

Hage, Ghassan. 2009. "Waiting Out the Crisis: On Stuckedness and Governmentality." In *Waiting*, edited by Ghassan Hage, 97–106. Carlton, Australia: Melbourne University Press.

Hall, Stuart. 1979. "The Great Moving Right Show." *Marxism Today*.

Han, Clara. 2012. *Life in Debt: Times of Care and Violence in Neoliberal Chile*. Berkeley: University of California Press.

Hardie, Ian. 2012. *Financialization and Government Borrowing Capacity in Emerging Markets*. London: Palgrave Macmillan.

Harvey, David. 1989. *The Condition of Postmodernity: An Enquiry into the Origins of Cultural Change*. Oxford: Blackwell.

———. 2003. *The New Imperialism*. New York: Oxford University Press.

———. 2005. *Paris, Capital of Modernity*. New York: Routledge.

———. 2007. *Limits to Capital*. New York: Verso.

Harvey, Penny, and Christian Krohn-Hansen. 2018. "Introduction: Dislocating Labour: Anthropological Reconfigurations." *Journal of the Royal Anthropological Institute* 24, no. S1: 10–28.

Haynes, John. 2003. *New Soviet Man: Gender and Masculinity in Stalinist Soviet Cinema*. Manchester, UK: Manchester University Press.

Helms, Elissa. 2013. *Innocence and Victimhood: Gender, Nation, and Women's Activism in Postwar Bosnia-Herzegovina*. Madison: University of Wisconsin Press.

Hemment, Julie. 2015. *Youth Politics in Putin's Russia: Producing Patriots and Entrepreneurs*. Bloomington: Indiana University Press.

Herzfeld, Michael. 2009. *Evicted from Eternity: The Restructuring of Modern Rome*. Chicago: University of Chicago Press.

Hilferding, Rudolph. 1910; 1981. *Finance Capital: A Study of the Latest Phase of Capitalist Development*. London: Routledge.

Hirsch, Francine. 2005. *Empire of Nations: Ethnographic Knowledge and the Making of the Soviet Union*. Ithaca, NY: Cornell University Press.

Ho, Karen. 2009. *Liquidated: An Ethnography of Wall Street*. Durham, NC: Duke University Press.

———. 2018. "Markets, Myths, and Misrecognitions: Economic Populism in the Age of Financialization and Hyperinequality." *Economic Anthropology* 5, no. 1: 148–50.

Hochschild, Ariel Russel. 2016. *Strangers in Their Own Land: Anger and Mourning on the American Right*. New York: New Press.

Holleran, Max. 2014. "'Mafia Baroque': Post-Socialist Architecture and Urban Planning in Bulgaria." *British Journal of Sociology* 65, no. 1: 21–42.

Holmes, Douglas R. 2000. *Integral Europe: Fast Capitalism, Multiculturalism, Neofascism*. Princeton, NJ: Princeton University Press.

———. 2013. *Economy of Words: Communicative Imperatives in Central Banks*. Chicago: University of Chicago Press.

Horvat, Robert, and Bojana Korosec. 2015. "The Role of Accounting in a Society: Only a Techn(Olog)Ical Solution for the Problem of Economic Measurement or Also a Tool of Social Ideology?" *Naše Gospodarstvo / Our Economy* 61, no. 4: 32–40.

Horvath, Robert. 2012. *Putin's Preventive Counter-Revolution: Post-Soviet Authoritarianism and the Spectre of Velvet Revolution.* London: Routledge.

Humphrey, Caroline. 1985. "Barter and Economic Disintegration." *Man*, New Series 20, no. 1: 48–72.

———. 2002. *The Unmaking of Soviet Life: Everyday Economies After Socialism.* Ithaca, NY: Cornell University Press.

Humphrey, Caroline, and Stephen Hugh-Jones. 1992. *Barter, Exchange and Value: An Anthropological Approach.* Cambridge: Cambridge University Press.

Ibrahim, Nur Amali. 2018. "Everyday Authoritarianism: A Political Anthropology of Singapore." *Critical Asian Studies* 50, no. 2: 219–31.

Ibroscheva, Elza. 2007. "Caught Between East and West? Portrayals of Gender in Bulgarian Television Advertisements." *Sex Roles* 57, no. 5: 409–18.

IEG. 2016. "Former Yugoslav Republic of Macedonia." Project Performance Assessment Report 106177, June 30. World Bank.

IMF. 2009. "Minutes of Executive Board Meeting 09/123-3. Former Yugoslav Republic of Macedonia–2009 Article IV Consultation." Washington, DC: International Monetary Fund.

———. 2013. "Country Report No. 13/178: The Former Yugoslav Republic of Macedonia. Staff Report for the 2013 Article IV Consultation." Washington, DC: International Monetary Fund.

———. 2015. "Country Report No. 15/242: The Former Yugoslav Republic of Macedonia. Staff Report for the 2014 Article IV Consultation." Washington, DC: International Monetary Fund.

———. 2016. "Country Report No. 16/356: The Former Yugoslav Republic of Macedonia. Staff Report for the 2016 Article IV Consultation." Washington, DC: International Monetary Fund.

Institute for Public Health of the Republic of Macedonia. 2015. "Information About the Air Pollution in Cities in the Republic of Macedonia and Possible Risks to Health." Accessed October 22, 2018. http://www.iph.mk/en/information-about-the-air-pollution-in-cities-in-the-republic-of-macedonia-and-possible-risks-to-health/.

Isin, Engin. 2004. "The Neurotic Citizen." *Citizenship Studies* 8, no. 3: 217–35.

Ivanovski, Jovan. 2008. "Decoding Postsocialist Transition on the Case of Skopje: Housing in the Arena of Private Interest and the Emergence of New Urban Prototypes." Master's thesis, Department of Architecture, Dessau Institute of Architecture.

James, Deborah. 2014. *Money from Nothing: Indebtedness and Aspiration in South Africa.* Stanford, CA: Stanford University Press.

Janchevska, Marjana. 2014. "The Importance of FDI in the Macedonian Economy." Master's thesis, Department of Economics, University of Ljubljana.

Janev, Aleksandar. 2017. "Fanfari za 3.8 Milijardi, Fabriki za Polovina Milijarda Evra /

Фанфари за 3,8 милијарди, фабрики за половина милијарда евра" (Fanfare for 3.8 Billion Euro, Factories for Half a Billion Euro). Призма (*Prisma*), January 23. Accessed October 26, 2018. http://prizma.mk/fanfari-za-3-8-milijardi-fabriki-za-polovina-milijarda-evra/.

Janev, Goran. 2011. "Ethnocratic Remaking of Public Space: Skopje 2014." *EFLA Journal* 1: 33–36.

Jansen, Stef. 2009. "After the Red Passport: Towards an Anthropology of the Everyday Geopolitics of Entrapment in the EU's 'Immediate Outside.'" *Journal of the Royal Anthropological Institute* 15, no. 4: 815–32.

———. 2010. "Of Wolves and Men: Postwar Reconciliation and the Gender of Inter-National Encounters." *Focaal*, no. 57: 33–49.

Jasarevic, Larisa. 2017. *Health and Wealth on the Bosnian Market: Intimate Debt.* Bloomington: Indiana University Press.

Jeffrey, Craig. 2010. "Timepass: Youth, Class, and Time Among Unemployed Young Men in India." *American Ethnologist* 37, no. 3: 465–81.

Jessop, Bob. 2019. "Authoritarian Neoliberalism: Periodization and Critique." *South Atlantic Quarterly* 118, no. 2: 343–61.

Johnson, Ericka. 2007. *Dreaming of a Mail-Order Husband: Russian-American Internet Romance.* Durham, NC: Duke University Press.

Jordanovska, Meri. 2015. "Todor Mircevski: Liceto Sto go Povrzuva 'Eksiko' so Kamcev Тодор Мирчевски — лицето што го поврзува „Ексико" со Камчев" (Todor Mircevski, the person who connects Eksiko with Kamcev). Призма (*Prisma*), March 31. Accessed October 26, 2018. http://prizma.mk/todor-mirchevski-litseto-shto-go-povrzuva-eksiko-kamchev/.

———. 2016. "Direktorot na Makedonski Telekom bil Sopstvenik na Misteriosnata 'Eksiko' / Директорот на Македонски Телеком бил сопственик на мистериозната „Ексико"" (The Director of the Macedonian Telekom Was the Owner of the Mysterious Company Eksiko). Призма (*Prisma*), May 27. Accessed October 26, 2018. http://prizma.mk/direktorot-na-makedonski-telekom-bil-sopstvenik-na-misterioznata-eksiko/.

Jordanovska, Meri, and Vlado Apostolov. 2016. "Od Tesorot na MVR 'Ispumpani' 860.000 evra / Од трезорот на МВР „испумпани" 860.000 евра" (From the Budget of the Ministry of the Interior 860,000 Euro Were 'Pumped Out'). Призма (*Prisma*), September 28. Accessed October 26, 2018. http://prizma.mk/od-trezorot-na-mvr-ispumpani-860-000-evra/.

Jovanovic, Branimir. 2015. "When Is There a Kuznets Curve?" 201550. Department of Economics and Statistics, Cognetti de Martiis. Working Papers. Turin, Italy: University of Turin.

———. 2016. "The Real Price of the Cheap Labour Force." Accessed October 26, 2018. http://www.isshs.edu.mk/the-real-price-of-the-cheap-labour-force/.

Jovanovic-Weiss, Srdjan. 2009. Paper presented at Forum Skopje 2009: *The Aftershock of the Postmodernism*, Mala Stanica, Skopje, Macedonia, June 8–14.

Jovanovikj, Biljana, and Danica Unevska Andonova. 2017. "The Optimal Level of Foreign Reserves in Macedonia." Working Paper, p. 5. National Bank of the Republic of Macedonia.

Kalaitzake, Manolis. 2017. "The Political Power of Finance: The Institute of International Finance in the Greek Debt Crisis." *Politics & Society* 45, no. 3: 389–413.

Kalb, Don. 2009. "Conversations with a Polish Populist: Tracing Hidden Histories of Globalization, Class, and Dispossession in Postsocialism (and Beyond)." *American Ethnologist* 36, no. 2: 207–23.

Kalb, Don, and Gábor Halmai. 2011. *Headlines of Nations, Subtexts of Class: Working Class Populism and the Return of the Repressed in Neoliberal Europe*. New York: Berghahn Books.

Kapferer, Bruce. 2005. "New Formations of Power, the Oligarchic-Corporate State, and Anthropological Ideological Discourse." *Anthropological Theory* 5, no. 3: 285–99.

Kar, Sohini. 2018. *Financializing Poverty: Labor and Risk in Indian Microfinance*. Stanford, CA: Stanford University Press.

Kar, Sohini, and Caroline Schuster. 2016. "Comparative Projects and the Limits of Choice: Ethnography and Microfinance in India and Paraguay." *Journal of Cultural Economy* 9, no. 4: 347–63.

Karajkov, Risto. 2007. "The End of a Bad Privatization." Osservatorio Balcani e Caucaso, October 5. Accessed October 26, 2018. https://www.balcanicaucaso.org/eng/Areas/Macedonia/The-End-of-a-Bad-Privatization-54625.

———. 2013. "Macedonia: Il Mattone dal Boom alla Crisi" (Macedonia: From Construction Boom to Crisis). Osservatorio Balcani e Caucaso, August 12. Accessed October 26, 2018. https://www.balcanicaucaso.org/aree/Macedonia-del-Nord/Macedonia-il-mattone-dal-boom-alla-crisi-140451.

Karim, Lamia. 2011. *Microfinance and Its Discontents: Women in Debt in Bangladesh*. Minneapolis: University of Minnesota Press.

Karwowski, Ewa, and Engelbert Stockhammer. 2017. "Financialisation in Emerging Economies: A Systematic Overview and Comparison with Anglo-Saxon Economies." *Economic and Political Studies* 5, no. 1: 60–86.

Kasmir, Sharryn, and August Carbonella. 2008. "Dispossession and the Anthropology of Labor." *Critique of Anthropology* 28, no. 1: 5–25.

Kennelly, Jacqueline, and Paul Watt. 2011. "Sanitizing Public Space in Olympic Host Cities: The Spatial Experiences of Marginalized Youth in 2010 Vancouver and 2012 London." *Sociology* 45, no. 5: 765–81.

Khalvashi, Tamta. 2015. "Peripheral Affects: Shame, Publics, and Performance on the Margins of the Republic of Georgia." PhD diss., Department of Anthropology, University of Copenhagen.

Ki, Youn. 2018. "Industrial Firms and Financialization in Late Twentieth-Century America." Presented at the 30th Annual SASE Conference, *Global Reordering: Prospects for Equality, Democracy, and Justice*, Doshisha University, Kyoto, June 23–25.

Kjuka, Deana. 2013. "Urban Renewal or Nationalist Kitsch? Skopje 2014 Stirs Controversy." *Radio Free Europe*, December 2. Accessed October 22, 2018. https://www.rferl.org/a/skopje-kitsch-renewal-statues/25187521.html.

Knight, Daniel M., and Charles Stewart. 2016. "Ethnographies of Austerity: Temporality, Crisis and Affect in Southern Europe." *History and Anthropology* 27, no. 1: 1–18.

Kofti, Dimitra. 2016. "Moral Economy of Flexible Production: Fabricating Precarity Between the Conveyor Belt and the Household." *Anthropological Theory* 16, no. 4: 433–53.

Kohn, Tamara. 2009. "Waiting on Death Row." In *Waiting*, edited by Ghassan Hage, 218–27. Carlton, Australia: Melbourne University Press.

Konings, Martijn. 2010. "Neoliberalism and the American State." *Critical Sociology* 36, no. 5: 741–65.

Kornai, Janos. 1992. *The Socialist System: The Political Economy of Communism*. Oxford: Oxford University Press.

Kowsmann, Patricia. 2015. "Portugal President Reappoints Prime Minister, Despite Lack of Majority." *Wall Street Journal*, October 22. Accessed October 26, 2018. https://www.wsj.com/articles/portugal-president-reappoints-prime-minister-despite-lack-of-majority-1445544988.

Krippner, Petra. 2011. *Capitalizing on Crisis: The Political Origins of the Rise of Finance*. Cambridge, MA: Harvard University Press.

Krueger, Anne. 1974. "The Political Economy of the Rent-Seeking Society." *American Economic Review* 64, no. 3: 291–303.

Kurtović, Larisa. 2018. "Conjuring 'the People.'" *Focaal* 80:43–62.

Kurtović, Larisa, and Azra Hromadžić. 2017. "Cannibal States, Empty Bellies: Protest, History and Political Imagination in Post-Dayton Bosnia." *Critique of Anthropology* 37, no. 3: 262–96.

Kusimba, Sibel. 2018. "'It Is Easy for Women to Ask!': Gender and Digital Finance in Kenya." *Economic Anthropology* 5, no. 2: 247–60.

Labanca, Nicola. 2007. *Oltremare: Storia dell'Espansione Coloniale Italiana* (Beyond the Sea: History of the Italian Colonial Expansion). Bologna: Il Mulino.

LaFont, Suzanne. 2001. "One Step Forward, Two Steps Back: Women in the Post-Communist States." *Communist and Post-Communist Studies* 34, no. 2: 203–20.

Lagna, Andrea. 2016. "Derivatives and the Financialisation of the Italian State." *New Political Economy* 21, no. 2: 167–86.

Lakicević, Mijat. 2017. "Makedonski Scenario 3" (The Macedonian Scenario 3).

Peščanik, May 25. Accessed October 26, 2018. https://pescanik.net/makedonski -scenario-3/.

Lambevski, Sasho. 1999. "Suck My Nation: Masculinity, Ethnicity and the Politics of (Homo)Sex." *Sexualities* 2, no. 4: 397–419.

Langley, Paul. 2008. *The Everyday Life of Global Finance: Saving and Borrowing in Anglo-America*. London: Oxford University Press.

———. 2010. "The Performance of Liquidity in the Subprime Mortgage Crisis." *New Political Economy* 15, no. 1: 71–89.

Lapavitsas, Costas. 2013. *Profiting Without Producing: How Finance Exploits Us All*. London: Verso.

Laszczkowski, Mateusz. 2011. "Building the Future: Construction, Temporality, and Politics in Astana." *Focaal* 60:77–92.

———. 2016. "'Demo Version of a City': Buildings, Affects, and the State in Astana." *Journal of the Royal Anthropological Institute* 22, no. 1: 148–65.

Laszczkowski, Mateusz, and Madeleine Reeves. 2015. "Introduction." *Social Analysis* 59, no. 4: 1–14.

Lazzarato, Maurizio. 2012. *The Making of the Indebted Man: An Essay on the Neoliberal Condition*. Cambridge, MA: MIT Press.

Ledeneva, Alena. 1998. *Russia's Economy of Favours: Blat, Networking and Informal Exchange*. Cambridge: Cambridge University Press.

Lefkov, Goran. 2016. "Samsonenko: Successful in Macedonia—Under Scrutiny in Russia." Scoop English, December 5. Accessed October 26, 2018. http://en.scoop .mk/samsonenko-successful-in-macedonia-under-scrutiny-in-russia/.

Le Normand, Brigitte. 2014. *Designing Tito's Capital: Urban Planning, Modernism, and Socialism in Belgrade*. Pittsburgh: University of Pittsburgh Press.

Lofranco, Zaira Tiziana. 2015. "Refurnishing the Home in Post-War Neoliberalism: Consumption Strategies in the Sarajevan Household Economy." *Human Affairs* 25, no. 1: 81–92.

Loftsdóttir, Kristín, Andrea L. Smith, and Brigitte Hipfl, eds. 2018. "Introduction." In *Messy Europe: Crisis, Race, and Nation-State in a Postcolonial World*, 1–30. New York: Berghahn Books.

Lóránd, Zsófia. 2016. "Socialist-Era New Yugoslav Feminism Between 'Mainstreaming' and 'Disengagement': The Possibilities for Resistance, Critical Opposition and Dissent." *Hungarian Historical Review* 5, no. 4: 854–81.

Luxemburg, Rosa. 2003. *The Accumulation of Capital*. New York: Routledge.

Lydall, Harold. 1989. *Yugoslavia in Crisis*. New York: Clarendon Press.

Magyar, Balint. 2016. *Post-Communist Mafia State: The Case of Hungary*. Budapest: CEU Press.

Mahmud, Lilith. 2016. "We Have Never Been Liberal: Occidentalist Myths and the Impending Fascist Apocalypse." Hot Spots, Cultural Anthropology (website).

Accessed October 26, 2018. https://culanth.org/fieldsights/981-we-have-never
-been-liberal-occidentalist-myths-and-the-impending-fascist-apocalypse.

Makstat Database. 2019a. "Completed Construction Works Abroad." State Statistical
Office. Accessed June 19, 2019. http://makstat.stat.gov.mk/PXWeb/pxweb/en/Mak
Stat/MakStat__Gradeznistvo__IzvrseniGradRabotiStanstvo/?rxid=46eeof64
-2992-4b45-a2d9-cb4e5f7ec5ef.

———. 2019b. "Employed by Type of Ownership of the Business Entities and Sectors of
Activities, by Year." State Statistical Office. Accessed June 19, 2019. http://makstat
.stat.gov.mk/PXWeb/pxweb/en/MakStat/MakStat__PazarNaTrud__Aktivnos
NaNaselenie/081_vrab_Sopst_Dejnost_ang.px/?rxid=46eeof64-2992-4b45-a2d9
-cb4e5f7ec5ef.

Malarek, Victor. 2004. *The Natashas: The New Global Sex Trade.* Toronto: Penguin
Books.

Malinowski, Bronislaw. 1978. *Argonauts of the Western Pacific: An Account of Native
Enterprise and Adventure in the Archipelagoes of Melanesian New Guinea.* New
York: Routledge.

Martin, Randy. 2002. *Financialization of Daily Life.* Philadelphia: Temple University
Press.

Marusic, Sinisa. 2013a. "Macedonians Divided over President's Support for Erdogan."
BalkanInsight, July 8. Accessed October 26, 2018. http://www.balkaninsight.com
/en/article/macedonian-president-s-whole-hearted-support-for-endogan-divides
-critics/2027/2.

———. 2013b. "Macedonian Divorce Rate Blamed on Women's Rights." BalkanInsight,
August 16. Accessed October 26, 2018. http://www.balkaninsight.com/en/article
/women-s-emancipation-blamed-for-divorces-in-macedonia.

———. 2014. "Macedonia PM Accused of Bribery over Bank Sale." BalkanInsight,
April 17. Accessed October 26, 2018. http://www.balkaninsight.com/en/article
/macedonian-pm-accused-of-corruption.

———. 2016. "Macedonia's SJO Says Secret Police Ran Illegal Wiretapping." Balkan-
Insight, November 18. Accessed October 26, 2018. http://www.balkaninsight.com
/en/article/macedonia-s-sjo-says-secret-police-ran-illegal-wiretapping-11-18-2016.

Massey, Doreen. 1984. *Spatial Divisions of Labour: Social Structures and the Geography of Production.* London: Palgrave.

Massey, Garth, Karen Hahn, and Duško Sekulić. 1995. "Women, Men, and the 'Second
Shift' in Socialist Yugoslavia." *Gender & Society* 9, no. 3: 359–79.

Matic, Davorka. 2007. "Is Nationalism Really That Bad? The Case of Croatia." In *Democratic Transition in Croatia: Value Transformation, Education, and Media*, edited
by Sabrina P. Ramet and Davorka Matic, 326–53. College Station: Texas A&M University Press.

Mattei, Clara Elisabetta. 2017. "Austerity and Repressive Politics: Italian Economists in the Early Years of the Fascist Government." *European Journal of the History of Economic Thought* 24, no. 5: 998–1026.

Mattioli, Fabio. 2014. "Unchanging Boundaries: The Reconstruction of Skopje and the Politics of Heritage." *International Journal of Heritage Studies* 20, no. 6: 599–615.

———. 2018. "Financialization Without Liquidity: In-Kind Payments, Forced Credit, and Authoritarianism at the Periphery of Europe." *Journal of the Royal Anthropological Institute* 24, no. 3: 568–88.

———. 2019. "Debt, Financialization, and Politics." In *A Research Agenda for Economic Anthropology*, edited by James Carrier, 56–73. Cheltenham, UK: Edward Elgar.

Maurer, Bill. 2006. "The Anthropology of Money." *Annual Review of Anthropology* 35, no. 1: 15–36.

———. 2012. "Payment: Forms and Functions of Value Transfer in Contemporary Society." *Cambridge Anthropology* 30, no. 2: 15–35.

Mayer, Till. 2013. "Macedonian Capital Skopje Gets Kitsch Makeover via Skopje 2014 Project." *Spiegel Online*, November 12. Accessed October 22, 2018. http://www.spiegel.de/international/europe/macedonian-capital-skopje-gets-kitsch-makeover-via-skopje2014-project-a-933154.html.

McDowell, Linda. 1991. "Life Without Father and Ford: The New Gender Order of Post-Fordism." *Transactions of the Institute of British Geographers* 16, no. 4: 400.

McRobbie, Angela. 2011. "Reflections on Feminism, Immaterial Labour and the Post-Fordist Regime." *New Formations* 70, no. 17: 60–76.

MEPP. 2017. *Air Quality Assessment Report for the Period 2005–2015*. Skopje: Macedonian Environment Information Center. Accessed June 19, 2019. air.moepp.gov.mk/wp-content/uploads/2017/07/AirQualityReport_EN.pdf.

Meta.mk. 2015. "Karpoš 4 Are Gathering Signatures to Save Their Parks, the Mayor 'Gives' His Support," September 23. Accessed October 26, 2018. http://meta.mk/en/karposh-4-sobira-potpisi-za-spas-na-zeleniloto/.

———. 2016. "'Transparency Macedonia': Tenders for Security Tailored Especially for SGS," February 10. Accessed October 26, 2018. http://meta.mk/en/transparency-macedonia-tenders-for-security-tailored-especially-for-sgs/.

Mikuš, Marek. 2018. *Frontiers of Civil Society: Government and Hegemony in Serbia*. New York: Berghahn Books.

———. 2019. "Contesting Household Debt in Croatia: The Double Movement of Financialization and the Fetishism of Money in Eastern European Peripheries." *Dialectical Anthropology* (May): 1–21.

Millar, Kathleen. 2015. "The Tempo of Wageless Work: E. P. Thompson's Time-Sense at the Edges of Rio de Janeiro." *Focaal*, no. 73: 28–40. https://doi.org/10.3167/fcl.2015.730103.

————. 2018. *Reclaiming the Discarded: Life and Labor on Rio's Garbage Dump*. Durham, NC: Duke University Press.

Mintz, Sidney. 1985. *Sweetness and Power: The Place of Sugar in Modern History*. London: Penguin Books.

Mitchell, Timothy. 1991. "The Limits of the State: Beyond Statist Approaches and Their Critics." *American Political Science Review* 85, no. 1: 77.

Miyazaki, Hirokazu. 2007. "Between Arbitrage and Speculation: An Economy of Belief and Doubt." *Economy and Society* 36, no. 3: 396–415.

————. 2013. *Arbitraging Japan*. Berkeley: University of California Press.

Mojsoska-Blazevski, Nikica. 2011. "Supporting Strategies to Recover from the Crisis in South Eastern Europe, Country Assessment Report: The Former Yugoslav Republic of Macedonia." Budapest: International Labour Organization. Accessed October 26, 2018. http://www.ilo.org/budapest/what-we-do/publications/WCMS_167032/lang—en/index.htm.

Mole, Noelle. 2011. *Labor Disorders in Neoliberal Italy: Mobbing, Well-Being, and the Workplace*. Bloomington: Indiana University Press.

Mollona, Massimiliano. 2009. *Made in Sheffield: An Ethnography of Industrial Work and Politics*. Oxford: Berghahn Books.

Monova, Miladina. 2015. "'We Don't Have Work. We Just Grow a Little Tobacco': Household Economy and Ritual Effervescence in a Macedonian Town." In *Economy and Ritual in Postsocialist Times*, edited by Stephen Gudeman and Chris Hann, 160–90. New York: Berghahn Books.

Mooslechner, Peter. 2012. "Management of Debt Challenges in Europe." Österreichische Nationalbank, April 27. Accessed October 26, 2018. http://www.nbrm.mk/WBStorage/Files/WebBuilder_2_1400_Peter_Mooslechner_P6_MOOS_Skopje_2011_04_27_final.pdf.

Morris, Jeremy. 2018. "Hauntology and the Trauma of Social Change: Deindustrializing Communities in Mumbai and Provincial Russia." *City & Society* 30, no. 1.

Mostov, Julie. 2000. "Sexing the Nation / Desexing the Body: Politics of National Identity in the Former Yugoslavia." In *Gender Ironies of Nationalism: Sexing the Nation*, edited by Tamar Mayer, 89–112. London: Routledge.

Muehlebach, Andrea. 2011. "On Affective Labor in Post-Fordist Italy." *Cultural Anthropology* 26, no. 1: 59–82.

Mujanovic, Jasmin. 2018. *Hunger and Fury: The Crisis of Democracy in the Balkans*. New York: Oxford University Press.

Musaraj, Smoki. 2011. "Tales from Albarado: The Materiality of Pyramid Schemes in Postsocialist Albania." *Cultural Anthropology* 26, no. 1: 84–110.

Narotzky, Susana. 2018. "Rethinking the Concept of Labour." *Journal of the Royal Anthropological Institute* 24, no. S1: 29–43.

Narotzky, Susana, and Niko Besnier. 2014. "Crisis, Value, and Hope: Rethinking the

Economy: An Introduction to Supplement 9." *Current Anthropology* 55, no. S9: S4–16.

National Archives. Telegram 102 from Belgrade to Foreign Office, March 15, 1966, FO371/189036. London, UK. https://discovery.nationalarchives.gov.uk/browse/r/h /C7685.

National Bank of the Republic of Macedonia (NBRM). 2000. *Annual Report 1999.* Accessed November 15, 2019. http://www.nbrm.mk/WBStorage/Files/II-a-1999 .pdf.

———. 2001. *Annual Report 2000.* Accessed October 26, 2018. http://www.nbrm.mk /WBStorage/Files/II-Ang-2000.pdf.

———. 2015. *Financial Stability Report for the Republic of Macedonia 2014.* October. Accessed October 26, 2018. http://www.nbrm.mk/ns-newsarticle-financial -stability-report-for-the-republic-of-macedonia-in-2015.nspx.

Neofotistos, Vasiliki. 2008. "The Balkans' Other Within: Imaginings of the West in the Republic of Macedonia." *History and Anthropology* 19, no. 1: 17–36.

———. 2010. "Cultural Intimacy and Subversive Disorder: The Politics of Romance in the Republic of Macedonia." *Anthropological Quarterly* 83, no. 2: 279–315.

———. 2012. *The Risk of War: Everyday Sociality in the Republic of Macedonia.* Philadelphia: University of Pennsylvania Press.

———. 2019. "The Rhetoric of War and the Reshaping of Civil Society in North Macedonia." *Slavic Review* 78, no. 2: 357.

Nesvetailova, Anastasia. 2010. *Financial Alchemy in Crisis: The Great Liquidity Illusion.* Chicago: University of Chicago Press.

Neveling, Patrick, and Luisa Steur. 2018. "Introduction: Marxian Anthropology Resurgent." *Focaal* 82: 1–15.

Nielsen, Christian. 2009. "The Symbiosis of War Crime and Organized Crime in the Former Yugoslavia." COST Action IS0803 Working Paper, presented at the *Money and the Shifting Locations of Eastern Peripheries* conference, October 16–17, Zagreb.

Norris, Pippa, and Roland Inglehart. 2019. *Cultural Backlash: Trump, Brexit, and Authoritarian Populism.* New York: Cambridge University Press.

Nova TV. 2014. "Gosev: Makedonska Banka Ne Smeese Da Mu Se Prodade na Gazda Nini / Гошев: Македонка Банка Не Смееше Да Му Се Продаде На Газда Нини" (Gosev: Makedonka Bank Should Not Have Been Sold to Gazda Nini). Accessed October 26, 2018. https://novatv.mk/goshev-makedonka-banka-ne-smeeshe -da-mu-se-prodade-na-gazda-nini/.

Oates-Indruchová, Libora. 2006. "The Void of Acceptable Masculinity During Czech State Socialism: The Case of Radek John's Memento." *Men and Masculinities* 8, no. 4: 428–50.

Ong, Aihwa. 1987. *Spirits of Resistance and Capitalist Discipline: Factory Women in Malaysia.* Albany: State University of New York Press.

———. 2011. "Hyperbuilding: Spectacle, Speculation, and the Hyperspace of Sovereignty." In *Worlding Cities: Asian Experiments and the Art of Being Global*, edited by Ananya Roy and Aihwa Ong, 205–26. London: Wiley-Blackwell.

Orazem, Peter F., and Milan Vodopivec. 1995. "Winners and Losers in Transition: Returns to Education, Experience, and Gender in Slovenia." *World Bank Economic Review* 9, no. 2: 201–30.

Orsi, Luigi, and Stefano Solari. 2010. "Financialisation in Southern European Economies." *Économie Appliquée* 63:5–34.

Ortiz, Fernando. 1995. *Cuban Counterpoint: Tobacco and Sugar*. Durham, NC: Duke University Press.

Ortiz, Horacio. 2017. "A Political Anthropology of Finance: Profits, States and Cultures in Cross-Border Investment in Shanghai." *HAU: Journal of Ethnographic Theory* 7, no. 3: 325–45.

Ost, David. 2018. "Workers and the Radical Right in Poland." *International Labor and Working-Class History* 93:113–24.

Ott, Katarina. 1988. *The Yugoslav Banking System*. Zagreb: Institut za Iavni Financii.

Otten, Justin. 2013. "Wine Mafia and the Thieving State: Tension and Power at the Crossroads of Neoliberalism and Authoritarianism in 21st Century Macedonia." *Anthropology of East Europe Review* 2:2–18.

Oustinova-Stjepanovic, Galina. 2017. "A Catalogue of Vice: A Sense of Failure and Incapacity to Act Among Roma Muslims in Macedonia." *Journal of the Royal Anthropological Institute* 23, no. 2: 338–55.

Palairet, Michael. 1997. "Metallurgical Kombinat Smederevo 1960–1990: A Case Study in the Economic Decline of Yugoslavia." *Europe-Asia Studies* 49, no. 6: 1071–1101.

Palomera, Jaime. 2014. "How Did Finance Capital Infiltrate the World of the Urban Poor? Homeownership and Social Fragmentation in a Spanish Neighborhood." *International Journal of Urban and Regional Research* 38, no. 1: 218–35.

Papic, Zarana. 1994. "From State Socialism to State Nationalism: The Case of Serbia in Gender Perspective." *Refuge: Canada's Journal on Refugees* 14, no. 3: 10–14.

Parry, Jonathan, and Maurice Bloch, eds. 1989. *Money and the Morality of Exchange*. Cambridge: Cambridge University Press.

Pedersen, Morten. 2007. "From 'Public' to 'Private' Markets in Postsocialist Mongolia." *Anthropology of East Europe Review* 25, no. 1: 64–71.

Peebles, Gustav. 2010. "The Anthropology of Credit and Debt." *Annual Review of Anthropology* 39, no. 1: 225–40.

Pellandini-Simányi, Léna, Ferenc Hammer, and Zsuzsanna Vargha. 2015. "The Financialization of Everyday Life or the Domestication of Finance? How Mortgages Engage with Borrowers' Temporal Horizons, Relationships and Rationality in Hungary." *Cultural Studies* 29, nos. 5–6: 733–59.

Petkovski, Mihail. 1989. "Deviznite Kursevi i Nacionalnata Ekonomska Politika

Девизните Курсеви И Националната Економска Политика" (Exchange Rates and the National Economic Politics). PhD diss., Department of Economy, University of Ss. Cyril and Methodius, Skopje.

Petrović, Tanja. 2013. "European New Colonialism." *Belgrade Journal of Media and Communications* 2, no. 4: 111–28.

Pezdir, Rado. 2008. *Slovenska Tranzicija od Kardelja do Tajkunov (The Slovenian Transition from Kardelj to Tycoons)*. Ljubljana: Časnik Finance.

Piketty, Thomas. 2014. *Capital in the Twenty-First Century*. Cambridge, MA: Harvard University Press.

Pine, Frances. 1998. "Dealing with Fragmentation: Consequences of Privatization for Rural Women in Central and Southern Poland." In *Surviving Post-Socialism: Local Strategies and Regional Responses in Eastern Europe and the Former Soviet Union*, edited by Susan Bridger and Frances Pine, 106–23. London: Routledge.

Pisarev, Aleksandar. 2014. "Cross and Crescent Divide Up Macedonia." BalkanInsight, October 1. Accessed October 26, 2018. http://www.balkaninsight.com/en/article /cross-and-crescent-divide-up-macedonia.

Pitluck, Aaron Z. 2014. "Watching Foreigners: How Counterparties Enable Herds, Crowds, and Generate Liquidity in Financial Markets." *Socio-Economic Review* 12, no. 1: 5–31.

Pitluck, Aaron Z., Fabio Mattioli, and Daniel Souleles. 2018. "Finance Beyond Function: Three Causal Explanations for Financialization." *Economic Anthropology* 5, no. 2: 157–71.

Plueckhahn, Rebekah, and Terbish Bayartsetseg. 2018. "Negotiation, Social Indebtedness, and the Making of Urban Economies in Ulaanbaatar." *Central Asian Survey* 37, no. 3: 438–56.

Pojani, Dorina. 2015. "Urban Design, Ideology, and Power: Use of the Central Square in Tirana During One Century of Political Transformations." *Planning Perspectives* 30, no. 1: 67–94.

———. 2018. "Cities as Story: Redevelopment Projects in Authoritarian and Hybrid Regimes." *Journal of Urban Affairs* 40, no. 5: 705–20.

Polanyi, Karl. 1944. *The Great Transformation: The Political and Economic Origins of Our Time*. Boston: Beacon Press.

Pollard, Jane. 2013. "Gendering Capital: Financial Crisis, Financialization and (an Agenda for) Economic Geography." *Progress in Human Geography* 37, no. 3: 403–23.

Poon, Martha. 2007. "Scorecards as Devices for Consumer Credit: The Case of Fair, Isaac & Company Incorporated." *Sociological Review* 55:284–306.

Poulantzas, Nicos. 1975. *Classes in Contemporary Capitalism*. New York: Verso.

———. 1978. *State, Power, Socialism*. New York: Verso.

Prizma. 2019. "Skopje 2014 Uncovered." Accessed June 19, 2019. http://skopje2014.priz ma.birn.eu.com/en.

Prva Arhi Brigada. 2009. *First Architectural Uprising, March 28.* [прво архитетонско востание 28.03.2009.] Accessed June 19, 2019. http://prvaarhibrigada.blogspot .com/2009/03/28032009_29.html.

Radhakrishnan, Smitha. 2018. "Of Loans and Livelihoods: Gendered 'Social Work' in Urban India." *Economic Anthropology* 5, no. 2: 235–46.

Raiffeisen RESEARCH. 2016. *CEE Banking Sector Report: New Normal and 10% Thresholds.* June 9. Accessed October 26, 2018. https://www.rbinternational.com /eBusiness/services/resources/media/829189266947841370-829189181316930732 -1162386883983662776-1-2-EN.pdf.

Rajković, Ivan. 2018a. "From Familial to Familiar: Corruption, Political Intimacy and the Reshaping of Relatedness in Serbia." In *Reconnecting State and Kinship*, edited by T. Thelen and E. Alber, 130–52. Philadelphia: University of Pennsylvania Press.

———. 2018b. "For an Anthropology of the Demoralized: State Pay, Mock-Labour, and Unfreedom in a Serbian Firm." *Journal of the Royal Anthropological Institute* 24, no. 1: 47–70.

Reactor–Research in Action, and Arhitektri. 2013. "Skopje Raste: Policy Study on the Effects of Urban Planning Methodology and Practice: Case Studies of Debar Maalo and Bunjakovec." Skopje. Accessed October 26, 2018. http://reactor.org.mk /CMS/Files/Publications/Documents/SkopjeRaste.pdf.

Redfield, Peter. 2012. "The Unbearable Lightness of Ex-Pats: Double Binds of Humanitarian Mobility." *Cultural Anthropology* 27, no. 2: 358–82.

Ricciardi, Raffaele. 2016. "Produzione Industriale, l'Italia Ha Perso il 22% dallo Scoppio della Crisi" (Industrial Production, Italy Lost 22% from the Outbreak of the Crisis). *La Repubblica*, September 23. Accessed October 26, 2018. http://www .repubblica.it/economia/2016/09/23/news/investimenti_produzione_industriale _crisi-148365722/.

Risteska, Sonja. 2018. "Macedonia: A New Russian Frontier." In *The Russian Economic Grip on Central and Eastern Europe*, edited by Ognian Shentov. Abingdon, UK: Routledge.

Ristova-Aasterud, Katerina. 2017. "The Gender Dimension of the EU Enlargement: Case Study of Macedonia as a Candidate Count." Presented at the ECPG Conference, University of Lausanne, June 8.

Roberts, Adrienne. 2013. "Financing Social Reproduction: The Gendered Relations of Debt and Mortgage Finance in Twenty-First-Century America." *New Political Economy* 18, no. 1: 21–42.

———. 2016. "Finance, Financialization, and the Production of Gender." In *Scandalous Economics: Gender and the Politics of Financial Crises*, edited by Aida Hozic and Jacqui True, 57–78. New York: Oxford University Press.

Rogers, Douglas. 2005. "Moonshine, Money, and the Politics of Liquidity in Rural Russia." *American Ethnologist* 32, no. 1: 63–81.

———. 2014. "Energopolitical Russia: Corporation, State, and the Rise of Social and Cultural Projects." *Anthropological Quarterly* 87, no. 2: 431–51.

Røyrvik, Emil. 2011. *The Allure of Capitalism: An Ethnography of Management and the Global Economy in Crisis*. New York: Berghahn Books.

Rubinstein, Alvin. 1972. "The Yugoslav Succession Crisis in Perspective." *World Affairs* 135, no. 2: 101–14.

Sacchioli, Michela. 2015. "Il Lavoro negli Anni della Crisi: L'Italia Paga il Conto, la Disoccupazione è Cresciuta del 108%" (Work During the Years of Crisis: Italy Pays a Steep Price as Unemployment Rises 108%). *La Repubblica*, April 29. Accessed October 26, 2018. http://www.repubblica.it/economia/2015/04/29/news/il_lavoro _negli_anni_della_crisi_l_italia_paga_il_conto_la_disoccupazione_e_cresciuta _del_108_-112996138/.

Sargent, Adam, and Gregory Duff Morton. 2019. "What Happened to the Wage?" *Anthropological Quarterly* 92, no. 3: 637.

Savezni Devizni Inspektorat, Macedonian National Archives, Skopje, Republic of Macedonia.

Savezni Zavod za Statistiku. 1987. *Statistical Yearbook of Yugoslavia* [Statistički godišnjak Jugoslavije]. Belgrade: Savezni Zavod za Statistiku.

Schatzberg, Michael. 1988. *The Dialectics of Oppression in Zaire*. Bloomington: Indiana University Press.

Schiffauer, Leonie. 2018. "Dangerous Speculation: The Appeal of Pyramid Schemes in Rural Siberia." *Focaal* 81: 58–71.

Schubert, Jon. 2017. *Working the System: A Political Ethnography of the New Angola*. Ithaca, NY: Cornell University Press.

———. 2018. "'A Culture of Immediatism': Co-Optation and Complicity in Post-War Angola." *Ethnos* 83, no. 1: 1–19.

Schuster, Caroline. 2015. *Social Collateral: Women and Microfinance in Paraguay's Smuggling Economy*. Oakland: University of California Press.

———. 2019. "Weedy Finance: The Political Life of Resilience in the Paraguayan Countryside." Paper delivered at the Seminar of Anthropology, University of Melbourne, May 1.

Schwenkel, Christina. 2013. "Post/Socialist Affect: Ruination and Reconstruction of the Nation in Urban Vietnam." *Cultural Anthropology* 28, no. 2: 252–77.

Scoop. 2016. "Key Players in the Media Business: Who Owns the Media in Macedonia?" April 21. Accessed October 26, 2018. http://en.scoop.mk/key-players-in-the -media-business-who-owns-the-media-in-macedonia/.

Searle, Llerena Guiu. 2016. *Landscapes of Accumulation: Real Estate and the Neoliberal Imagination in Contemporary India*. South Asia Across the Disciplines. Chicago: University of Chicago Press.

Sekretarijat za Stoki i Promet. 1956. Macedonian National Archives, Skopje, Republic of Macedonia.

Sekulić, Dubravka. 2017. "Energoprojekt in Nigeria." *Southeastern Europe* 41, no. 2: 200–229.

Shaikh, Anwar. 2016. *Capitalism: Competition, Conflict, Crises.* Oxford: Oxford University Press.

Sherif, Khaled, Michael Borish, and Alexandra Gross. 2003. "State-Owned Banks in the Transition: Origins, Evolution, and Policy Responses." Washington, DC: World Bank.

Shevchenko, Olga. 2008. *Crisis and the Everyday in Postsocialist Moscow.* Bloomington: Indiana University Press.

Shore, Chris. 2000. *Building Europe: The Cultural Politics of European Integration.* New York: Routledge.

Shoshan, Nitzan. 2016. *The Management of Hate: Nation, Affect, and the Governance of Right-Wing Extremism in Germany.* Princeton, NJ: Princeton University Press.

Simić, Ivan. 2017. "Gender Policies and Amateur Sports in Early Yugoslav Socialism." *International Journal of the History of Sport* 34, no. 9: 848–61.

Skidelsky, Robert. 2014. "Cameron Is Right to Warn of Another Recession, but Wrong to Blame the World." *The Guardian*, November 18. Accessed October 26, 2018. https://www.theguardian.com/commentisfree/2014/nov/18/david-cameron-recession-policies-cut-deficits.

Slaveski, Trajko. 1997. "Privatization in the Republic of Macedonia: Five Years After." *Eastern European Economics* 35, no. 1: 31–51.

Smith, Neil. 1987. "Gentrification and the Rent Gap." *Annals of the Association of American Geographers* 77, no. 3: 462–65.

Snajdr, Edward. 2007. "Ethnicizing the Subject: Domestic Violence and the Politics of Primordialism in Kazakhstan." *Journal of the Royal Anthropological Institute* 13, no. 3: 603–20.

Sneath, David. 2012. "The 'Age of the Market' and the Regime of Debt: The Role of Credit in the Transformation of Pastoral Mongolia." *Social Anthropology* 20, no. 4: 458–73.

Sobranje Na SRM (1945–1990), Macedonian National Archives, Skopje, Republic of Macedonia.

Sofos, Spyros. 1996. "Inter-Ethnic Violence and Gendered Constructions of Ethnicity in Former Yugoslavia." *Social Identities* 2, no. 1: 73–92.

Solari, Stefano, and Giandemetrio Marangoni. 2012. "The Making of the New European Periphery: The Evolving Capitalisms Within the Monetary Union." Presented at the 17th Workshop on Alternative Economic Policy in Europe, September 16–18, 2011, C3—Center for International Development, Vienna, Austria.

Sopranzetti, Claudio. 2017. *Owners of the Map: Motorcycle Taxi Drivers, Mobility, and Politics in Bangkok.* Berkeley: University of California Press.

Souleles, Daniel. 2019. *Songs of Profit, Songs of Loss: Private Equity, Wealth, and Inequality*. Anthropology of Contemporary North America. Lincoln: University of Nebraska Press.

Spaskovska, Ljubica. 2018. "Building a Better World? Construction, Labour Mobility and the Pursuit of Collective Self-Reliance in the 'Global South,' 1950–1990." *Labor History* 59, no. 3: 331–51.

Ssorin-Chaikov, Nikolai. 2003. *The Social Life of the State in Subarctic Siberia*. Stanford, CA: Stanford University Press.

State Statistical Office. 2007. *Employees and Net Wages, Statistical Review: Population and Social Statistics*. Skopje: State Statistical Office.

State Statistical Office. 2015. *Employees and Net Wages, Statistical Review: Population and Social Statistics*. Skopje: State Statistical Office

Stefoska, Irena, and Darko Stojanov. 2017. "A Tale in Stone and Bronze: Old/New Strategies for Political Mobilization in the Republic of Macedonia." *Nationalities Papers* 45, no. 3: 356–69.

Stockhammer, Engelbert. 2011. "Peripheral Europe's Debt and German Wages: The Role of Wage Policy in the Euro Area." *International Journal of Public Policy* 7, no. 1: 83–96.

Stojanovksi, Vlatko. 2017. "Sašo Mijalkov stanal gazda na 'sofija Gradna,' 'Žito Luks,' i na 'Zdravje Radovo,' / Сашо Мијалков станал газда на „Софија Градба", „Жито Полог", „Пелагонија" и на „Здравје Радово"!" (Sašo Mijalkov became the owner of "Sofia Gradba," "Zito Polog," and "Zdravje Radovo"). *Fokus*, November 16. Accessed June 19, 2019. http://fokus.mk/fokus-express/sasho-mijalkov-stanal-gazda-na-sofija-gradba-zhito-polog-pelagonija-i-na-zdravje-radovo/.

Stone, Marla. 1993. "Staging Fascism: The Exhibition of the Fascist Revolution." *Journal of Contemporary History* 28, no. 2: 215–43.

Storm, Servaas, and C. W. M. Naastepad. 2015. "Europe's Hunger Games: Income Distribution, Cost Competitiveness and Crisis." *Cambridge Journal of Economics* 39, no. 3: 959–86.

Stout, Noelle. 2016. "Petitioning a Giant: Debt, Reciprocity, and Mortgage Modification in the Sacramento Valley." *American Ethnologist* 43, no. 1: 158–71.

Strazzari, Francesco. 2007. "The Decade Horribilis: Organized Violence and Organized Crime Along the Balkan Peripheries, 1991–2001." *Mediterranean Politics* 12, no. 2: 185–209.

Susser, Ida. 1982. *Norman Street: Poverty and Politics in an Urban Neighborhood*. Oxford: Oxford University Press.

Teovski, Sveto. n.d. "Neizkoristenite IPA-fondovi, pokazatel za zabavena EU inbtegracija?" (Unused IPA Funds, Evidence of a Slower EU Integration?).

Thiessen, Ilká. 2007. *Waiting on Macedonia: Identity in a Changing World*. Toronto: Broadview.

Thompson, E. P. 1963. *The Making of the English Working Class*. New York: Random House.

Tischer, Daniel, Bill Maurer, and Adam Leaver. 2018. "Finance as 'Bizarre Bazaar': Using Documents as a Source of Ethnographic Knowledge." *Organization* 26, no. 4: 1–25.

Todorov, Petar. 2013. "Skopje, od Pochetok na XIX Vek do Krajot na Osmanlinskoto Vladeenje / Скопје Од Почетокот На XIX Век До Крајот На Османлиското Владеење" (Skopje, from the Beginning of the XIX Century Until the End of Ottoman Rule). PhD diss., Institute of History, University of Ss. Cyril and Methodius, Skopje.

Todorova, Maria. 1997. *Imagining the Balkans*. New York: Oxford University Press.

Tolic, Ines. 2011. *Dopo il Terremoto: La Politica della Ricostruzione negli Anni della Guerra Fredda a Skopje* (After the Earthquake: The Politics of Reconstruction during the Cold War Years in Skopje). Reggio Emilia, Italy: Diabasis.

Torsello, Davide. 2012. *The New Environmentalism? Civil Society and Corruption in the Enlarged EU*. London: Ashgate.

Trampusch, Christine. 2019. "The Financialization of the State: Government Debt Management Reforms in New Zealand and Ireland." *Competition & Change* 23, no. 1: 3–22.

Tridico, Pasquale. 2013. "The Impact of the Economic Crisis on EU Labour Markets: A Comparative Perspective." *International Labour Review* 152, no. 2: 175–90.

Troebst, Stefan. 2003. "Historical Politics and Historical 'Masterpieces' in Macedonia Before and After 1991." New Balkan Politics 6. Accessed on November 16, 2019. http://www.newbalkanpolitics.org.mk/item/Historical-Politics-and-Historical-"Masterpieces"-in-Macedonia-before-and-after-1991#.Xdcl2_FdKiUl.

Tsing, Anna. 2000. "Inside the Economy of Appearances." *Public Culture* 12, no. 1: 115–44.

Tsingou, Eleni. 2015. "Club Governance and the Making of Global Financial Rules." *Review of International Political Economy* 22, no. 2: 225–56.

Tullock, Gordon. 1989. *The Economics of Special Privilege and Rent Seeking*. Studies in Public Choice. Amsterdam: Springer.

UNDP. 2016. "Strengthening Women's Political Participation," Istanbul. Accessed November 14, 2019. https://www.eurasia.undp.org/content/dam/rbec/docs/undp-rbec-strengthening-womens-political-participation-final.pdf.

UNWOMEN. 2012. "Writing Women into the Budget: FYR Macedonia Welcomes Its First Strategy on Gender-Responsive Budgeting." Accessed October 26, 2018. http://www.unwomen.org/en/news/stories/2012/8/writing-women-into-the-budget-fyr-macedonia-welcomes-its-first-strategy-on-gender-responsive-budget.

Vahabi, Mehrdat. 2015. *The Political Economy of Predation*. Cambridge: Cambridge University Press.

van der Pijl, Kees, Otto Holman, and Or Raviv. 2011. "The Resurgence of German

Capital in Europe: EU Integration and the Restructuring of Atlantic Networks of Interlocking Directorates After 1991." *Review of International Political Economy* 18, no. 3: 384–408.

van der Zwan, Natascha. 2018. "Finance and Democracy: A Reappraisal." Presented at the 30th Annual SASE Conference on Global Reordering: Prospects for Equality, Democracy, and Justice, Doshisha University, Kyoto, June 23–25.

Vangelov, Ognen. 2017. "Stalled European Integration, the Primordialization of Nationalism, and Autocratization in Macedonia Between 2008 and 2015." *Intersections: East European Journal of Society and Politics* 3, no. 4: 17–40.

Vasovic, Aleksandar. 2017. "Russia Accuses NATO, EU and Albania of Meddling in Macedonia." Reuters, March 2. Accessed October 26, 2018. https://www.reuters .com/article/us-russia-macedonia/russia-accuses-nato-eu-and-albania-of-med dling-in-macedonia-idUSKBN169262.

Veblen, Thorstein. 1934. *The Theory of the Leisure Class: An Economic Study of Institutions* (1899). New York: Modern Library.

Verdery, Katherine. 1991. *National Ideology Under Socialism*. Berkeley: University of California Press.

———. 1996. *What Was Socialism, and What Comes Next?* Princeton, NJ: Princeton University Press.

———. 2003. *The Vanishing Hectare: Property and Value in Postsocialist Transylvania*. Ithaca, NY: Cornell University Press.

———. 2018. *My Life as a Spy: Investigations in a Secret Police File*. Durham, NC: Duke University Press.

Veron, Ophélie. 2016. "Contesting the Divided City: Arts of Resistance in Skopje." *Antipode* 48, no. 5: 1441–61.

Vesentini, Ilaria. 2014. "In Italia Chiudono Due Imprese Ogni Ora. In Cinque Anni Perse 60mila Aziende" (Every Hour, Two Italian Companies Shut Down. In Five Years, 60,000 Companies Have Disappeared). *Il Sole 24 Ore*, January 23. Accessed October 26, 2018. https://www.ilsole24ore.com/art/impresa-e-territori/2014-01-23 /in-italia-chiudono-due-imprese-ogni-ora-cinque-anni-perse-60mila-aziende-17 4528.shtml?uuid=ABjyzjr&refresh_ce=1.

Vetta, Theodora. 2011. "Nationalism Is Back! Radikali and Privatization in Serbia." In *Headlines of Nations, Subtexts of Class: Working Class Populism and the Return of the Repressed in Neoliberal Europe*, edited by Don Kalb and Gábor Halmai, 37–54. New York: Berghahn Books.

Vliegenthart, Arjan. 2010. "Bringing Dependency Back In: The Economic Crisis in Post-Socialist Europe and the Continued Relevance of Dependent Development." *Historical Social Research / Historische Sozialforschung* 35, no. 2: 242–65.

Walley, Christine. 2013. *Exit Zero: Family and Class in Postindustrial Chicago*. Chicago: University of Chicago Press.

Waters, Hedwig Amelia. 2018. "The Financialization of Help: Moneylenders as

Economic Translators in the Debt-Based Economy." *Central Asian Survey* 37, no. 3: 403–18.

Watson, Peggy. 1993. "Eastern Europe's Silent Revolution: Gender." *Sociology* 27, no. 3: 471–87.

Watts, Holly, and Saska Cvetkovska. 2015. "Tory Chairman Refuses to Name Macedonian Business Partners." *The Guardian*, May 25. Accessed October 26, 2018. https://www.theguardian.com/politics/2015/may/25/tory-chairman-refuses-to-name-macedonian-business-partners.

Watts, Jacqueline. 2009. "Leaders of Men: Women 'Managing' in Construction." *Work, Employment & Society* 23, no. 3: 512–30.

Weiss, Hadas. 2015. "Financialization and Its Discontents: Israelis Negotiating Pensions." *American Anthropologist* 117, no. 3: 506–18.

Whitehead, Judy. 2008. "Rent Gaps, Revanchism and Regimes of Accumulation in Mumbai." *Anthropologica* 50, no. 2: 269–82.

Wigan, Duncan. 2009. "Financialisation and Derivatives: Constructing an Artifice of Indifference." *Competition & Change* 13, no. 2: 157–72.

Wigger, Angela. 2012. "The Political Interface of Financialisation and the Regulation of Mergers and Acquisitions in the EU." *Journal of European Integration* 34, no. 6: 623–41.

Wilkis, Ariel. 2017. *The Moral Power of Money: Morality and Economy in the Life of the Poor*. Culture and Economic Life. Stanford, CA: Stanford University Press.

Williams, Brett. 2005. *Debt for Sale: A Social History of the Credit Trap*. Philadelphia: University of Pennsylvania Press.

Wilson, Dave. 2015. *Music Making Space: Musicians, Scenes, and Belonging in the Republic of Macedonia*. PhD diss., Department of Ethnomusicology, UCLA.

———. 2019. "Shaping the Past and Creating the Future: Music, Nationalism, and the Negotiation of Cultural Memory at Macedonia's Celebration of Twenty Years of Independence." *Music and Politics* 13, no. 2: 1–38.

Wolf, Eric. 1982. *Europe and the People Without History*. Berkeley: University of California Press.

Wolff, Larry. 1994. *Inventing Eastern Europe: The Map of Civilization on the Mind of the Enlightenment*. Stanford, CA: Stanford University Press.

Woodruff, David. 1999. *Money Unmade: Barter and the Fate of Russian Capitalism*. Ithaca, NY: Cornell University Press.

Woodward, Susan. 1995a. *Socialist Unemployment: The Political Economy of Yugoslavia, 1945–1990*. Princeton, NJ: Princeton University Press.

———. 1995b. *Balkan Tragedy: Chaos and Dissolution After the Cold War*. Washington, DC: Brookings Institution Press.

World Bank. 2015. "FYR Macedonia Partnership Country Program Snapshot April 2015." Washington, DC: World Bank.

World Economic Forum. 2015. *The Global Gender Gap Report 2015*. Geneva: World Economic Forum.

Yates, Douglas Andrew. 1996. *The Rentier State in Africa: Oil Rent Dependency and Neocolonialism in the Republic of Gabon*. Trenton, NJ: Africa World Press.

Zaloom, Caitlin. 2006. *Out of the Pits: Traders and Technology from Chicago to London*. Chicago: University of Chicago Press.

Zarkov, Dubravka. 2003. "Feminism and the Disintegration of Yugoslavia: On the Politics of Gender and Ethnicity." *Social Development Issues* 24, no. 3: 59–68.

Zazzara, Gilda. 2018. "'Italians First': Workers on the Right Amidst Old and New Populisms." *International Labor and Working-Class History* 93: 101–12.

Zerilli, Filippo M., and Julie Trappe. 2017. "Expertise and Adventure: In/Formalization Processes Within EU Rule of Law Capacity Building Programs." *Anuac* 6, no. 2: 103–8.

Zivkovic, Marko. 2006. "Ex-Yugoslav Masculinities Under Female Gaze, or Why Men Skin Cats, Beat Up Gays and Go to War." *Nationalities Papers* 34, no. 3: 257–63.

Zoli, Edda. 2001. "Cost and Effectiveness of Banking Sector Restructuring in Transition Economies." IMF Working Papers WP/01/157, October 1.

Index

Page references in *italics* refer to figures and photos.